Secrets to Living Younger Longer

The Self-Healing Path

of

Qigong, Standing Meditation and Tai Chi

Other Books, Articles, Audio and Video Tapes by Michael Mayer

The Mystery of Personal Identity
ACS, 1985

Trials of the Heart: Healing the Wounds of Intimacy
Celestial Arts, 1994

Psychotherapy and Qigong: Partners in Healing Anxiety,
The Psychotherapy & Healing Center, 1997

Qigong and Behavioral Medicine: An Integrated Approach to Chronic Pain
Qi Magazine, Winter 1996/97

Qigong and Hypertension: A Critique of Research,
The Journal of Alternative and Complementary Medicine, Vol 5 (4), August 1999

Qigong Clinical Research,
ED: Dr. Wayne Jonas, Healing Intention and Energy Medicine,
Elsevier Science Limited, U.K., 2003

Find your Hidden Reservoir of Healing Energy: A Guided Meditation for Cancer
Audio Tape, 2002

Find your Hidden Reservoir of Healing Energy: A Guided Meditation for Chronic Disease
Audio Tape, 2002

Bodymind Healing Qigong, Video Tape (1 Hour)
Bodymind Healing Center, 2000.

Bodymind Healing Qigong, DVD (1 Hour)
Bodymind Healing Center, 2004.

Secrets to Living Younger Longer

The Self-Healing Path

of

Qigong, Standing Meditation and Tai Chi

Michael Mayer, Ph.D.

Orinda, California

Secrets to Living Younger Longer: The Self-Healing Path of Qigong, Standing Meditation and Tai Chi by Michael Mayer, Ph.D.

Copyright © 2004 by Michael Mayer, Ph.D.
Cover Design by Jamon Walker of Mythic Studios

First American Edition
ISBN: 0-9704310-6-6

Printed in the United States of America
10 9 8 7 6 5 4 3 2 1

Library of Congress Control Number: 2004093380

Book Design by Karin Kinsey, Dolphin Press, CA

Published by Bodymind Healing Publications
Orinda, California

This book is dedicated to my cherished parents Abraham (posthumously) and Freda Mayer, and to all those who go beyond the first famous sentence of Kipling's quote, in order to take to heart, the entirety of his quote, which honors the union of Eastern and Western cultures. For the benefit our common humanity, may we all experience the multifaceted spiritual traditions of the world as the truly great Treasures they are.

Oh, East is East and West is West,
and never the twain shall meet,
Till Earth and Sky stand presently at God's great judgment seat;
But there is neither East nor West,
border, nor breed, nor birth,
When two strong men (and women) stand face to face,
though they come from the ends of the earth.

— Rudyard Kipling, *The Ballad of East and West*, 1889

The energy of the human body is the foundation of our health.
When our energy is at its peak, our immune system is at full strength.
When our energy declines we become vulnerable.

All healing depends on energy.
This energy can come to us in many ways,
but ultimately it is our own reserves of energy
that provide the inner strength, which keeps us healthy
and enables us to overcome illness.

Energy is the foundation of life. Without energy we die.
All the cells in our bodies depend on energy for their existence.
It is energy, which keeps them constantly at work,
reproducing and renewed.

If we learn how to increase our energy to higher levels,
we can use it to support others and ourselves
when we are hurt or unwell.

—Yi Chuan Master Lam Kam Chuen
The Way of Healing: Chi Kung

Table of Contents

List of Illustrations

Preface:

Chapter 1:

Chapter 3:

Appendix II:

Acknowledgments

A golden thread has run throughout the history of the world,
consecutive and continuous,
the work of the best men and women in successive ages.
From point to point it still runs,
and when near, you feel it as the clear and bright and searchingly irresistible light
which Truth throws forth when the great minds {and hearts} conceive {and live} it.

—Adapted from Walter Moxon, *Pilocereus Senilis* and other papers, 1887

This book brings into form a spiritual practice, a lineage, a lifestyle, a tradition and the collective learnings of a community. Without this wider whole of which I am a part, I could not have taken the steps forward that I have on this pathway that has so deeply transformed my life and those around me.

First, and foremost, I wish to express the greatest appreciation to Master Fong Ha for his magnetic force, drawing into the center of the circle in which he stands, such talented teachers and dedicated students. Many of them have met regularly over a period of twenty-five years, to drink from the endless well of his teachings in the meditative internal martial arts. I am grateful for his lack of ego in bringing to us some of the greatest Chinese masters of the tradition of Standing Meditation, including Han Xingyuan, Cai Song Fang and Sam Tam. This gave us the opportunity to study with a broad range of teachers, and access knowledge long held secret behind the Great Wall of China. I will forever be thankful for the opportunity to study with them, and to absorb their embodied wisdom.

Among the other teachers and masters of Qigong, acupressure and the internal martial arts that have been an important part of my learning and the creation of the Bodymind Healing Qigong system are: Ken Cohen (friend and fellow traveler on the path), Luke Chan, Dr. Alex Feng, Kumar Francis, Michael Gach, Chungliang Al Huang, Brian O'Dea, Zhi Gang Sha, Marek Wajsman, Zishen Wang, Stacey Barros and Larry Wong.

In my extended family of Qigong, Standing Meditation and Tai Chi practitioners are my own students and the students of Fong Ha's classes. Thank you all for being part of our internal arts circle that has kept me learning through practicing with you (apologies to those who I may be unintentionally omitting): Stacey Barros, Uma Bhatnagar, Deborah Wood Campbell, Delores Clark, Chris Geiser, Rick Konlin, Michlene Ha, Nancy Larkin, John Lebourgeois, Bob Lee, Higgie Lerner, Mark McKenna, Jennifer McKeever, Scott Moressi, Tim Muscovitch, Laura Nownes, June (Kozuko) Onodera, Eric Olsen, Mildred Partansky, Elsie Sink, Rebecca Spalton (posthumously,) Terry Rockwell, Harold Rossman (posthumously), Marc Schuler, Patrick Sheehy, Tomer and Leigh Steinberg, Barbara Stevensen, Louis Swaim, Mitch Tsao, Fred and Katrina Van Den Berg, Katie Wesdorf and

Bruce Wolfe. Special appreciation goes to my Tai Chi brothers Jan Diepersloot and Sandy Rosenberg for countless hours of shared learning and collaboration. What a treasure it is to have shared this path together!

I appreciate all those, too numerous to mention, who have helped me evolve on the Path where Western and Eastern healing practices meet. I am grateful to Dr. Wayne Jonas, former Director of the National Institute of Health Office of Alternative Medicine, for recognizing the value of my peer-reviewed article on Qigong and Hypertension by including a revised version of it for his edited book on Healing, Intention and Energy Medicine. Among my teachers of Western approaches to psychotherapy, I am particularly appreciative of Eugene Gendlin, Ph. D., originator of Focusing, for whom I served as the East Bay Coordinator for ten years. Likewise to the conference settings, and universities that gave me a forum to present my Bodymind Healing Qigong method, I owe much gratitude. Some of these include: The National Qigong Association, and particularly, Joanne Coyle who helped to get my workshop on Bodymind Healing Continuing Education credits for nurses. The World Qigong Conference, sponsored by Effie Chow gave me the honor of inviting me to teach a Master's level workshop. The California Institute of Integral Studies gave me the opportunity to train doctoral level psychologists, in perhaps the first course in the country, in the integration of Psychotherapy and Qigong. San Franciso State University, Ken Burrows and Eric Pepper, Ph.D., enabled me to expand my offerings to undergraduate students in Holistic Health in a course in Eastern Perspectives on Healing. Finally, John F. Kennedy University, Sanjen Miedzinski, Ph.D., and Bryan Wittine, Ph.D., had the foresight in the 1980's to allow me to train master's level Psychotherapy students in a three-semester course in Tai Chi, Qigong and Psychotherapy. To all of these people and institutions, and to the students of these workshops and classes, I am appreciative of being given the opportunity to teach about the bodymind healing methods that are in this book. You helped my ideas and practice to grow.

Regarding the integration of Eastern, Western, and indeginous healing practices, I have had the good fortune to help to co-found and be a staff psychologist and Qigong teacher at the HealthMedicine Institute in Lafayatte, California. My gratitude goes to our whole multi-disciplinary treatment team, including Len Saputo, M.D. - internist, Collette Devore - Acupuncture, Phillip Scott - Native American healing practices, Lorenz Schweitzer - Rolfing, Steve Milligan, D.C. - Chiropractor, Bill and Cathy Kneebone, D.C. - Chiropractors, Rex Wilson - Naturopath, Will Friedman, Ph.D. - Psychologist, Meg Jordan, Ph.D. - Guided Imagery and Linda Chrisman - Trauma Resolution Bodywork. Equally important to our practitioner team is our executive staff Kay Sandberg - Executive Director, our administrative staff, and supporters - Anne Miller, Margo Power, Gay Pierre and Janice Lum and Bob Leppo - benefactor. I feel blessed to be working with all of you, past practitioners, and the patients at HMI, who helped to give me a place to practice the healing ways that have come from my gifted teachers, my explorations of ancient and modern healing traditions, and from my inner journeys.

I am grateful to the scholarship which led me to develop the thesis that the ancient arts of Standing and Moving Meditation have roots in pre-history, and are long-lost holistic methods which incorporate: self-defense, health and longevity practices, changing the elements of one's life stance, as well as being a spiritual path. Thanks to Joseph Campbell, Ken Cohen, Catherine Despeux, Jan Diepersloot, Mircea Eliade, Felicitas Goodman, Belinda Gore, Livia Kohn and Shifu Nagaboshi Tomio.

I feel blessed to have such good friends who have been there for me for feedback on my writing and other details: Katie Carrin, Tarra Christoff, Joanne Coyle, Ellen Demel, Mark Fromm, Jean Hayek, Raphael Rettner, Sandy Rosenberg and Cynthia Yaguda Gould. Also much thanks goes to Temple Chochmat Halev (Wisdom of the Heart) for inspiring services which helped to maintain my connection to sacred space during difficult times in my writing process.

I am grateful to Carol Hansen, Victor Grey and Kandy Petersen for the earlier design phases of this book. In the later phases of the design, great appreciation goes to photographer David Lehrer, administrative assistant Tracy Chocholousek for copy editing and indexing. Much appreciation goes to award winning cover designer, Jamon Walker of Mythic Studios, for his creative cover design of this book. Thanks to MyLinda Butterworth of Day to Day Enterprises for creating the final PDF for this book. Greatest thanks for the overall design of the book goes to Karin Kinsey who mid-wifed the birth of this book. All these people brought Qi to the design of this book with great skill and open hearts.

AUTHOR'S NOTE

The techniques, ideas and suggestions in this book are not intended as a substitute for medical advice. Though there is much research documenting the healing effects of qigong, and Standing Meditation, these arts may activate an alchemical healing process of activating old blockages, physical or emotional, in order to work them through at a deeper level. As part of this healing process you may discover, through your practice, ways to Self-heal or you may choose to go to an appropriate medical professional. Do not substitute the practice of these movements for necessary medical attention. It is advisable to do these practices with the guidance of a trained teacher. In choosing to practice these methods you are taking responsibility for working with what arises in you. Before doing any of these practices, please consult with your physician and other allied health professionals.

Prologue

This book was born during a confusing time in my life when I was in my first semester of my doctoral Psychology program. I was in the dark about what to focus on for the subject of my dissertation. I decided to go out into the woods for forty nights to see if I could find my Path, and at the same time, to see if I could cure my phobia of being out in the woods alone in the darkness of night. The following experience happened:

After about three weeks of sleeping in the woods, about three miles from the nearest mark of civilization—it came. I was asleep alone on top of a ridge with a water hole nearby; and I was in a lucid, dream-like state where I was conscious of my surroundings, while, at the same time, aware of being in a dream. I noticed that a group of seven deer were approaching me. I was particularly aware of the leader, who had very large, golden, glowing antlers, and eyes so emblazoned that I was not sure if it was really a deer, or a Shaman wearing a mask trying to trick me. I was afraid that the deer might attack me, but I thought that if I pretended to be asleep perhaps he would just pass me by. My left eye started to quiver however, and I thought that surely this was going to give me away. The deer approached, and gently kissed my eye. A warm, energized ecstasy filled me like nothing I had ever experienced before. A moment later, I was terrified as I realized that my eye was not longer in its socket…it was in the deer's mouth. In my panic, the first thought that came to mind was that my parents would say, "I told you so. We always told you something like this would happen when you slept out in the backyard in New Jersey, Why do you have to do things like this? Why can't you just sleep inside like everyone else? If you had only listened to us, you wouldn't have lost your eye." This thought of my parents' "I told you so," was as bad as the image of crawling back to civilization with only one eye.

Even amidst these horrifying fantasies I somehow realized that, regardless of the consequences, all this had a place in my destiny…I breathed, letting go to my fate. Then, I noticed the deer in a new way. I realized that he was doing something with my eye that was not malevolent. He was rolling my eye around in his mouth, like some kind of ritual, as if washing it. He then placed my eye back in its socket…but it was not an eye, it was some kind of jewel—a green emerald, or a piece of jade. I was awestruck.

My next recollection was waking at dawn and feeling for my eye. To my surprise it was just an eye again. I then noticed a large number of fresh deer tracks around me. Had the deer actually been there? Was it a dream, a vision? For many days thereafter (and even to this day) I was filled with a sense of wonder.

When I returned to my doctoral advisor and group after the forty-day period someone suggested I read the book *Seven Arrows* which is about the process of Vision Questing among the American Plains Indians. Here amongst the legends of the native people of this land, I found a beginning place on my personal path.

From reading *Seven Arrows*, I discovered, many years before the movie *Dances with*

Wolves became popular, that taking a symbolic name associated with an element of nature helped to give Native Americans a sense of their life's meaning in connection with nature. I began to explore the symbology of this experience, and thought that perhaps my purpose laid in becoming like the deer of my vision. What a quest it would be to "kiss the eyes of others" like the deer had kissed mine, to help people to transform their fears and life issues and see the sacred gems of life. If I could do this gently, then I could be like a "Deer Kissing Eyes."

Influenced by my vision of the deer, my first book, *The Mystery of Personal Identity,* showed how to re-vision the way we look at our ways of Being using the metaphors of nature and the celestial sphere to re-sacralize our personalities. My second book, *Trials of the Heart: Healing the Wounds of Intimacy,* took ancient myths and stories and applied them to our relationships so that we could more clearly see the sacred purpose involved in our struggles. It showed how ancient sacred wisdom stories could help bring healing to the wounds of intimacy, and how relationship is an initiation through the elements of fire, earth, air and water.

Now in this latest book on *Qigong,* I hope to initiate the reader into how the ancient sacred wisdom tradition of Qigong can help us change our ways of seeing, and being in, our bodies. The healing secrets encoded in the Animal Qigong movements, in Standing Meditation and in the sets of Bodymind Healing Qigong are a gift from the times that humans lived in tune with primordial energies and natural rhythms. By following the deer, other animals and Shamanic practices into the dark forests of the times of old, ancient tools are uncovered to heal the bodymind. We are all like Snow White needing to be kissed on the eyes by the wisdom of our ancestors; and their ancient sacred wisdom traditions help us to wake to our natural and spiritual Selves.

As you go through this book you may find some exercises more fitting for you than others, due to your own Medicine Animal Way. There are an extensive amount of practices in the book; take due care not to overdose on them by trying to do too much at once. Since these movements took me 25 years to synthesize, you might do best to incorporate them gradually into your lifetime preventative medicine program. Be attuned to what your deepest Self needs as you walk through the forest ahead; and I hope you find some practice, set of movements, concept or new way of Being that will become "dear" to you, and that will kiss your eyes.

This book is the first of a two-volume set on Bodymind Healing Practices. Volume II will focus further on the integration of Psychotherapy and Qigong.

Preface

In this era of high stress, terrorist threats and managed health care, consumers want to learn self-healing methods to practice preventative medicine and become more self-reliant about their own health treatment. Qigong is one of the key methods that the holistic doctor prescribes to fulfill this need.

I. Overview

There is a rising tide of authors bringing Eastern traditions to help with the Western health care crisis. Dean Ornish's use of yoga with heart disease has achieved national recognition, John Kabat Zinn brought Buddhist mindfulness meditation to many hospitals, Deepak Chopra and Mahareshi Mehesh Yogi have brought the wisdom of mantra, Transcendental Meditation and Ayurveda into many American households, and Michael Gach introduced Acupressure to unlock Eastern secrets of healing touch. As these authors take the commonplace activities and spiritual traditions of lying down (Yoga), sitting (Vipassana Meditation), touch (Acupressure) and sound (mantra yoga) and linked them to health, so does this book link health with *Qigong* (pronounced *chee gong*), which includes Standing and Moving Meditation, and Tai Chi.

Qigong is a many thousand-year-old way to cultivate the vital energy of the universe (*Qi*) using breath, posture, movement, touch, sound and awareness. Qigong is a rising star on the Eastern horizon…a healing tool for the healthcare crisis, a time-proven method to help us live younger longer. Though Qigong literally translates as "work" (Gong) with cultivating Qi (pronounced *chee*), I like to say that Qigong means "play" with Qi. Though not a technically correct translation, it may fit better with the original intention of Qigong practice which is to loosen up the constrictions which come from trying so hard in life. As we play with the energy of life, then the relaxing and enlivening effects of Qigong are discovered. True, for most of us this first requires some holding of forms, and learning some new ways to move the body which initially may seem difficult. May you find the play in the work of Qi cultivation.

Long before Dr. Andrew Weil popularized the term "living younger longer,"[1] Taoist adepts practiced longevity methods and wrote about them extensively in various texts with names such as Compendium of Essentials on Nourishing Life (*Yangsheng Yaoji*), Record on Nourishing Inner Nature and Extending Life (*Yangsing Yanming Lu*), and Great Clarity Scripture of Gymnastics and Nourishing Life (*Taiqing Daoyin Yangsheng Jing*). These are some of the names of texts in the Taoist Canon (*Daozang*), which were written as far back as the later Han dynasty in the second century B.C. Anonomous Taoist adepts compiled this sixty volume set, which included longevity techniques long before amazon.com's thirteen titles on living younger longer were conceived. The pursuit of long life and immortality, and practices for living younger longer are a cornerstone of Taoism and are the subject of innumerable well-researched books.[2]

One of the key ingredients in the Taoist methods for increasing longevity were the methods of *daoyin,* (leading and guiding the life force of the universe), now called *Qigong.* The term "Qigong" was first mentioned by Taoist Master Xu Sun (died 374 A.D.). But the term was not used in its specialized sense as "the art of Qi cultivation" until the twentieth century. According to Taoist scholar Catherine Despeux the term Qigong appears in the titles of two works in 1915 and 1929 where it "designates the force issued by the working with the Qi and martial applications of this force." The therapeutic use of the term dates only from 1936 in a work by Dong Hao entitled *Special Therapy for Tuberculosis: Qigong.* Since that time, the term "Qigong" has been widely used in the medical sense representing all Chinese self-healing exercise and meditation disciplines from ancient times to the present.[3]

Qigong is now known world-wide as a method for enhancing health for people of any age, and ameliorating the effects of aging. Growing older is usually associated with hardening of the arteries, hypertension, rigidity in the body and mind, locked and immobile joints, atrophy of muscles, falls from losing balance, stagnation of energy and lethargy. Qigong is a time-tested antidote for the effects of aging. It increases blood flow and circulation, reduces hypertension, increases flexibility, oxygenates the brain, balances the brain's left and right hemispheric functions, increases helpful neuro-chemicals, adds spring to the joints through exercises using expansion and contraction, naturally develops muscles, reduces falls, increases balance, and leads to energy flow throughout the body. There is now much scientific research to support these claims (some of which is reviewed in the Appendix II and III of this book). Here we have a way to practice living younger longer and to enhance vitality. But this is a small part of what this time-tested treasure-house has to offer. As we shall see, Qigong is a body-mind-spirit practice for "Self-healing" in the broadest sense of the word.

The term *Self-healing* has a depth of meaning behind it. The term *Self* with a capital "S" was initially coined by Carl Jung to mean a "Self" broader than the ego—a Self that incorporates the archetypes of the collective unconscious. Thus, the path of *individuation,* according to Dr. Jung, is to form an ego-Self axis, whereby the personal ego is connected with the transpersonal elements of the psyche. Later in Dr. Jung's work, he spoke of the importance of the *psychoid* (body-centered) elements of the psyche in the individuation process. When the term *Self,* in Self-healing, is used in this book, it is meant to convey not only the psychoid dimension of the Self, but also the incorporation of the healing elements of the surrounding universe into the sphere of the Self. The healing powers of the Self blossom when the archetypal possibilities of embodied life are brought to fruition. This follows the viewpoint that in order for the Self to be whole, the mind-body-universe split needs to be resolved, which can be accomplished through incorporating bodymind healing practices from the East such as the ones outlined in this book.

Here, we should also stop for a moment and clarify the term *healing* in Self-healing. When ill, we all would like our disease to be gone. With any Self-healing practice or technique we need to be careful that we don't produce a personal sense of shame when a cure doesn't come as quickly as we might like. Hence the distinction between *cure*—the absence of symptoms—and *healing*—an attitude that whatever life presents us with is a *divina afflictio* (divine affliction) which gives us the opportunity for psycho-spiritual growth, soul-making and finding the source of healing. With this in mind, although suffering and death are inevitable parts of life that can not always be "cured" through healing practices, in the Eastern belief, it is possible for one to be "healed" even as one suffers or dies.

Every symptom of illness or disease that we experience is a call from our body to learn to read its language. The awareness of our primordial Self is tested with each pain or body block. When tuning in to our symptoms, is our body telling us to let go of our self-healing arrogance and rely on the advice of a medical professional who can help us deal with a an early warning sign of cancer or liver disease? Or on the other hand, are we giving away our innate healing powers to the medical propaganda machine that benefits from convincing us that every ache is a call to go to the temple of Western medicine for relief? At those times when our own inner temple has the resources to heal us, it is empowering to activate these Self-healing abilities and avoid the side effects of modern medications. If this path fails, then we may choose to move up the hierarchy toward the resources of modern medicine.

Modern neuroscience, psycho-neuroimmunology and energy medicine have demonstrated that many chemicals of the outer world are produced in our brains and bodies, and can effect healing, as is discussed more fully in Appendix II. The question becomes, how, and to what extent, can we increase our abilities to unlock our natural powers? In a culture like ours, so oriented to the outer world, we oftentimes forget our inner resources and the old traditions, which existed long before the advent of Western medicine, that held knowledge of how to effect Self-healing.

In this book we will focus on Qigong as an age-old method of bodymind healing. The first use of the term "bodymind" in Western thought came from Ken Dychtwald whose book, *Bodymind,* was written in 1977. There are now 124 books on amazon.com with the word "bodymind" in their titles. Joining the two words, "body" and "mind" into one word expresses the core philosophic belief of Eastern thought that body, mind and spirit are one inseparable whole. Mind, body and spirit may seem separate, but if we stop and reflect on them, all three levels exist as one inseparable whole in our everyday experience. For example, when we are embarrassed, our face flushes, thoughts of not being the "way we should be" fill our minds, and we become out of harmony with our higher Self-accepting nature. "Bodymind Healing" is a term that emphasizes the need to activate all aspects of ourselves to achieve optimal mental, emotional and spiritual health. The journey of this book will explore how the practice of Standing and Moving Meditation Qigong is such a path, and it exists as a quintessential part of the ancient root system of the tradition of "bodymind healing."

The original pictogram of Qi shows a character divided into two parts—on top is a square resembling a pot with a handle, and underneath the container are four strokes representing a fire. Water heated by fire, along with the vapor rising from the liquid, is a powerful representation of the alchemical transmutation of the fire and water elements in the human body that take place when Daoyin (Qigong) is practiced. Maybe the symbol means that bubbles of feeling rise through the liquid inside of ourselves and turn into vapor as our life energy joins cosmic energy when we practice this ancient art.

Figure 1: Original pictogram of Qi

The traditional pictogram for Qi in Chinese is a pictogram which has "rice" as its lower trigram, and "air" as its upper trigram. This Chinese character of Qi symbolizes steam rising from cooking rice. It implies the movement of breath and its ability to nourish us. Also, the ancient Chinese said that Qigong helps to "cook" our internal Qi by stoking the inner fire of energy in the body, mixing it with the appropriate amount of internal water, and thereby leading us to rise up from our earthly existence to heavenly realms. The Chinese believe we inherit Qi from our ancestors, and that there are sources inside the body and in the external environment from which we can absorb energy, including the sun, moon, and elements of the earth.

Figure 2: Official character of Qi

In this book, the spelling will be *Qi*, not so much because it is the most current Pin Yin method, versus the older Wade-Guile spelling "chi." But rather because of the symbolic and pictoral representation and meaning of that specific spelling.[4] The letter "Q" is a circle with roots going below the line, into the Earth—just like the Taoist tradition teaches us that Qi may be first contacted by sinking the Qi into our roots. The circle in the "Q" represents the circle of all creation, the unity of things and wholeness of the universe that the Qigong tradition says we may contact if we work (Gong) on cultivating the life force of the universe (Qi). We can look at the dot above the "i" in Qi as a representation of contacting the subtle energy of heavenly space. I also like how the Westerner who first looks at the word says, "There is something different here; there is always supposed to be a "u" after a "Q "in the English language." And so, in choosing the path toward finding this energy involved in Qigong, we need to let go of our old habitual ways of looking at life—and let go of the identification with ourselves, i.e., "you," or "u." This certainly was true for me when I was first introduced to Qigong.

I was brought up to be a lawyer, and then trained in psychological research methods; I was a skeptic. Yet I was curious about this "Qigong thing." I had to let go of many of my preconceptions as I began to study Tai Chi and Qigong. In time, my natural curiosity led me to wonder about the deeper dimensions of these arts. To tell you the truth, it wasn't so much curiosity as it was "necessity"—when I was doing my Doctoral dissertation in Psychology my body was so tense that I needed something to loosen me up as an every-day practice. I couldn't afford to keep seeing massage practitioners, acupuncturists and chiropractors. And those relaxation techniques that I was learning as part of my Doc-toral training only went so far. Then I saw someone practicing Tai Chi and Qigong—this became an answer to some of my deepest needs.

In the pages that follow are the Standing and Moving Meditation Qigong practices that I have been doing for 25 years, along with my perspective on them. The book is divided into three sections. Section I explores Standing Meditation. The Standing prac-tices in this book are the center post of a system of Qigong, called *Bodymind Healing Qigong* which I developed over the last two decades by integrating the gifts of my teach-ers with my background in the Western healing arts. Section II illustrates the "Bodymind Healing Qigong" practices for health and longevity. And Section III resurrects the tradi-tion into modern life.

Section I explores Standing Meditation Qigong, with the hope that this book will help this valuable tradition to find rightful stance along with more well-known path-ways that use sitting or lying down to develop our connection with the spiritual dimen-sion of life. Ask any Qigong Master and they will tell you that the secret of Qigong lies in Standing Meditation, a long lost art that was kept as a closely guarded secret in Chinese families. We are indeed fortunate to have access to this great tradition that would have otherwise taken lifetimes to discover, even if we had the chance to wander around an-cient China. As Westerners, we are so used to being sold things, so used to needing boundaries to defend ourselves from gimmickry, particularly spiritual and health gim-mickry, that it is hard to be open to receiving treasures when they are presented. One way to know if the treasure is real is to bite into the Gold, and test its metal. According to one's taste and needs, what is a treasure for one person may not be for another.

The Overview to Section I is an introduction to my experience with Standing Medi-tation. It contains background information on my initial resistance to this practice, and the transformative process that took place when I worked with various Masters of the tradition. In Chapter 1, The Historical Roots of Standing Meditation, the thesis of this book will be introduced—that at one time Standing was a holistic practice that inte-grated self-defense, health and longevity practices, self-transformation and spiritual development. Then, in Chapters 2 through 6 you'll learn "how to do it," along with learning about the theoretical and spiritual basis of Standing as a Path. You'll discover for yourself some of the experiences that derive from Standing; and you'll find a blend of imagery techniques and related Qigong practices that in my, my students' and my patients' experience enhance the ability to feel and cultivate Qi. In Chapter 2 the question will be posed whether *The Lost Golden Ball,* belonging to the king's son in the Grimm's fairy tale, "Iron Hans," relates to the cultivation of the Golden Ball of the Eastern Standing and Moving Meditation Qigong traditions. The metaphorical will be blended with the practical as you, the reader, get a chance to discover for yourself whether you find the Golden Ball from these practices; and hopefully you will discover deeper levels of "what you Stand for." It will be suggested that many spheres of development are encompassed by the symbolic expansive meaning of the Golden Ball spoken of through this book. Standing Meditation helps us to hold the Golden Ball, develop its spiritual base and dissolve into the source from which the creative energy of life arises. The Bodymind Healing Qigong practices help us to cultivate the ability to energize, heal and move with the Golden Ball. Two-person exercises help us to play with, test, roll with, and develop the substance of the Golden Ball and share our practice with another. The alchemical transmutation of the leaden emotional and mental issues that cloud us from glowing gold in life are another essential part of the sphere of the Golden Ball. In Chapter 3 and 4 you'll learn about various Standing postures, breathing methods and energy centers that can open from doing the practice. In Chapter 5, you'll find practices to change your stance towards life and death. In Chapter 6, some of the deeper spiritual dimensions of the practice will be explored.

In Section II you will be introduced to the illustrated "Bodymind Healing Qigong" practices for health and longevity. Standing Meditation is enhanced by Qigong movement practices; they prevent "stagnation of Qi," and are the second member of the double key that unlocks the healing powers of your bodymind and spirit. Both are an integral part of the family of Qigong practices. The Bodymind Healing Qigong system is an integration of ten systems of Qigong which developed from over two decades of practice with some of the most respected teachers and masters of Qigong with whom I have had the blessing to meet and practice. In this section you'll find Self-healing methods for specific common ailments, and for living younger longer. Hopefully some of the methods will become part of your lifetime practice of preventative medicine. You'll learn age-old methods to cultivate and balance your energy, activate healing trance states, vitalize your internal organs, increase flexibility and stamina, disperse stagnant Qi and develop grace and power. You may never say hello and good-bye the same way again after seeing the greeting method of the Wild Goose.

In the Tai Chi and Animal Forms sections a secondary hypotheses of this book will be explored—that the popular art of Tai Chi has roots in the Shamanic tradition of Healing Animal Movements. Mythic tales will be blended with examples to elucidate this theme. You'll see the similarities between the Tai Chi movement "Push" and the First Century A.D. Chinese Physician, Hua Tuo's Animal Frolic Movement, "Bear Pushes the

Tree." Another example is that "Brush Knee Forward" in Tai Chi is very similar to "Tiger Pawing" in Hua Tuo's Animal Frolics. Even more important than discovering the roots of some Tai Chi movements in earlier Shamanic practices is discovering the particular healing technologies for organs and meridians that Hua Tuo and others carrying the Shamanic lineage brought as a timeless gift to help people of all ages. Understanding these Shamanic roots of our modern practice can deepen the healing potential of Tai Chi. For example, you'll see how the popular Tai Chi movement, "Cloud Hands," is a practice for clearing away negative emotions from the clouded heart; and "Grasping the Bird's Tail" is a method for finding "magnetic Qi," as well as for "Gathering Starlight," a Shamanic practice to bring light to your dark times. Section II concludes with a description of *Tai Chi and Yi Chuan Joining Hands, Self-development Practice,* a method for two people to practice embodying various Taoist principles and the healing qualities of the elements of creation (fire, earth metal, water and wood); as well, it is a way to practice dual-cultivation of the "Golden Ball of Qi."

In Section III the theme of this book is revisited—the ancient arts of Standing and Moving Meditation have roots in pre-history and are long-lost holistic methods which incorporate: self-defense, health and longevity practices, transformation of the totality of the practitioners life stance, and is a spiritual path. Over time this tradition was broken into isolated fragments; we now have an opportunity to resurrect the tradition in modern life. In Chapter 8, you will see how the broken pieces of the ancient arts of Tai Chi and Qigong can be reunited in modern times to change your stance in life. To illustrate how the Standing Practice can once again be reunited with the psychological dimension, you'll see examples of how the Standing practice has helped me in my life, and how it has helped some of my students and patients. Finally, Chapter 9, The Tao of Everyday Life, illustrates ways to bring this ancient tradition into modern life. You'll see how these practices will change your way of standing in grocery lines, open new ways to deal with being stuck on the highway in rush hour traffic, make fun out of being stuck in boring conversations at parties, influence your ways of eating and perhaps even change the way you make love. Don't overlook the sections on walking in the woods and sleeping outside at night to reactivate your Primordial Self.

For those who are scientifically inclined, in Appendixes II and III I have included a discussion and some of the research that supports the case for energy oriented practices increasing health and longevity. I begin with Western research on "energy medicine," and then summarize some of the studies on Qigong and Tai Chi.

The Standing and Moving Qigong practices in this book are not direct replications of the movements learned from my esteemed teachers. The particular integration here comes from my own experimentation on my own healing journey, and has been refined by my work with my students and patients, to whom I am eternally grateful. I believe one of the marks of a Master teacher, like the ones I have had, is giving the student room to find their own way, and their own intention in practicing.

My overall orientation to Standing and Moving Meditation Qigong is influenced by my experience as a psychotherapist, hypnotherapist and practitioner of many systems of

Qigong. As well, regarding the purposes of the postures, I draw from various cross-cultural healing traditions including acupressure, shamanism, mythology and alchemy. The names and meanings of some of the postures and movements have been renamed along the lines that fit with these traditions. I believe that "the Standing and Moving Meditation Qigong Traditions," as is implied by the term *Yi* (intention) *Chuan,* means that the practice leads to what each individual intends. There are self-defense, meditative, self-healing, healing of others, spiritual and alchemical intentions which can guide the direction of this practice, depending upon our orientation and purpose in practicing. They are all an important part of the Energy Mandala, in the center of which we all stand at each moment, whether we are conscious of it or not. Ultimately, Standing and Moving Meditation Qigong is a way of transforming the physical body into an energy field that is one with the Tao.

SECTION I:

STANDING MEDITATION:

WHAT DO YOU STAND FOR?

When I stand, the earth is in my hands. The universe is in my mind.

You are free. You are a great fire. If anything comes toward you,
it will be consumed in the fire.
If it does not approach the fire, it will not be burned. You are merely the fire.
You remain where you are, content to be alight.

You are the sea. Whatever anyone gives you, you can take. They can also take from you
anything they want. The sea is vast; it can give up anything and still remain the sea.
Like the sea, you are endless and unceasing. This is the true freedom.

—Standing Meditation Grandmaster
Wang Xiangzhai

Overview to Section I:

My Experience Standing

There are experiences in life that change us, and the people around us, at our core. Such an experience happened for my teacher Master Fong Ha (who I shall refer to as *Sifu*, or respected teacher) in the mid 1970's when I had been studying Tai Chi Chaun with him for about six months. When Sifu Ha returned from one of his many exploratory trips to China, he told the story of meeting a great master of an art that would change the direction of his Tai Chi Chaun practice. The teacher he met there was Han Xingyuan, a Master of one of the Standing Meditation traditions called the *Yi Chuan*.[1] This art involved simply standing still.

I have to admit that I was skeptical when Sifu Ha suggested that I try standing for a hundred hours over the next few months, and that by doing so, my development would be enhanced. I felt much resistance to "just standing." I associated Standing with my childhood experience of being told to "stand in the corner" when I was disobedient in school. As an adult, one of the things I most detested was standing in line at various public places, being forced to stop my life and stand still when I needed to get "important things" done. To tell you the truth, I had secretly believed all my life that there was something wrong with me. At parties, I noticed that most people could spend longer times standing with one person than I could. I felt mounting tension in my body when I stood in one place for longer than I wanted. If there was anyone who wouldn't be a good candidate for this "Standing Meditation thing," I believed it was me.

In the Tai Chi class with Sifu Ha, I had come to learn to move as I had seen him move—with grace and power. I didn't want to waste my time just standing there, "doing nothing." But I figured I'd just do this as I had done so many other things in life—by pushing my way through and getting it over with, then I could get onto "the real thing"--the graceful movements of Tai Chi and Qigong. Little did I know at that time, that this simple method would change me at my core.

From Sifu Ha, and from each of the different masters of Qigong and Standing Meditation that he brought to the United States from China over the next two decades, I went through a gradual process of initiation into a world for which my Western education had not prepared me. In the pages that follow, we will explore the methods that were imparted to me, and how I integrated them into an wide range of spiritual traditions.

Through practicing these methods, I hope that the reader will begin to find renewed energy, peace and "contentment from being alight" in everyday life. The beauty of this method lies in our many opportunities to practice this simple posture in our everyday activities. Standing meditation can be done in bank lines, in the grocery store, or waiting at the Department of Motor Vehicles. Tapping into the roots of this tradition can change everyday life in the way we stand, walk, talk, eat, sleep, relate to others and make love.

Some Background on My Teachers

I was indeed fortunate when Sifu Ha brought Master Han Xingyuan to this country to study with us throughout two summers in 1976 and 1977. As I will discuss in greater detail in the first chapter, I learned that Master Han had been trained by one of the grandmasters of Standing Meditation, Wang Xiangzhai, who lived in Beijing in the early 1900's. He called his system the *Yi* (pronounced ee) *Chuan,* meaning the mind, or intentionality behind the various systems of Chuan.[2]

One of the things I learned from Master Han was concentration. I remember one day going to Golden Gate Park at five in the morning to "just stand." When a car accident happened nearby and people stopped their meditation and started talking, he ended the class. Though it seemed cruel to deprive us of a class after having driven so far, so early in the morning, I got a lesson in discipline and concentration. Han's Standing was an intense ordeal, like a trial by fire—or I should say, a trial by ice cold San Francisco air. Standing in the cold, for periods of up to an hour, was, at first, hard for me and the other students to bear. I remember one student who wore gloves and a hat. Master Han took them off. If this was a public school, he might have been fired, sued or accused of cruel and unusual punishment. But by going through the rigors of his training, I learned that through this "tough love" came a soft loving feeling that was to transform my cerebral stance in life.

I had always suffered from coldness in my hands and feet, and doing Standing Meditation in this freezing cold temperature didn't help. At first, my hands and feet became colder, but this coldness that had been so much a part of the constriction of my early years, began to change. By staying with the coldness and just experiencing it, the coldness gradually changed to smoothness—my skin felt like baby's skin. Red blotches appeared on my hands; and then my whole body became warm. I became initiated into a practice that is common in shamanic initiation traditions to cultivate "inner heat."[3] Now when the coldness comes, I have found a way to turn the coldness to warmth. We'll learn more about other aspects of the alchemical processes of change that can be a part of this tradition in the pages that follow.

In 1987, Sifu Ha brought another Standing Meditation teacher to the United States to train us. His name was Master Cai Songfang and he developed the school of Wuji Standing Meditation which is related to the Standing Like a Tree style of Qigong.[4] Master Cai was chosen in 1987 as the representative of Guangdong Province to the National Committee on Qigong Research. Though many of us who had studied with Sifu Ha for over a decade were proficient in using the ball of energy to neutralize and bounce off the aggressive force of others (*Fajing*)[5] as we played "Push Hands" together, working with Master Cai was a humbling experience for us all. I also watched teachers and students of other martial arts traditions test his skill, and bounce off of him, as if he were a ball. The amazing thing was that he was hardly doing anything; he was just standing there. From Master Cai, I learned about the power of stillness.

In the pages that follow we will explore various aspects of the Standing practices I have been doing now for about 30 years. Though I have studied with recognized Masters of various Standing Meditation traditions such as Masters Han Xingyuan, Fong Ha, Cai Songfang and Sam Tam for two decades, the exercises imparted here are not duplications of their teachings. From the two decades that I have been teaching Qigong and Standing Meditation, I have developed my own unique synthesis from my life experience, as does each practitioner.

For example, all of the above Masters say to just "be" with the natural breath. Although I also have found that this is the best place to start, I have added other forms of breathwork from a broader range of sources. Though the Yi Chuan has its roots in Buddhist meditation methods, I add techniques that come from both Taoist and Buddhist meditation, as well as techniques from my training in modern hypnotherapy. When I use these breathing methods, I honor the wisdom in my teachers' advice that breathing techniques be used as they arise out of natural breathing, and that they not be forced. Likewise, I use a method called "Finding the Circle that Arises out of Stillness" as both a healing and a spiritual practice. It stems from my work with Yi Chuan Master Han Xingyuan, though he never conceptualized it as a healing or spiritual practice—there were no words imparted from him regarding this dimension of it. In general, words were not used very much in my initiatory experience from the four teachers listed above, I "just stood."

THE HISTORICAL ROOTS OF STANDING MEDITATION

*We cannot recreate the original wilderness man.
But we can recover him because he exists in us.
He is the foundation in spirit or psyche on which we build,
and we are not complete until
we have recovered him.*

—Laurens Van der Post,
After time spent with the Kalahari Bushmen

A Mythic Journey: "Trance-forming" your Posture through Shape-Shifting

What if you took a monkey, removed him from the forest, and for many generations trained him in taking the shape of alien postures? Imagine, if you will, this monkey's ancestors sitting in ninety-degree angle chairs in their formative years in school and in their later work lives. Imagine these monkeys walking on flat pavement for thousands of generations. Then, imagine that you are this monkey and that one day, towards the end of your life, you take a class in tree climbing. You experience a new Self, awakening within you, and a sense of *re-memberance*—"re-membering" is putting back together split off "members" (parts of oneself) into an original wholeness. Your monkey pelvis opens; flexibility and multidirectional, angular movements emerge as your feet are placed at climbing angles that are in your long-lost body memory. Your arms, as they grasp the tree limbs, rediscover a long-lost functionality. Pelvic blockages loosen and latent muscularity develops from forgotten pathways. Postural and structural realignment takes place by moving in accordance with your essential nature. And, your whole Monkey Way of Being becomes revitalized as a primordial energy opens, and you return to who you are in your deepest essence.

Then imagine that you are a fish. As part of a scientific experiment your ancestors were taken out of water, and put into a laboratory where they adapted to survive in air for many generations. Your great grandparent fishes adapted and developed new lungs and ways of moving. After tens of thousands of generations even the stories that you were once a water creature had been relegated to the realm of mythology. Then one day you are put in the water—a Self-awakening happens, and a returning to some deep part of your Self occurs. A healing takes place as joints that were stiff discover a fluidity of movement. A sense of separateness that always felt alien dissolves. And, you melt into some awesome sense of Being that connects you to all things.

It is one thesis of this book that, not only are we monkeys and fish—as prenatal research of the phylogenetic development of humans proves; but we have the essential nature of all animals, and all life forms. And, when we return to Being and moving like them, a remembering, awakening and healing of our minds and bodies takes place as long-lost energy is activated.

Human Beings, in our deepest essences, are "shape-shifters." We are the elements of creation: fire, earth, metal, water and wood. We are empty space, as modern physics shows us. This book will show how we can change our life stances by becoming like a tree. We can move like a silk-worm reeling silk, and thereby transform our identities with a lightness of Being that can be as colorful as that of a butterfly. We can transform our linear bodies into the likeness of a ball of energy. And, if current research is accurate, when we shape-shift into the appropriate element for the occasion, and return to our primordial selves, natural health is restored and we live younger longer.

The Primordial Language of Posture

Postural stance is the original human alphabet. Through a stance, the human body takes the shape of a postural letter which communicates who we are at that moment. Our bodies change their character and become more erect as we "stand up" for our ideals. Our shoulders cave-in, our backs pull back and our eyes change shape as we "shrink back" in fear. Our hands go on our hips when we feel defiant. We touch our hearts when we are moved to compassion.

Creation itself is linked with forming thought and spiritual intention into words and letters. According to John in The Gospel, "In the beginning was the word and the word was God." According to the Kaballah, the world came into Being through the letters of the Hebrew alphabet.[1]

Human speech is, in its fullest expression, composed of both words and postural gestures. We become aligned with "the creator of life" when we incarnate the many-faceted spirit of life into form. When we make an intelligent point, energy manifests in our heart or head, and is directed outward as our finger points. When our anger surfaces, our faces flush with blood-red color and our hands form fists. Paradoxically, sometimes the deepest story is told when we say nothing and become still.

States of consciousness are expressed in postures; and just as an actor practices "stances" to enhance the expression of feeling, so does a Qigong practitioner practice his or her stance to maximize power, healing and the expression of intention. Both actors and Qigong practitioners know that anger may be less effective with out-of-control flailing hands than with a powerful stance. The intricacies of cultivating stances of power, healing and spiritual unfoldment have been matters of inquiry for Qigong practitioners over the last many thousands of years.

The Spiritual and Shamanic Roots of Posture

> *What is the work of works for man if not to establish in and by each one of us,*
> *an absolutely original centre in which the universe reflects itself*
> *in a unique and inimitable way?*
> *And those centres are our very Selves…"*

—Teilhard de Chardin

Ancient sacred wisdom traditions teach that the very purpose of human evolution is to become all things; and that this is one thing that makes human beings unique amongst the animals. In the Kaivalya Upanishads it says, "by seeing oneself in all beings and all beings in oneself, enlightenment is obtained." The Old Testament, according to the teachings of ancient rabbis, heralds the human being not as an anthropocentric creature superior to all creation, but as a creature comprised of all creation. "The creator addressed all that had been made in the sky and in the earth and said unto them, '…let us all join together in this final creature's creation, and make this Earth Being in our image.… All of you join in making its body, and I will join you in making its spirit.'" Thus, according to this teaching each of us contains the attributes and powers of all the creatures and elements of the earth, as well as qualities of the spirit of the Infinite One, Creator of Life.

In shamanic literature, postural forms are linked to becoming all things, animal and human. A story from the Pacific Northwest, tells it this way: [2]

> *A Native American fisherman paddles his kayak into an unknown bay. As he walks, exploring into this untouched new territory, he hears uproarious laughter and cautiously follows the sound until it leads him to the mouth of a cave. After carefully creeping through a great cavern, he sees, gathered around a great roaring fire, animals of all varieties, large and small, playing a game that makes them laugh from the depths of their different souls. The game is "shape-shifting" and they are embodying the postures of different forms, then changing into those forms. The fisherman is in awe as the animals turn into human form, and the human turns into animal forms.*

On one level, this mythical story brings us in touch with those times when humans and animals lived in harmony with the natural world. On another level, it tells the story of the cave of our everyday lives where we shape-shift from one state of consciousness to another fueled by the fire of our intention.

By assuming different postures we become the archetypal energy potentials inherent in life's aliveness; we transform one state of Being into another. Each posture speaks a language of becoming one of the forms of creation…of our creation…of the universe's creation.

When you are in fear, try imagining and assuming a cowering stance, tucking your head in like an ostrich. Then try imagining that you are standing up straight on your hind legs, with claws extended, like a powerful grizzly bear.

Shape-shifting from one stance to another breaks fixated life stances and activates the healing power of "the universe of possibilities." The primordial healing gift of being human is being a consciousness-shaping animal. When we do so, we return to "the mythical cave of human creation."

In Epidaurus in ancient Greece, at the oldest holistic healing center of the Western world from where Western medicine originates, shape-shifting into another identity was one of the essential elements of rituals to create healing. The Aesclepian Priest would advise the sick to go to the Dionysian theater. Instructions were given to play a particular part in a play, or to wear a mask so that a new energy would be activated in the Psyche of those in need of healing. These masks, or *personae*, are the root of our contemporary word "person." So, by assuming the face and adopting the stance of another person, or animal, a pathway to healing could emerge.[3]

Recent modern research into multiple personality disorder adds to our understanding of how the power of changing our life stance and state of consciousness affects health and healing. It was discovered that a multiple personality diabetic had one or more separate personalities that did not suffer from the disease.[4] Allergies present in one multiple personality were often not present in other ego states, for example, allergies to orange juice, and cats. Research by various doctors has shown that in different identity states extraordinary bodily changes take place in visual acuity, brain wave patterns and changes in slowing down the aging process. This has supported the belief by researchers that dissociative and altered states facilitate healing.[5]

Not just in multiple personality states, but in other states of consciousness as well, many health conditions are associated with "state-specific" states of consciousness. When shifting our consciousness, health conditions oftentimes disappear. For example, Milton Erikson, a famous hypnotherpaist, cured a woman from her orange juice allergy by age regressing her to the time of the negative association to orange juice. As the "state dependent memory hypothesis" and psycho-neuroimmunological research evolved it was shown that when we use the powers of the imagination, and enter into an altered state, we can create another reality in which disease, and general imbalances of body, mind and spirit can be healed.[6] For example it is now common knowledge that by activating the relaxation reponse and imagining we are someone, something or somewhere else that immune response is activated and healing oftentimes occurs. For example, for a taste of this experience, take a few slow natural breaths, imagine you are sitting in a beautiful spot in nature with your back against a tree overlooking a river, and feel the changes that come to your Self and body.

Regarding Qigong, embodying various postures and using appropriate visualizations evokes correlated specific states of consciousness; and the practice opens an age-old pathway which enables us to tap into the energy of our Primordial Selves. This has the potential for healing our imbalances.

The Anthropology of Standing Postures

The roots of the Standing Meditation Qigong postural practice grew from the time of the earliest humans. Hunters naturally discovered postures of stillness while stalking animals. In stillness they became one with their surroundings. What was felt and perceived inside, was the key to survival outside. From a Darwinian perspective, those who were best at keeping still and being aware of their surroundings had the best chance at survival.

But, in addition to early hunters assuming various postures as a practical survival method, postural stances were used by members of early hunter-gatherer societies, and particularly by *shamans* (the earliest "religious leaders" of the tribe) as a method to enter into a trance-state for the purposes of healing, divination, and metamorphosis.[7] These "spirit journeys are an inherent part of the religious practices of the gathering hunters," according to the tradition of "psychological archeology" of whom Dr. Felicitas Goodman is the best known representative.[4] Below we see a Deer Dancing posture:

Figure 3: Dancing Deer Posture

From Dr. Goodman's research, over fifty postures were gleaned from ethnography books, museum exhibits, etc. that provide a route to finding "a balance and harmony with the natural world, not just with animals, but with all life forms, including wind and thunder, rocks and insects."[8] Posture returns us to our primordial origins, and connects us to pre-technological sacred cosmologies.

The statues, totems and rock and cave paintings left to us from those times display a wide variety of uses of posture. The stance of the "Standing Bear Posture" is one of the most common; it arose almost simultaneously at many places in the world during the sixth to fifth millennium B.C. On the Greek Cycladic Islands alone, thirty-four examples were found.[9]

Figure 4: Standing Bear Posture

Other examples of body posturing for ritual purposes involved using various hand positions (known in the East as *mudras*) for healing and transformation. For example, statues of the Chiltan Spirit Posture depicted below show standing figures that have one hand on the heart and the other on the belly.[10] This posture has been found in Alaska, Arizona and Tennessee, on the Northwest coast of America, among the Olmecs in Central America, in Bolivia, as well as in Asia in the valleys of Uzbekistan.[11]

Figure 5: Chiltan Spirit Posture   *Figure 6: Chiltan Totem*

The tradition of Psychological Archeology has experimented with imitating various postures from these indigenous sources. At the Cuyamungu Institute near Santa Fe, New Mexico, when the students of Dr. Goodman explored these postures, they discovered that the postures induced various trance states.[12] Before I learned of her work, I explored the use of posture and hand movements with my patients at the Psychotherapy and Healing Center who suffer from a wide variety of psychological issues, including anxiety disorders, chronic pain, hypertension, insomnia, etc.[13] Without even knowing the anthropological tradition that I was following, for many years I had my patients touch their hearts and bellies, as in the Chiltan Spirit postures above, to practice self-soothing. In some sense, this book may be considered an exploration in the realm of what we might call "Psycho-spiritual Postural Anthropology."

From cave paintings and inscriptions on rocks, it is common knowledge that various stances were part of initiation rituals. These rituals have purposes about which we can only guess. Cave paintings of the bushman and other indigenous cultures show the use of posture as a path to metamorphosis of humans into various animals—perhaps to gain power for hunting, or perhaps for broader reasons. It has been hypothesized that particular angles are associated with different types of trance states. For example, the 32,000 year-old Venus of Galgenberg at the Cave of Lascuax in France (whose posture inclines 37 degrees—the same degree of incline as the great Pyramid) may be communicating postural angles at which particular trance states are induced, according to Dr. Goodman.[14]

Figure 7: Rock Painting, Cave of Lascaux showing figure at 37 degree angle.

Modern scientific research has made valid the notion that trance has healing effects. This is given substance by psychological and psycho-neuroimmuniligcal research.[15] From the "copper wall experiments," we know that electricity in the brain increases when healers go into "trance states."[16] Blood levels of stress-related hormones like cortisol, epinephrine, and norepinephrine initially rise, then drop dramatically, the blood pressure drops, and then the pulse rate increases—a rare combination of reactions that are usually associated with the preliminary stages of dying.[17] Standing Meditation traditions have been shown to normalize synchronization between left and right hemispheres of the brain.[18]

The Adena Pipe posture, shown in the picture below, represents the posture of a standing figure that's been formed into a smoking pipe, which would be smoked through a hole at the top of the statue's head. This statute was unearthed from a funeral mound belonging to the Adena Indians, the mound-builders who lived in central and southern Ohio 2000 years ago.[19]

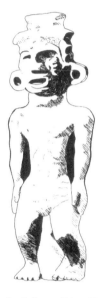

Figure 8: Adena Pipe Posture

It may not be too great a leap of the imagination to wonder whether this statue is a symbolic representation of the Adena Shamans' spiritual experience with the pipe. Perhaps the figure standing here represents the trance state that was activated as these Native Americans stood in this Standing posture and smoked the pipe which induced an altered state. Did they imagine the divine presence drawing them up to the heavens as they inhaled and "the spirit of the sky" filled them with divine energy as they exhaled? Though we may never know definitively whether the Adena Shamans actually imagined themselves being "smoked by the Gods," as this statue may represent, speculation turns into phenomenological metaphor in Psycho-spiritual Postural Anthropology when life is breathed into anthropological remnants.

Chinese Shamanism, Posture, Health and Longevity

In ancient China, animal postures were used to improve health and enhance longevity. Daoyin (guiding and pulling the Qi) practices were used by Pengzu, a long-lived sage who was called a master of fire, wind and rain, who, along with other shamans of that era, taught special dances to resolve congestion and stagnation of vital energy. Crane dances were used to expel evil demonic influences, which were thought to cause serious diseases. "Yin," in the term Daoyin in this context, meant "to pull close and expel" evil from the body. According to another legend, Yu the Great regulated the waters with a Bear dance.[20]

Scholarly evidence shows that the animal postures and movements were used by shamans in the Zhou dynasty (1028–221 B.C.). During a New Year's ritual known as the Great Exorcism (Da No), a shaman danced through the village followed by a procession of villagers wearing masks of the zodiacal animals in order to drive out pestilence and demons.[21]

Animal stances and movements were used by early Chinese doctors as part of disease treatment. In the King Ma tomb, (Mawangdui, 168 B.C.), in one of the coffins, a piece of silk, called the Daoyin Tu, was found which showed forty-four figures representing nearly all the major categories of modern Qigong, including breathing, stance and movement. Among the captions, under some of the figures are the names of animals including hawk, wolf, crane, dragon, cat and bear. The captions name specific medical disorders such as kidney disease, flatulence, painful knees, and anxiety, suggesting that by 168 B.C. specific exercises were used to treat specific illnesses.[22]

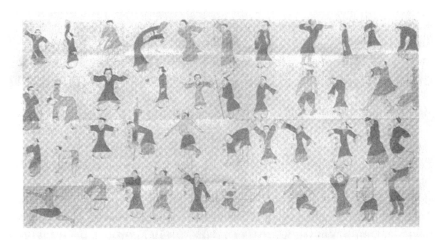

Figure 9: King Ma Tomb 168 B.C.—Daoyin Pictures for Specific Disorders

Hua Tuo (110 A.D.–207 A.D.) was the first Taoist physician who synthesized earlier Taoist methods into the *Five Animal Frolics*, which include bear, crane, monkey, tiger and deer. His system had clearly delineated methods—preventative and prescriptive—to treat the elements and functions of the organs.

In these days of early Chinese history it was said that by,

> *...spitting out the old breath and drawing in the new, practicing bear hangings and bird stretching...the man who so nourishes his body... may live to be as old as Pengzu, for more than eight hundred years.*

> —Zhuanngzi, Fourth Century B.C.

The Taoist Canon (Daozang) is a literary treasure reduced into a sixty volume set, compiled by nameless Taoist adepts who inscribed their wisdom regarding meditation, posture, visualization, and health and longevity practices. The material from the Daozang texts dates back to a variety of early Chinese dynasties, some texts dateback to the Han dynasty in the second century B.C. The Daozang provides a lens into ancient times when Taoist adepts practiced *daoyin* to tap into the natural movements of the Ways of nature in order to relax and cultivate vital energy—a juxtaposition to our modern lives where we tune into television to relax and get information we feel is vital. These texts give us a sense of the kind of knowledge that may have been lost in the destruction of the ancient Library of Alexandria in our Western world. Among the many texts is one called, "Formulas on Nourishing Life of the Highest Venerable Lord (Laojun Jue)," which includes the Five Animal Frolics as well as procedures for absorbing the Qi with the help of visualizations, methods for retaining the Qi, and methods for distributing Qi to the members and organs of the body.[23]

Among the early Chinese physicians who implied a link between Animal postures and healing was Pien Chhio; he is dated to the period between the 6th to 4th Century B.C. He was reported to have brought a crown prince out of a coma with an acupuncture needle. In the picture below, from a stone relief associated with Pien Chhio by scholars, he is shown as a bird-like figure treating a patient with a needle and holding the patient's pulse.[24] The ornitho-android figure suggests the hypothesis that the origins of acupuncture and the Chinese meridian system may both lie in the movements of the earlier shamanic masters of the animal Daoyin practices. Did these practitioners who led and guided the Qi find the acupuncture channels through their stances and movements thereby healing themselves and their fellow human beings? It is difficult to determine which came first Qigong or Aupuncture; but in depictions like in the one below, and in the close-up in the Crane Animal Frolic section later in this book, we can see there seems to be a correlation between acupuncture and the healing ways of animals and birds.

Figure 10: Ornitho-Android Figure Treating a Kneeling Patient with other patients queuing up to be treated.

When you read and then practice the Animal Movement section of this book, you may discover how the animal postures and movements help with your Self-healing and the healing of others. Perhaps you will join the lineage of cross-cultural shamanic healers, from the *gandarvas*, human-headed avian inhabitants of the Indian Vedas who were supposed to be good physicians, and the Chinese physicians like Hua Tuo and Pien Chhio. For example, when you practice Hua Tuo's Crane movement, called Crane Soaring, or his Bear Pouncing posture, notice whether you experience healing for your heart (love, joy, etc.) and liver (anger, toxicity, etc.) issues.

Hindu and Buddhist Roots of Standing Meditation

By the time of the Buddha, the shamanic practices of early humans had evolved into holistic kinetic practices involving body, mind and spirit. The Buddha (Shakyamuni) was born around 623 B.C. into the *Ksatreya,* or warrior class, which was an elite force of noble-born warriors who studied literature, history, religion, esoterica and philosophy, as well as a wide variety of martial arts.[25] These were not street ruffians, but warriors in the spiritual sense. These "Bodhisatva Warriors" were like Western "Knights of the Round Table" who adhered to a strict code of ethics.

Figure 11: Shiva Nataraja—Deity of Martial Arts and Forms Making Circular Movements

According to the research of Shifu Nagaboshi Tomio, a fundamental part of the practices into which the Buddha was initiated involved *Nataraja* practices whereby the initiate awakened wisdom through mental and physical concentration.[26] The term *Nataraja* comes from Shiva Nataraj, whose dance has a threefold purpose according to classical Hindu scholarship: to replicate the rhythmic play of movement of the Cosmos, to release the souls of men from the state of illusion, and to activate the Centre of the Universe within the heart. In addition, classical scholarship says that the fire around dancing Shiva Nataraj symbolizes burning away the ego, purification and overcoming those personal characteristics that could end the cycle of rebirth.[27] The Hindu God Shiva predated the Buddha by many years; early references to Shiva go back to approximately 2000 B.C. The student of Tai Chi will notice the similarity between the "double butterfly kick" of Tai Chi Chaun, and the dancing Shiva Nataraj, underlining the hypothesis that there has been a long-standing historical tradition that links static posture and circular movement with multifaceted transformational purposes.

The term *nata,* at the root of dancing Shiva Nataraja's name, refers to sequences of attack and defense. They were practiced by the Ksatreya. When he was seven years old, various Nata Masters, including the famous Kshantideva, instructed Shakyamuni Buddha in nata fundamentals of the physical arts, including stances and movements of the animals, Ksatreya fighting and healing sounds, and techniques for grappling, gymnastics and weaponry.[28] At the core of these practices was the method of *Vajramukti,* or thunderbolt hands (*vajra* meaning thunderbolt, *mukti* meaning spiritual liberation.[29] Myths of the Buddha's childhood, told in the *Lalitavistara,* say that he was able to discharge an elephant with such power that the depression made by its falling body was named *Hastatigarta* (elephant ditch), and was used afterward as a water channel.[30] Another legend tells of the Buddha firing arrows with such power that one of them hit a rock and opened an artesian spring. Whether such stories are literally true, or are metaphors to excite the initiate's imagination to cultivate the powers stemming from the practices, is not the most important point. We do know that these highly secret, bodymind practices into which the Buddha was initiated were used not only for self-defense, but for health purposes and also to practice the self-control befitting of the royal class.[31]

The traditions of the *Chuan Fa,* for example, involved not only the closed hand (Chuan), but all of the arts (Fa) associated with them. The purposes of the *Vajramukti* and Chuan Fa traditions involved a totality of body, mind and spiritual practices. Giving health (*Agadakayasiksa*) was fundamental to practicing these exercises.[32] The totality of the student's life stance and unconscious mental patterns (*sthana*) were also a focus of the training. One area of attention was addressing the *klesas,* the mental obstructions that are part of the initiate's process of self-transformation—such as greed, ill will, delusion, conceit, fearfulness and restlessness.

Practices such as these contained kinetic keys to open the elemental doors to consciousness. They rest on the assumption that the "Self" is projected into the physical being of the body where the elements of life and consciousness (fire, earth, metal, water and wood) manifest in embodied metaphors. Chuan Fa practices had the advantage over other spiritual practices, in that the teacher could test the psychophysical development of the student in concrete ways. For example, picture a student of today saying, "I feel clear and centered after that spiritual, inspirational lecture." Chaun Fa practice removes the intellectual façade of thinking that our mind is clear and our body is centered, because the issues potentially inhibiting the acolyte's psycho-spiritual progress would be felt in the body, and could be tested by practices such as Pushing Hands, called *shili.*[33] When the teacher pushes on us, do we fight back or do we yield? When pushed on by the forces of life, do we become rigid or do we roll with the life force? According to many of the most advanced practitioners, Standing Meditation is the key to developing proficiency in these arts.[34]

According to the research of Shifu Nagboshi Tomio,[35] the tradition of Chuan Fa was holistic, and originally incorporated all of the following: work on characterological fixations, self-awareness training, auto-physiotherapeutic healing, balancing the five elements, reviving the dead, teaching the aggressor through circular forms of defense, circumventing the ego's power for self-deceit and work on the totality of the mind-body stance (*sthana*).

Figure 12: Master Cai teaching Fajing— Note the discharge of force uprooting the second student's front foot, and the blurring of the students, showing they are moving while Master Cai is still.

Figure 13: Master Cai using Fajing, discharging the author.

When we hear stories of the Buddha throwing an elephant, our Western skepticism becomes active. Though the tradition of *Yi Chuan* Standing Meditation is known to help cultivate the ability to issue *Fajing*, which involves circling back an attacker's force and bouncing them away, doing this with an elephant seems a farfetched leap of the imagination. From the viewpoint of the wider psycho-spiritual purpose of the Chaun Fa tradition, the throwing of the elephant is a metaphor for transforming the base aspect of one's psyche into something lighter. In Western alchemy, this is called *sublimatio*. The metaphor of the arrow opening a well symbolizes the opening of the well of vital energy through the clearly directed use of intention. In this sense, the metaphor speaks to the alchemical process that is part of the Western mystery tradition whereby the initiate transforms lead into gold, i.e. takes the base elements of our Selves and transforms them into lighter ones. Thus the story is similar to the teaching stories of the Greek mysteries where the mythical hero, Thesues, defeats the Minotaur, who represents the bullheaded aspects of ourselves that are in need of transformation.[36] All this said, we must not forget that within the training of the Buddhist and Taoist kinetic arts, the balance between the martial, health and spiritual dimensions are all seen to be part of an integral whole.

The Static Chuan Fa Tradition

One of the deepest-kept secrets in these bodily "movement" traditions was the important practice of static postures. We see these translated in Sitting or Standing postures involving *mudras*, or divine gestures of the hands; one example is holding the hands clasped in front of the heart. These postures were passed on from the time of the Buddha and are known to have existed in the Tien T'ai school called *Za* (meaning static) in around 550 A.D.[37]

Some of these practices came to be known as *dissolving practices*, or in the terms of *The Srimalasimhanada Sutra*, "exchanging your body for the body of the Buddha." Each part of the body was a vehicle for the transformation of the human spirit. In the *Avadana Sataka*, referring to the Buddha it said that, "the sky and the palm of his hand are the same in his mind." These quotes allude to the state of consciousness that is cultivated from the practice of doing "no-thing." The body becomes a vehicle for transforming into all of the elements of creation.

I have put forth the opinion elsewhere [38] that the esoteric meaning of Chuan (fist) may mean the ability to grasp and hold, without clenching, the power of the five elements (fire, earth, metal water and wood). *Fire* may symbolize and be associated with general energy (Qi), *earth* with the ability to stay grounded when a force presses against you, *metal* with the ability to cut through and penetrate with intention, *water* with the ability to yield and *wood* with the ability to move into another's space while maintaining one's central equilibrium. Working with a teacher in circular forms of movement is a way to help assist the initiate in the process of character transformation of the *klesas*, and test the initiate's ability to embody the lessons of the different elements.

There is a danger in static practices that the first Chinese Buddhist patriarch Bodhidharma, also know as Ta Mo, knew well. When he came to China in around 520 A.D. and saw the monks' bodies atrophying from long periods of static Sitting practice, he set out to find a solution. According to the myth, nine years after retreating to a cave, he came out and taught various *Vajramukti* practices to the Shaolin monks that emphasized both body and mind.[39] He taught the Mahayana (Great Vehicle) Buddhist emphasis on the balanced practice of mind and body, Stillness Meditation (*Jing Gong*) and Movement Meditation (*Dong Jing*).[40] In this sense, the practices in this book are part of a wider sphere of Qigong practices that emphasize dynamic stillness, and stillness in movement. In the classics, it is said that, "the stillness that you think is stillness is not true stillness;

only when you find the stillness in movement and the movement in stillness is enlightenment found."

Through the upright Standing posture, we lift ourselves up from the world of nature, with the mind raised straight above the feet. Thus, our Standing Posture makes on the vertical plane, a connecting rod linking heaven and earth; and, on the horizontal plane we stand for a gathering place for all of the elements of creation. We become aware of our true nature by doing "no-thing," just being aware of what is under our feet, above our heads and in our bodies.

Destruction through Dispersion: The Diaspora of the Chuan Fa

The *nata* practices continued until the time of the Muslim invasions during the Pala Dynasty around 750 A.D. As a result of the invasions, the tradition dispersed and many of its teachers were slain.[41] The subsequent slaughter of Buddhist monks caused many to flee to Southern India, China and elsewhere. Though remnants of the forms remain today in such places as Dravidian folk dance, for the most part, the psycho-spiritual and martial aspects of the Chuan Fa were separated into disparate forms and were lost as an initiatory, holistic, bodymind transformational system.

Author's Lineage

The particular lineage that I was trained in for the last twenty-five years came from Wang Xiangzhai. He was born in 1885 and was sickly in his youth, suffering from asthma and stunted growth. When he was eight years old, his father made him study Xing Yiquan, which emphasizes static and moving postures embodying the healing powers of the five elements. He then traveled around China studying with some of the best martial artists in the country. Not only did he heal his body, but he became one of the best martial artists of China.

Figure 14: Wang Xiangzhai Standing—Holding Ball of Energy

Wang Xiangzhai said that his skill came from "just standing." His method is called the *Yi Chuan*, the mind or intention behind the various systems of Chuan.[42] One of Wang Xiangzhai's main influences came from Huang Muqiao, who learned a certain "health dance" that descended from the time of the Sui and Tang dynasties (581–907 C.E.). This health dance was depicted on wall pictures at the archeological site of Dunhuang. Huang reconstructed the techniques and recovered the spirit of the ancient dance. So we may imagine that Wang Xiangzhai was initiated into some of the deepest methods that descended from the Buddhist Chuan Fa traditions. Wang Xiangzhai wrote that Bodhidharma combined the Five Animal Frolics, created in the Han Dynasty (206 B.C.– 220 C.E.) by Hua Tuo, the "first Chinese doctor," with the methods for changing the ligaments (*yi jin jing*) and washing the bone marrow (*Shi Soei Chin*) to create the system of Yi Chuan (also spelled Yi Quan), mind or intention boxing.[43]

Figure 15: Master Fong Ha

As mentioned in the Overview to this section, I learned the Yi Chuan originally in 1976 and in 1977 from my Sifu, Master Fong Ha. He learned it from Master Han Xingyuan, a descendent of the lineage of Grandmaster Wang Xiangzhai—neither of them overtly discussed the healing, psychological or spiritual dimensions of the practice. After ten years of practicing Yi Chuan, I was introduced in 1987 to the tradition of Wuji Standing Meditation from Master Cai Songfeng. The essence of the spirituality of the tradition was there in name, since Wuji means the undifferentiated, the mother of Qi, and the void prior to movement.[44] But the wider idea of healing and psycho-spiritual unfoldment was not specifically discussed by either of these teachers, nor was it discussed by other Standing Meditation Masters with whom I have studied including Masters Fong Ha and Sam Tam.

Figure 16: Master Sam Tam

Lying beneath my teachers' silence, beneath the stance of Standing, were the roots of an age-old holistic transformative tradition. In this sense, the tradition is more like Zen Buddhism, where the teacher opens the door to possibility by "not talking about it" but manifesting "it" through nonverbal means. There is something useful about this "non-talking about it" that I have received in studying with my teachers for many years. As a scholar, too much thinking about it in my early years may have taken away from the act of cultivating Qi. But now, after over two decades of Standing, I want to share the broader range of my experience and bring forth the case that remembering the wider ancestral roots of the tradition of Chuan Fa can also be important. *Re-membering* means to put back disintegrated members of something "dis-membered." It is my hope that this book will bring to practitioners of this art, a way to hold in their hands, this wider sphere of intentionality while Standing.

In the modern world of martial arts, even in so-called internal schools,[45] the psycho-spiritual aspects of the tradition, the healing elements of the tradition and the intent of cultivating the Qi, "to dissolve into the body of the Buddha," are rarely discussed in their totality. We often hear arguments from practitioners of Tai Chi (one of the best-known systems of Qigong) that it is only a martial art and there is no historical proof of its spiritual or healing roots. And yet at the beginning of the Tai Chi set, the discerning student will see that the first movement is a Standing Meditation of "doing nothing." This Standing practice was known by some of the greatest practitioners of Tai Chi, such as Yang Lu Chan and Yang Cheng Fu, to be one of the deeply guarded secrets of the art. But even here, the significance of the secret is seen to be in developing great martial abilities, not, to my knowledge, to develop the whole Self in the sense of our historical perspective regarding the Chuan Fa associated arts.

Likewise in the other popular sources on Standing Meditation the whole tradition of the *Chuan Fa* is not addressed. Some sources address the martial arts dimension, others incorporate aspects of the spiritual or healing traditions; however, none of them address the holistic use of the art as a practice for health, longevity, spiritual unfoldment, self-defense and alchemically transforming the practitioner's personality.

Plato's Loss: Western Traditions of Stillness and Postural Initiation

The theme of the loss of the importance of postures of stillness in activating altered states is a long forgotten part of the Western esoteric tradition. The Western scholar, Peter Kingsley, argues that the tradition from which Plato derived used such methods as an essential part of their initiatory methods. According to Kingsley, the founding hero of Plato's tradition was Paramenides, who stemmed from a tradition of healers (*Oulios*) who were Masters of Stillness, and Masters of Altered States (*Iatromantis*). Parmenides gives credit to his lineage forebearer, Ameinias, for "leading him to stillness" (*hesychia*); and built a shrine to him in appreciation. This was because Paramenides recognized that stillness was an essential "method for coming as close as possible to the divine world." Epimenides, an initiate of this tradition, was said to have slept in a cave in Crete for years, and used "rituals demanding patience, involving watching animals and following them in their movements." He was called to Athens to heal people from a plague.

But Plato, though deriving from this tradition, is mostly remembered as a purveyor of truth and reason in Western Philosophy. As in the East, lineages of knowledge have been disconnected from their deeper roots in a wider tradition of healing. The Greek God who represented this tradition, Apollo, was changed into a solar God of reason contrasted with Dionysian ecstasy. Kingsley argues that Apollo was a god of both lightness (the sun) and darkness (the underworld journey of incubation), representing the mastery of states of awareness and of silence, not merely a god of reason as he has been portrayed. He was a god of healing (*Apollo Oulios*) whose initiatory tradition involved "recipes for immortality," among which involved snakes, travelling in the path of the sun, music, cave incubation, and making sounds like a snake hissing. (When I led two trips to the ancient healing sites of Greece, my students reported the Delphic Cave of Apollo was their favorite place to practice Qigong.) Apollo's son, or lineage descendent, Aesclepius is the founding father of the Western Hippocratic medical tradition. So in the West, as in the East, traditions of stillness and postural initiation and incubation were a fundamental part of the root system of healing; and in the West, as in the East, humanity has become disconnected from these vital roots.[46]

In summary, I am reminded of an old Jewish story:

> *Once there was a great Rabbi. When his congregation was ill and suffering, he would take the secret Book of Prayers and go out to a special place in the woods. There, he would sing a special prayer of healing while rocking back and forth in special ways. The people were healed. In the next generation, his lineage holder did not have the book because it was destroyed, but he still knew the prayer, the movements and the sacred spot in the woods. He was able to heal the people thereby. In the following generation, the place in the woods was destroyed through fire, but the next Rabbi could still heal the people with the prayers and movements. Today, the prayers and the movements are lost, but the story of the old ways, and the "re-membrance" it evokes, may still be enough to heal the people.*

STANDING MEDITATION:
The Million Dollar Secret of Ancient Sacred Wisdom Traditions

If I had to choose one Qigong technique to practice, it would undoubtedly be this one. Many Chinese call Standing Meditation "the million dollar secret of Qigong." Whether you are practicing Qigong for self-healing, for building healing Qi, for massage or healing work on others, Standing is an essential practice. Acupuncturists feel that by practicing Standing Meditation they can connect with the Qi of the universe, and be able to send it through their bodies when they hold the acupuncture needle ... Standing is probably the single most important Qigong exercise. One of the reasons that Standing is such a powerful way to gather and accumulate fresh Qi in the body is that during the practice of Standing the body is in the optimal posture for Qi gathering and flow.

—Ken Cohen
The Way of Qigong

Cross-Cultural Perspectives on Standing

Standing: A Buddhist Path to Enlightenment

The Buddha said that there were four noble postures through which one could discover enlightenment: Lying, Sitting, Standing and Walking. When the idea of enlightenment was translated to the West, what was originally a felt experience became a concept. *Enlightenment,* in its primordial meaning, was an experience of light and energy in the human organism that came as a natural gift to those who had found the Way to simply and fully *be* with their Selves.

Many know about Sitting Meditation (Zazen, Vipassana, etc.) and Lying Down Meditation (such as practiced in Yoga); but the practice of Standing is less known as a base for cultivating the human spirit and the light that mystics say is to be found within the human being.

The Lost Golden Ball of Western Fairy Tales: Is Standing Meditation Qigong a Path to Discovering the Lost Golden Ball of Energy?

In the famous fairy tale, *Iron Hans*, written by the Grimm's Brothers and popularized by Robert Bly in his best-selling book, *Iron John*, the King's son loses his golden ball when it rolls into the cage of the wild man. The loss of the golden ball became a symbol in the men's movement of the 1990's for the Western man's loss of connection with his instincts due to a variety of factors including: a lack of male initiation rituals, being overly civilized and overly feminized, and living in an industrialized society where the father was not present. In the tale, the King's son got back the golden ball when he gave the wild man the key to his cage, which led to the King's son leaving the castle and being initiated by the wild man. As one part of the his initiation, he dipped his finger and hair into the wild man's pond and they turned to gold.

In the Grimm's Brothers' tale of the *Frog Princess*, the golden ball is lost in a well.[1] Many women today may also feel a disconnection with their instincts due to such factors as media-driven portrayals of beauty, wearing high heel shoes, which disconnect women from their sense of groundedness in the earth, and moving according to mechanized, rather than natural, rhythms.

What is this "Golden Ball" that is spoken of in mythic and esoteric traditions? It is well-known that many secret practices and traditions were hidden in the form of myths, images and fairy tales.[2] Robert Bly interprets the lost golden ball as the unity of personality that we had as children, a kind of radiance or wholeness, before we split into male and female, rich and poor, bad and good.

In the following chapters, we will be putting forth the viewpoint that not only can a deeper wholeness be found by following the Golden Ball into the Western forests, with the Western wild man, but that a transformative initiatory process can also be found by leaving our familiar Western ways and following the rolling ball to the East. This book will take you on an odyssey exploring specifically how the Golden Ball can be found through the cultivation methods of Eastern Standing and Moving Meditation Qigong traditions. Hopefully, by following the practices suggested, the King's son in you will experience how Standing and Moving Meditation Qigong are keys that open the cage in the King's court where the Golden Ball of energy lies locked away. As you dip your bodymind into the Eastern pond of these practices, perhaps you will experience a Golden glow as the King's son did when his finger and hair turned to gold.

For a woman, the Frog Princess metaphor might work better; hopefully you will find some new ways to retrieve the Golden Ball that has been lost in the well of your Being. Whether you journey to a distant forest or a deep well, the willingness to explore unfamiliar territory leads to transformative possibilities.

The Taoist Practice of Cultivating the Golden Ball

The Golden Ball as a vital concept in the East was first introduced to the West by the Chinese scholar Richard Wilhelm. After extensive research in rare Taoist texts such as the *Book of the Yellow Castle,* he discovered ancient practices for "cultivating golden light in the body." In his book, *The Secret of the Golden Flower,* with an introduction by psychologist Carl Jung, he revealed to Westerners these practices, associated with finding the "Elixer of Life." He synopsizes these secret methods of Taoist Alchemy with the term "Golden Flower (*Chin-tan*)"—in Chinese, *Chin-tan,* literally translates as "Golden Ball" or Golden pill.[3]

Tai Chi Chuan is one method of embodying Taoist philosophy, and a practice to cultivate Qi, the vital energy of life. It is the best-known system of Qigong. Anyone who takes an introductory course in Tai Chi will learn that a central aim of the practice is to learn to move like a ball, hold postures like a ball, and change the contours of the body into being rounded like a ball, rather than being stiffly linear. These practices are meant to transform the body from a straight, rigid or broken line into a radiating ball of energy. Later in this book we will explore how an advanced practice of Tai Chi and Yi Chuan Standing Meditation Qigong is to "become a ball," so that when someone pushes on you, they bounce off of your sphere and may even spring up into the air (Fajing.)

In esoteric training traditions, before beginning the movements of Tai Chi Chuan, a person first practices *Standing Meditation.* Beginning in stillness embodies the classic Taoist notion that energy comes from the void, or the mother of Qi, called *Wuji,* and that the movement of opposites, like yin and yang, are born from non-movement. It also reflects the central notion of cross-cultural healing traditions that "healing derives from returning to the origin of things."[4]

Yang Lu Chan and Yang Cheng Fu, the founders of the Yang style of Tai Chi Chuan, kept the Standing Meditation practice a carefully guarded secret—though the discerning student will realize that the Tai Chi set begins with the standing still posture and ends with it. Only on rare occasions was the secret practice of Wuji Standing Meditation shared with outsiders. One person who learned it from Yang Cheng Fu in the late 1920's in Shanghai, was Mr. Ye Dami. Mr. Dami, in turn, transmitted the knowledge to Master Cai Songfang in the 1950's. I shall have more to say about Master Cai in the following pages.[5]

What is Standing Meditation?
Standing as a Method of Qigong: Cross-Cultural Dimensions

Standing Meditation is a form of meditation, a system of Qigong, and a way to cultivate Qi. Not only in China, but throughout the world, indigenous peoples have appreciated energy as a sacred and fundamental part of life and of healing. It was called by many names.

In Japan this energy is called *Ki,* and we see the powerful effects of its use in the art of Aikido. In India it is called *Prana,* and in ancient Tibetan Vinaya texts of

Budd-hism, *Kum Nye* is used to cultivate it.[6] In ancient Greece, it was called *archaeus*, the vital life force. In Judiasm it is called *Chai* or *Ruach,* and in Kabbalah it is called *Chiyyut.*

The Kung tribesmen of the Kalahari call this healing energy *Num,* and say it was given to them by the Gods. They use this energy to heal their spouses and their community through dance and massage. Being a healer is part of normal socialization, not the function of a special class. One central event in this regard is the all-night healing dance that takes place approximately once a week and activates *Num.* "Num resides in the belly and is activated through trance dancing and the heat of the fire. It ascends or boils up the spinal column and into the head, at which time it can be used to pull out the sickness afflicting others." The rock paintings of their ancestors show that this dance has origins that go back far into their culture's past.[7]

Among Native Americans, the activation of energy is an intrinsic part of healing. A common ritual used by various tribes treats the person who falls ill by calling on *Wakantanka* (the Great Mystery) and the energies of the four directions to restore the person to harmony with the forces of nature. In sweat lodges, the medicine person leading the sweat often sprays or throws water into the face of the person doing the sweat to produce a mild shock, thereby raising the level of emotion.[8] According to Ken Cohen, author of *The Way of Qigong,* writing in *Bridges Magazine,* "The Seneca medicine man, Moses Shongo, would hold one hand up, fingers pointed toward the sky, and imagine that healing power was flowing directly from the Creator's 'Light of Love.' He simultaneously used the other hand to heal, sometimes with light touch, sometimes without touch … Keetoowah Christie, great grandson of the famed Cherokee warrior Ned Christie…warms the hands over a ceremonial fire and then, while praying, circling his palms on or over a diseased area. Clockwise circling is used to add energy, to fill depleted areas. Counterclockwise circling is used to remove congestion, fever, infection and inflammation…. The renowned Blackfoot Holy Man, Eagle Plume, healed his son's knee injury by pushing dried rose thorns into his son's leg… and then burned them right down to the bottom." This is similar to what the Chinese acupuncturist's do when heating the needle by burning moxa (mugwort). When Medicine Man Rolling Thunder was asked by Ken Cohen, recognized master of the Taoist arts, about acupuncture points, he responded incredulously, "You mean the Chinese know about that? That's Cherokee Medicine! "[9]

I had the honor of introducing and teaching Yi Chaun Standing Meditation to my colleague and brother on the path, Ken Cohen. From the quote at the beginning of this chapter, we see that he places great importance on Standing Meditation amongst the many systems of *Qigong* he has learned. He describes it as "the million dollar secret of Qigong."

Standing: Mysteries and Realities of the Posture

The Standing position expresses the culmination of the human posture's evolution from lying to sitting, and finally to its full upright stance. This posture also expresses humanity's evolution from the animal kingdom. Unlike four-legged animals whose anatomy protects the vulnerable underpart of their bodies, we raise our head upward and expose our hearts to our fellow humans, and to the world. The question is, can we really embody the gift of this posture, and find "the heart of standing?"

The gifts that emerge from Standing Meditation are multifaceted. They come from tapping into the vital energy of our most human posture. As we learn to cultivate this energy and the consciousness that derives therefrom, our stance in life may become transformed on physical, emotional, mental and spiritual levels. But the best starting point is to let go of seeking any purpose, and to let the posture initiate us in its own way.

If we can relax and "just be" in the posture doing "no-thing," we have a chance to experience the mudra (divine gesture) that is expressed through "just standing." When we say "stand and do "no-thing," we do not literally mean "do nothing." What we want is to transform the stance of "trying to do" something into letting go and simply Being. In that Being, we experience the magic and sacredness of our human posture. When we do "things," life can become an effortful, reified state of being. Postures lose their mystery—we've stood so many times before, and we do it again, getting up and going through the same, meaningless act. Standing Meditation gives us a practice to remember our stance in the lightness of Being.

Standing upright on our feet is a remarkable feat. Remember when we were small children and didn't take standing for granted; we felt appreciation and even awe in not falling down. Though we may not have had the words to express it, we knew balance was an evolutionary event that expressed the uniquely human gymnastic of bringing right and left, yin and yang, into balance in our upright posture. Nowadays when we practice Standing, we similarly seek to become like children again and appreciate the balancing act of standing. Here we have a practice to find the stance of such appreciation.

As adults we have learned to live in a world where spiritual and material, heaven and earth are separate. But when we practice Standing Meditation, we have an opportunity to unite opposites. Here is a practice that may lead to the end of this separation between our earthly and our spiritual Selves. Our two feet speak symbolically of that balance that can be found in the center of seemingly disparate realms—right and left, spiritual and material, yin and yang. We may become aware of how our spines, and our Selves, are a link connecting heaven and earth. Here we have a practice to find the stance of such balance.

On the path to a spiritual state of balance, we first experience "what is." When we stand still, we discover the truth of where we are in this moment. The felt experience of our bodies calls us to notice our embodied truth. Maybe we are held up off the ground in anxiety. Maybe we become mindful of the gripping sensation in our stomachs which lets us know that we are frozen in fear. Perhaps we become aware of how our bodies hold on to the things we need to accomplish in a day. Many of us clutch onto images of the identities we want to be, and judge ourselves for not being there yet. In Standing we may experience how our hearts constrict when we don't embrace our vulnerabilities.

While Standing, we become mindful of our tensions; we feel how we carry the events of the day in our bodies. When we haven't stood up for ourselves on a given day, this may be held in the body in a variety of ways. We may experience a sense of collapse in our chest area, or perhaps a pent-up anger manifesting as a feeling of overcharge in the body—like a river pent-up against a dam. Or maybe it feels like a sense of disconnection from the ground that is associated with an energetic break, and discomfort in the lower back (Ming Men—known as the Gate of Life Energy, below the second lumbar vertebra), or an overall feeling of being "held back."

Our Standing practice helps us to get in touch with our "felt experience" at a given moment.[10] While we are Standing we may become aware that this pattern of not standing up for ourselves relates to a sense of not being at home in the world—that we will be rejected if we speak up. We may become aware of how this pattern has dissociated us from our bodies, and disconnected us from life and the peace that comes from being connected to the energy of the universe. Once we can experience where we are, Standing, like many other forms of meditation, may lead to a path of letting go of whatever we are holding. The gateway to Self-transformation is found through having the courage to stand where we are.

In Sections II and III of this book, we will see how specific practices of Bodymind Healing Qigong, in conjunction with our inner work, can help us find our real Selves regarding such issues. In Holding the Golden Ball of the Heart, the reversal of collapsed energy in the chest can take place. In Yi Chuan and Wuji Standing Meditation a connection to the ground is restored; and a filling out of the lower back (Ming Men) may take place, opening the "Gate to Life's Energy."

Standing Meditation is a pathway to transform our habitual life stances, and who we identify ourselves as being. The energy that is activated through Standing helps us to transform the ego-bounded skin that separates us from our environment and from others. In addition to changing personal patterns, a transpersonal transformation my take place. The word *transpersonal* is here defined as opening our personal experience to discover the experiential link with the wider whole of which we are a part.

The word "transpersonal" is given currency by the current field of Transpersonal Psychology. This is often called "the fourth force of psychology," along with the Cognitive/Behavioral, Freudian and Humanistic/Existential. The Transpersonal Psychology field believes that by drawing on ancient sacred wisdom traditions and combining them with modern psychology that a more integrative and healing psychology can be formed.[11]

We may find a place where who we are is more than our everyday roles. Maybe while we are Standing there, we will discover the sensation of letting go and opening ourselves to the energies of the cosmos that can fill us with relaxed vitality. Every exhalation gives us a chance to let go of the physical container that we identify as ourselves, and to "dissolve" it. Our joints eventually loosen…space opens. It is as if we let go of our identification with being separate droplets of water and return to the ocean of Being that we are.

Some believe that this is the experience into which we are initiated at the moment of death, i.e., we let go of our separate existence and become one with the energy of the cosmos. When we feel tension arising in our bodies while Standing, we can begin our practice of letting go of tension and melting into a oneness with all that is—an experience we may all face in the final hours of our lives. Various meditation traditions, including Standing, seek to find peace in letting go of the separate Self during life, and use meditation as a vehicle to take us to this place. Here we have a practice to find this stance of "no stance."

In Standing Meditation, we let go of our control of the universe, and find universal energy as we melt into our original nature in luminous emptiness—nothing special, just standing there. We reverse the messages that may have been told to us by our elders that began the constriction—"Don't just stand there, do something." After practicing Standing for some time, we might change this message to "Don't just do something, stand there." After all, if we are a microcosm of the universe, and the light of the universe was born from the void in a big bang or a gentle glow of light, then perhaps we can give birth to a universe of light by emptying ourselves and returning to the stillness from which we were born. The field of quantum physics now gives theoretical ground and scientific evidence to support the belief of ancient sacred wisdom traditions that human beings are frozen light.[12]

Comparison Between Sitting, Yoga and Standing Meditation

Many people are familiar with Sitting Meditation. As every tradition has its own unique gifts, Standing Meditation has its own treasures, some of which are different from those of Sitting Meditation.

First, there are obvious distinctions between the Standing posture, Lying down and Sitting. Each is a different postural statement and energetic expression. From Lying, to Sitting, and up to Standing, our heads take another step in the long journey of evolution to reach for the heavens. The elongated human being is stretched and opened upwards to the fullest. In Standing, we are closer to the light of the sun than in any other posture. Can we go beyond this verbal and conceptual distinction, experience this blessing of Standing and find a consciousness that is closer to the light?[13]

Secondly, and most to the point, Standing Qigong is specifically oriented to cultivating Qi (the healing energy of life). In Standing, the body is in the optimal posture for Qi gathering and Qi flow. In Sitting Meditation, the legs are usually crossed under the practitioner in a half or full lotus pose; in Standing, the feet are straight on the ground. Having the feet uncrossed creates less of a blockage in the vital energy of the body. Energy can arise from the ground and connect with the sky without encumbrance. The Bubbling Well points at the bottom of the feet (Kidney 1) are on the ground, allowing the Qi of the earth to more easily be drawn into the body on the inhalation. With the weight of the whole body over these points, they are activated to either draw up healing energy from the ground, or to let go of stress and return it to the earth, depending upon our intention. In the Standing Meditation Qigong tradition, we focus our awareness on this intention, which becomes infused by the energy that emerges as a result of the practice.

The postural statement of Standing, compared to Sitting, is that in Standing, the pelvis—the seat of the life energy—is free to move. By unbridling the pelvis, the energy of the whole body is more easily activated. In later chapters, the reader will begin to see how, in the *Yi Chuan* tradition, Standing still is the beginning of a sophisticated system of fixed postures and powerful movements for opening the pelvic (Tan Tien and Ming Men) energy centers of the body. [14]

Obviously, all forms of meditation—Standing, Sitting and Lying down—lead us on the path to finding the glowing golden energy that radiates from the bodymind that is in alignment with the earth and the heavens. Of course, Standing Meditation, as a tradition, doesn't necessarily take us closer to being in an "enlightened state" of consciousness, any more than the Sitting posture does. Finding such awareness is not just a matter of posture, it's a matter of consciousness. Depending upon the state of our mind and body, encumbrances can block our access to altered states in any given posture.

When we have blockages or chronic diseases, we must tap into the appropriate place on the evolutionary continuum of healing meditative postures inherent in the human form. For those whose Qi is weakest, it is best to start our practice of reconnecting with our vital energy by first lying down (in Yoga postures), then gradually progressing to Sitting Meditation, and finally to Standing. The more our bodies suffer from chronic debilitation, the better it is to return to lying down in Yoga postures. We thereby honor the ancient dictum, "healing comes by returning to the origin of things."

Standing, Sitting, Yoga and Qigong are part of a spiritual family, all of which have their own unique contribution to the path of Self-realization. Elements of the Standing practice can easily be transposed to other meditative postures and compliment these practices. For example, when Sitting, practitioners often experience their energy becoming stagnant and their muscles atrophying. As we shall see in Chapter 3, by placing the intention on the centerline of the body and circulating Qi around this line while in the Standing or Sitting posture, a deeper level of energized relaxation may develop. When Taoist and Buddhist practitioners who have stood for quite some time practice Sitting Meditation, they often favor a sitting posture on the edge of a chair, with their feet are uncrossed and the Bubbling Well points of the feet (Kidney 1) on the ground. This prevents the energy in the legs from being cut off, or blocked.

Practitioners of Yoga and Sitting Meditation who also practice Standing Meditation report that Standing has helped them to become more aware and appreciative of the energy in their respective postures. In particular, the awareness of the centerline, so important in Standing Meditation, gives new meaning to the importance of alignment in Yoga postures. Likewise, various Yoga postures and Qigong movements can help to *disperse stagnant Qi*[15] that can become constellated in Sitting and Standing practices. And, various techniques of Sitting practices, including visualizations, breathing, mantras and mindfulness, can be transposed to Standing.

Finally, another gift of Standing Meditation is that it can be practiced anywhere—in bank lines, in grocery stores, even at the department of motor vehicles. It is a direct, wireless link-up to meditative and healing practice in everyday life. Many people associate Qigong with methods of movement; but actually, some of the deepest states of relaxation and energy found through the practice of Qigong can be experienced in static postures.

My Experience Standing: An Alchemical Initiation

If we are looking to find golden light before we are willing to descend into darkness, we will be sorely disappointed.

> *There is an old teaching story of a young man who was looking for a key he lost in a well-lit area next to a street lamp. An older man, from the crowd that had gathered to help him, asked, "Where did you lose the key, lad?" The young man replied, "Over there in the darkness." The old man asked, "Then why are you looking here in the light?" The young man replied, "Because it's brighter here and easier to see."*

We are all like this young man who wants to find the key to the energy of life in the well-lit corridors of everyday life. This story may be telling us that to find the key to our vital energy, we need to look into our dark places. In virtually all meditative traditions—Yoga, Sitting or Standing—a period of pain is often a necessary step on the path to finding the bliss and harmony that is found at later stages of the meditative process. Alchemical traditions teach that becoming aware of this "dark stuff (*the nigredo*)," whether it be physical pain, past emotional blocks or old distorted beliefs, is necessary to transform lead into gold.[16]

The first step in alchemy is a return to *the prima materia*, or the primal material from which we are made. It is from this new beginning that the alchemical process of transformation begins.

When my teacher Fong Ha first suggested that I stand still for 100 hours, I felt much resistance to this idea. After all, I had come to the Tai Chi class to learn a spiritual "movement" tradition. As I was Standing, I remembered that I never liked "just standing." It brought back childhood memories of grade school and having to "stand in the corner" as punishment for my disobedience. (If I had only known about Standing Meditation, I would have been able to turn a punishment into a ritual of pleasure.) Other painful images of early life experiences came up as I was Standing and focusing on particular blocks in my body. Along with these memories, I experienced many of the signs of Qi stagnation mentioned in the literature—itchiness, aching, shaking, coldness in my extremities, blocked energy, imbalances between right and left sides of the body, and sudden jolts of something like electrical energy moving through areas of blockage.

I was experiencing a *regressus ab uterum*, a regression back to the origins of my energy blockages in order to heal them. I had long suffered from an asymmetry in my neck. Many photographs from my childhood showed my neck tilted to one side—probably due to being born a "forceps baby." For years, a significant portion of my time was spent with a stiff neck, which at times immobilized me. An orthopedic specialist said, "there is nothing wrong," but my body told a different story when I was lying on the floor, many a weekend, while others were out having fun.

Standing became a core part of my multifaceted method of practice that evolved gradually over the years. It became a core part of learning how to bring my neck into balance.[17] The Western Newtonian scientist in me wants to find a single cure to all that is, but as indigenous healers know well,[18] we can never separate one thing from the whole of which we are a part.

For me, Standing Meditation became the center of a practice that incorporates many parts of a healing mandala—psychotherapy, Yoga, Tai Chi, Tai Chi Push Hands, acupressure and diet. One element cannot be isolated from another. For example, if I drink excess coffee, an imbalance and swelling in my hip may occur, and I can draw from one or more of the above traditions to bring myself back into balance. I may never be able to say to what degree Standing Meditation, isolated from the rest of my life, "causes healing."

It is said in the tradition of alchemy and homeopathy that healing often moves backwards to earlier and earlier layers of our body in order to work through the deeper layers of its encoding. In this process, healing often moves from the upper parts of our bodies to the lower ones.

Along these lines, as I found the way to bring the pain on the right side of my neck into balance, I noticed my right hip was blocked and felt as if it was twice the size of my left one. As I "just stood," my right leg started to shake uncontrollably. This intense shaking—a sign of the release of blocked Qi—was the beginning of a process of working through areas of blockage in my body that had been in a state of imbalance for years. Standing helped me to become aware of how my hip was related to my neck imbalance. The hip and neck are parallel gateways—one to the lower and the other to the upper body, or as the Hermetic aphorism states, "as above so below."

Below our blockages are the roots of our familial energy patterns. Through Standing, I was being initiated into a process of reversing the multigenerational encoding that led to health problems for many of my relatives in their advancing years. There had been blockages in the hip area through many generations in my family. My 87-year-old uncle had hip replacement surgery, and my father had chronic problems in his right hip.

Standing is no cure-all. Many other traditions compliment the practice, and add to it. Blockages often come from an incarnated thought form, are translated into the human energy field, manifest in the muscular system and pull out the spine. So, for example, Gendlin's *focusing*[19] technique can help us to be conscious of the felt meaning of the blockages in our body armor. For our energy blockages, a variety of Chinese energy healing techniques can help, such as: Qigong, acupuncture, Tai Chi Chuan, two partners pushing hands, acupressure and Chinese herbal medicine. There are many methods that are useful to the process of characterological transformation of our psychophysiological muscular holdings, including polarity therapy, Rolfing and other deep tissue work. For the spine, chiropractic and osteopathic traditions can be useful for aligning the body. All of these techniques belong to the same family of healing traditions and have been helpful to me in working on my energy blockages.

Though a multiplicity of methods may be helpful to our healing process, the simplicity of doing "no thing" may be the primordial healing method. In stillness, we travel to the source of all streams of healing techniques. As it is put in the classic Tao te Ching, "from the Tao comes the one, from the one comes the two, from the two comes the five elements and from the five elements come the myriad of things." Thus, healing is found by going from the myriad of things back to the one, and back to the stillness before the multiplicity of things. From here, deep healing arises from the unfathomable depths of the sea of all Being. This stillness is called *Wuji*, which translates as the void, the undifferentiated, the sea of all Being, the mother of Qi.

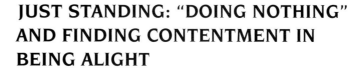

JUST STANDING: "DOING NOTHING" AND FINDING CONTENTMENT IN BEING ALIGHT

What lies behind us and what lies before us are tiny matters compared to what lies within us.

—Oliver Wendell Holmes

Look at these worlds spinning out of nothingness, That is within your power.

—Rumi

Wuji Standing Meditation Practice[1]

Basic to rites of renewal in cross-cultural healing is a "returning to the origin of things."[2] The *Wuji tradition*, likewise, tells us that if we seek to be healed through movement, we would do well to first regress back from the myriad of potential movements to their origin in Standing. In Wuji Standing Meditation we return to movement's "mother"—stillness. In stillness, a reservoir of Qi is discovered. We bathe in it like a fetus takes a bath in the amniotic fluid in the womb of his or her mother. The initiate of the tradition thereby undergoes an alchemical *regressus ab uterum*, a regression to the womb from which energy and healing are born.

Many who practice movement meditation traditions have not heard of "Standing in the Womb of Stillness" as a method to enhance the energy of movement. The theory behind *Wuji Qigong* is very simple, yet different from the more common Qigong practices based on the movement back and forth, from yin to yang in Tai Chi. Tai Chi Chuan also emphasizes the point where yin and yang meet. But in the classics, it says that Tai Chi originates from *Wuji*—the undifferentiated state before the separation into opposites. It is said by masters of movement meditation traditions like Tai Chi that unless one first connects with the source of Qi (Wuji), movement will be less beneficial. Thus, in the classics, the practitioner is directed to find "the movement in stillness and the stillness in movement." Masters of the tradition of Wuji say that if a practitioner does a lot of movement without first paying respect to this still place inside, he or she may get carried away spending money from a bank account without having the necessary resources to draw upon (an idea from which our credit card culture and our nation, with its multi-billion-dollar deficit, could gain much benefit.) In Standing Meditation practice the first step is to develop the inner bank account of Qi. Not spending enough time in stillness, while doing any form of exercise, can lead to a depletion of Qi and a feeling of tiredness.[3]

As an aside, it was reported that Socrates was seen standing in total stillness when the Greek armies went to battle. When they returned hours later, Socrates was in the exact same position, seemingly to have not moved at all.[4] Had the greatest philosopher of ancient Greece discovered the power of stillness found in Standing Meditation?

The Practice of Wuji Standing Meditation[5]

A Note of Caution before Standing

Before beginning Wuji Standing Meditation practice, a note of caution is in order: The process of opening the natural flow of our Primordial Self in Standing Meditation may activate a psychophysiological alchemical initiation process that can bring up memories of earlier emotional wounding, deep-rooted energy blocks, and/or a regression back through layers of our earlier diseases.

Some of the bodily symptoms that may arise include: a feeling of numbness in the hands, feet, one side of the body or even the whole body; tingling, vibrating, shaking, and even intense sudden jumping; aching in various parts of the body, particularly in the areas of old injuries; sensations of temperature are common, including warmth, sweating, or cold; a sense of asymmetry arising in various parts of the body, for example, one hand or leg may feel higher or longer than the other. All of these are signs of the activation of Qi to heal old areas of blockage. As the light of the sun gradually melts ice in a river, so may the light of our Qi in time melt away our blocked areas.

If we are looking for instant changes to deep-seated medical problems, we may be on the path of searching for fool's gold. Though there have been many reports of spontaneous remissions and healings taking place with the practice of Qigong,[6] the changing of long-standing blockages often takes time and practice. It is by keeping with the Taoist tradition to have a non-attached attitude toward change that healing can begin. Expectations bring constriction and "trying;" being open to the truth of our experience, and having compassion for the way things are, is the path of the true "heart of gold." On the other hand, keeping our intention open to possibilities allows the possibility of spontaneous remission to happen. Psycho-neuroimmunological research supports the notion that biochemical changes and healing are associated with changes in cognition. And according to ancient Chinese wisdom, "Qi follows Yi (intention)."

There are times when our blockages are greater than the current ability of our Qi to transform. This may be a sign that we need to take a break for a while, take a walk or sit down. We need to be able to read our own bodies to know when it's necessary to call on appropriate medical personnel or healers such as acupuncturists, chiropractors, psychotherapists or Western medical doctors. Just as the pebble can irritate the inner membrane of the oyster, so can our practice irritate us in the process of creating a pearl of great value.

Structure of the Practice

Setting

Really, any place will do because finding our stance in everyday life is the key to spiritual development. However, during the early phases of practice it's beneficial to find a quiet, well-ventilated place inside to practice; or ideally, to find a beautiful place outside in nature on a nice warm day where there is no wind and a minimum of distraction. Peaceful, environmentally-friendly conditions help our sensitivity to flower, and help us feel the Qi. Also, wait about an hour after eating so that your energy is not being used for digestion.

Length of Practice

The quality and the correctness of the posture is more important that the amount of time we Stand. Begin by Standing for about 5 minutes at a time, once or twice a day for your first week of practice. The next week, increase to 10 minutes once or twice a day. Gradually increase to 20 minutes once or twice a day. Use common sense regarding the length of time you Stand. Find that balance between not stopping too soon, and not continuing too long after a block appears. It is important not to overdo your practice. Though some advanced practitioners stand for up to 45 minutes or longer at a time, it may be best during the first year of practice to follow the Taoist dictum "less is more" to prevent burnout.

Dealing with Discomfort

If there is discomfort, don't change your posture immediately. If you change immediately you may lose the opportunity for transformation. Allow yourself to work with places of discomfort. Various breathing methods will be discovered as we Stand. For example, as we relax and breathe, our awareness may move to our exhalation which is associated with "sinking the Qi." One of the Taoists favorite ways to sink and cultivate Qi is a type of breathing called *long-breath*. To experience this type of breathing, first pay attention to how long and deep your breath is without trying to force it to be calm. Allow the breath to naturally rise up on the inhalation; on the exhalation it is as if you are pressing down on a tire with a slight hole in it. A "short breath" on the other hand, is like a blowout in a flat tire.

Another way of letting go of tension is to imagine the tension flowing downward into the ground on the exhalation. With each practice session new awareness emerges about how you are programming tension, and how to let go of the tension. You'll get to know yourself by seeing where you are tense and where you are more relaxed.

If you have a lot of tension or pain, it may be time to take a break. "Standing your ground" in this tradition does not mean "forcing through," but rather learning to take the stance in life of *Wu Wei*, or effortless effort. Pain can be a danger signal that is asking your body to listen and respond appropriately, as mentioned above.

Posture: Are You a Pushover?

Position of the Feet

Standing Meditation brings awareness to unconscious Standing patterns. Wuji Standing Meditation practice is done by keeping both feet parallel, pointing straight forward, shoulder width apart. Notice your feet; see if one is turned outward or inward further than the other, which may be a sign that the pelvis is out of balance. Another sign of off-centeredness is that many of us have a tendency to stand on the sides of our feet or put too much weight on the inside; some of us favor our toes or our heels. Shift your weight a little until you are Standing with your weight over the center of your feet, or slightly forward (over acupoint Kidney 1). For internal martial arts purposes, and to have a more solid base, according to Master Tam, it is important to first focus on the inside of the feet being straight, rather than the outside of the feet. This will make the toes point slightly inward, which gives a more solid base. The solidity of your base can be tested by having someone try to push you over from in front of you, as will be discussed in more detail at the end of Section II. Experiment with this in both positions, with your toes pointed outward and with them slightly pointed inward. Standing Meditation is a way to find your ground and cultivate the ability to not be a pushover in life.

The knees are unlocked and approaching being over the toes. For more advanced practitioners, the spiritual isometrics of the tradition can be felt by slightly expanding the knees toward the outside, as if pressing against elastic bands around the knees, while simultaneously intending to press them inward as if holding a balloon between them.[7] If the knees hurt, adjust your stance by not bending them so low. As long as they are not locked you will be on the right path; locking them, or any other joints of the body, blocks the Qi.

Figure 17:
Master Fong Ha
"just standing"
at 60 years of age

The pelvis is slightly rotated forward as if you are beginning to make love, and the lower back is slightly pushed out so that the lumbar curve begins to disappear and the back is straight in the location of the Ming Men, the area of the lower back behind the Tan Tien.

The tongue is touching the top of the palate just behind the teeth to connect the *Jen Mei* channel down the front of the body and the *Tu Mei* channel up the back. Master Tam at times advises putting the tongue more forward, resting right behind the upper teeth. Can you feel the energetic difference from each different placement of your tongue?

The eyes can either be open in a soft gaze, half open or can be closed "looking" straight ahead. Keeping the eyes level and the chin slightly tucked will naturally straighten the cervical vertebrae in the spine. If you are Standing inside, you might begin by looking out a window; the Taoists believed that by gazing out into the distance, *Shen,* or spirit, is developed. The mouth is gently closed, or maybe a half-smile will feel natural. The Taoists believed in the balance of yin and yang; thus, experiment with keeping the eyes half open or the mouth in a half smile when it feels natural.[8]

Position of Chest, Shoulders and Hands

The chest and shoulders are relaxed, causing a slight rounding of the upper back. The arms hang loosely at the sides. The hands can be at the sides or slightly rolled forward, with the palms facing backward. Some of the teachers with whom I have practiced, advise positioning the hands slightly rolled forward toward the front of the thighs. We shall have more to say about the position of the hands in the next chapter in the section on Opening the Door of the Heart and the Sphere of the Self using the Chest, Shoulders and Hands.

Awareness and Alignment

One focus of our awareness is to learn to align the body's centerline. Master Cai emphasizes "Three points in a straight line" which means (a) the midpoint of the line connecting the two Bubbling Well acupuncture points of the feet, (b) the *hui yin point,* or perineum between the anus and genitals, and (c) the *bai hui point* on the crown of the head.[9] This helps us to find our central equilibrium.

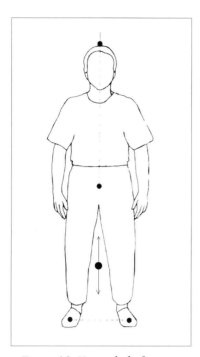

Figure 18: Your whole frame is suspended as if you are a puppet hanging from a star in the heavens above.

Eventually we get a sense of the spine stretching up through the top of the head, and the lower spine being pulled down to the ground. We thereby experience, "raising the spirit and sinking the Qi." The vertebrae of the spine may gradually feel like they are hanging from a star in the heavens like a string of pearls.

Corrections in posture and Qigong exercises by an experienced teacher helps to facilitate the process of Self-transformation. If you don't have a teacher, you may want to check your posture in a mirror to see whether you are Standing correctly because sometimes our imbalances are ingrained and unconscious. For example, the neck may be tilted to one side or the chin may not be tucked slightly in to straighten the spine and let the Qi flow properly. Gradually there is a refinement of alignment, your awareness of the centerline grows, and you may experience being at the center of a ball of energy.

The cultivation of the ball of life energy is not just a matter of imagination, but a practice to be played with and tested, as will be seen at the end of Section II. *Shili* (testing strength) and *fajing* (the essential force that can discharge another) are a part of Tai Chi and Yi Chaun Two Person Self-development Practice and helps us to transfom our linear postures into spheres of energy.

SECRETS OF CULTIVATING INTENTION THROUGH STANDING

4

*"Oh, I've had my moments, and if I had to do it
over again, I'd have more of them. In fact,
I'd try to have nothing else.
Just moments,
one after another, instead of living so many
years ahead of each day."*

—Nadine Stair, eighty-five years old, Louisville Kentucky

Yi Chuan: The Mind of Standing

We have already discussed in the preface how the *Yi Chuan* system began with Grandmaster Wang Xiangzhai, and was passed on to Master Han Xingyuan in turn to my Sifu, Fong Ha. But the central idea of the Yi Chuan, its essence, is the cultivation of intention. Yi Chuan can be defined as the mind or intention behind the various systems of Chuan (Tai Chi Chuan, Xingyi Chuan and Paqua Chuan.) The concept of Yi Chuan allows our focus to shift between martial arts, self-defense, healing purposes, alchemical transformation of the personality and spiritual unfoldment.

The outer meaning of *Chuan* means fist. The esoteric meaning of fist is taking the five elements: fire, metal, earth, water and wood, and bringing them into a whole, such that they are within our grasp. Adding the concept of *Yi* (intention), we have the idea of using the elements of the universe in alignment with our intention.

When we add this central idea behind the Yi Chuan Standing Meditation method to our Wuji Standing Meditation practice—the practice changes depending upon our awareness and intention. One example is with the breath.

The Intention Behind Various Types of Breathing

*The Lord blew into Adam's nostrils the breath of life,
and Adam became a living Being.*

—Genesis

Awareness of the Breath

Student, tell me, what is God?
He is the breath within the breath.

—Kabir

Just as Master Cai of the Wuji school advises us to be with the natural breath, so did Master Han as he taught Yi Chuan. But after the stillness and the gentle power that comes from the natural breath is honored for some time, other methods may be practiced to further develop our intention.

Crane or Diaphragmatic Breathing to Sink the Qi to the Tan Tien

One common type of breathing that is practiced in Standing is diaphragmatic or abdominal breathing. This type of breath is very good for cerebrally-oriented people who want to shift their energy center downward to "get out of their heads." This type of breathing has been shown to increase the relaxation response and reduce the blood pressure. This simple method is of great help to the many people who incorrectly pull the stomach in on the inhalation causing the Qi to rise, thereby increasing our tension level. *Crane breathing,* according to Ken Cohen, as learned from his teacher B.P. Chan is a classic Taoist variation on diaphragmatic breathing in the Standing posture to sink the Qi to the Tan Tien.

Crane Breathing Exercise	While Standing in the basic stance, place your hands on your belly. As you inale, the stomach expands, and your hands are pressed outward. As you exhale, the stomach contracts inward, and your hands follow the belly inward. Make sure that this type of breathing is relaxed and natural, not forced.

"Rock and Roll," Taoist Style: Ocean Wave Breathing

After months of practicing "just standing," you will begin to feel a natural rocking movement that synchronizes with your breathing. You may notice that the weight shifts back to the heels as you inhale, and the weight naturally shifts onto the balls of the feet as you exhale. From our earliest experiences of being rocked in the cradle, and then incorporated by shamanic traditions, rocking is a primordial way to energize, heal and soothe the bodymind.

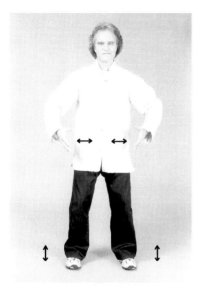

Figure 19: Ocean Wave Breathing

Experiment with synchronizing your hand movements outward and inward from your belly with your breath. It is as if you are blowing up a balloon and then allowing it to naturally inflate and deflate. As the body rocks backward, the breath goes in, and your hands go outward expanding your ball. As the body rocks forward, the hands come in and the breath goes out, collapsing your ball. As you continue to inhale and exhale, make the arm motions larger and larger.

Meditative Breath and Awareness

One intention in Sitting Meditation or Yoga is to develop "the observing self" and cultivate equanimity so that we don't get carried away with the cross-currents of life. To do this, a practitioner focuses on the breath, notices the thoughts and feelings that arise, and goes back to the breath. In Standing Meditation the intention is the same. The Standing posture can give additional postural support to finding our ground.

Elevator Breathing to Develop our Connection to Ground

One method of raising and lowering the Qi, I call *elevator breathing.*[1] By focusing on the up and downward movement of the breath, we "raise the spirit and sink the Qi."

Elevator Breathing Exercise

Notice your exhalation, the pause after the exhalation down in your belly, and the inhalation that comes from there. As your breath comes in, imagine your energy rising up from the ground, in the basement below your navel, to the crown of your head and connecting to the heavens above. As you exhale, imagine an elevator descending down from the head to a point just below the belly (the Tan Tien). At first you may not be able to sense your energy going down further than where an energy block stops it. Perhaps it stops in the heart or in a fearful place in your belly.[2] If you don't try to force the energy through, eventually, with each succeeding exhalation, you'll sink a little deeper down into yourself. Notice how many floors you go down on each breath. How low and how high does your elevator travel? Allow your breath to take your elevator to the level it wants to go to without trying or forcing. Can you feel the sense of peace from "having arrived" when your elevator rests on the ground floor?

> *The length of the breath that is associated with the development of Qi is called "Long-breath."*

The length of the breath that is associated with the development of Qi is called *long-breath*, which we discussed earlier with the tire metaphor. Another way to experience Long-breath is to imagine that you are in a body of water, and as you inhale your hands float up to the surface; as you exhale your hands press slowly down, feeling the resistance in the water. Don't try to force the breath in and out, just notice your natural breathing. As the number of breaths increase, the length of time of each part of the process will increase as well. For instance, you may count to four for the first inhalation, pause, and exhale. After doing a few cycles, the count may increase to seven. Pause longer after the exhalation than the inhalation to sink the Qi.

This exercise can be adapted to an individual's health issues. For example, the focus of our intention on the exhalation is particularly useful for those who suffer from various stress-related conditions, particularly hypertension. The focus on the exhalation brings our energy down to connect us with the earth.

Microcosmic Orbit Breathing for Healing

Microcosmic Orbit Breathing[3] is excellent for developing our healing powers.[4] The Taoists view breathing systems that use forced breath to direct the energy straight up the spine, such as is sometimes practiced in Kundalini Yoga, as potentially dangerous.[5] From the Taoist perspective it is important to keep up and down, yin and yang in balance in our practice. Thus Microcosmic Orbit Breathing emphasizes the circulation of Qi. It consists of the following steps:

> *Microcosmic Orbit Breathing Exercise*

1. Begin by focusing on the breath coming up the spine from a point at the bottom of the spine at the perineum (the *hui yin* point between the anus

and the genitals). Imagine the breath coming over the top of the head (to the *bai hui* point) where the lines of the ears converge at the top of the head (the soft spot on babies).

The tongue touches the palate in the hollow on the roof of the mouth; this connects two of the major meridian lines in the body. The one up the back, the Governing Vessel, is called the *Tu Mei*; the one going down the front of the spine, the Conception Vessel, is called the *Jen Mei*.

2. On the exhalation, focus on the breath coming down the front of the body until it reaches the Tan Tien. Feel the pause after the exhalation.

3. The movement of the breath downward continues to the perineum. Here our exhalation pauses until it naturally arises for a new cycle up the *Tu Mei*.

There are many other types of breathing that can be practiced with Standing Meditation, they go beyond the scope of our discussion. From the viewpoint of the Wuji and Yi Chuan traditions, it is best not to do any type of forced breathing, for this can contribute to serious physical and mental health problems.

Awareness on the Energy Centers of the Body

Since so much energy is activated in the process of Standing, it is natural for our awareness to go to various energy centers. It is best when the whole bodymind leads our awareness to one of these areas rather than to some concept in our heads. *Wuji* means that we allow "no-thing, the void, the mother of Qi" to lead our awareness. *Yi Chuan* adds the idea of focus of intention. Actually, these two traditions are brother and sister traditions...part of the same family. They represent the yin (Wuji) and yang (Yi Chuan) of Standing traditions. They are within one another; for without stillness, the direction of intentionality is forced; without intentionality, stillness may be less purposeful. After Standing for a period of time "doing nothing," if you feel filled with energy, you may want to direct your intention in one of the following ways:

Focus on the Tan Tien

This breathing center of the body in the lower abdomen, three fingers below the navel, has been called the field of elixir or the Tan Tien. As you focus on this energy center you may notice that the type of breathing that evolves naturally is diaphragmatic breathing. When our awareness is led here, we may notice a feeling of being in touch with the center of our body-self. When the breath is centered here, many people report finding a pathway to the depths of the waters of life found beneath the surface tensions that occur in daily life. Just be aware of the thoughts that arise from within and go back to your focus on the Tan Tien.

Focus on the Bubbling Well Points

By bringing our focus to the bottoms of our feet, we find a way to activate the macrocosmic orbit and cleanse the body by letting go of tension through the feet. The Taoists also believed that healing energy is drawn in from the earth through these points (called Kidney 1).

Awareness on the Heart and other Energy Centers

In the following section on "developing the golden ball of the heart," we shall have more to say about the Yi Chuan perspective on cultivating this energy center. It is beyond the scope of this book to say more about the postures for developing other centers in the body, but in the Yi Chuan system there are eight primary postures used for cultivating the ball of energy in different areas of the body.

Developing Integration of the Bodymind: The Sphere of the Embodied Self

The integral force developed in Standing can be a way to heal mind/body splits. The Tai Chi Chuan classic texts speak of transforming the body from a straight line into a sphere by "eliminating the hollows and protuberances of the body" with Qi. For example, by making sure that the chin is tucked slightly in, the cervical vertebrae of the spine straightens and fills out, and the spine is more able to channel the Qi from the upper body, up through the neck and out the head. Likewise, when we place our awareness on the *Ming Men*, the gate of life in the lower back behind the navel, gradually and over time, the Qi fills this area and can aid in integrating the lower body with the upper body. The main protuberances to be flattened are the abdomen and buttocks.

Figure 20: Developing the Sphere of the Embodied Self

We usually think of the standing posture of a human being in a linear sense, but when we "eliminate the hollows and protuberances" with Qi, a sense of a bodily sphere develops. The Yi Chuan is a sophisticated method for transforming the body into a sphere. Through our intention, we practice cultivating a readiness to meet a force being applied to us from many different directions. For example, we can imagine that we are standing in a river pointing downstream; as we feel the force directed at us from the back, the hollow in our lower back fills out, ready to meet that force. Simultaneously, we can imagine facing upstream; our connection to the ground manifests in a different way now as we imagine the water flowing against the front of our bodies. The parts of our body that are excessively protruded forward, in our normal rushing-around everyday lives, return to center so that we can meet the force of the river and maintain our balance in the most centered way. We can further develop the sphere by imagining the river pushing against us from all sides. Hopefully the stance we are practicing comes back to us when the everyday forces of the river of life comes roaring at us.

In general, when we feel fragmented by modern life, by our psychological complexes or by our relationships with others, Standing can help us to find our ground, our stance in who we are. The awareness of different parts of our body become connected, and the individual notes of the body come together in natural harmony.

Oiling the Hinge to the Door of the Heart, Cultivating the Sphere of the Self and Reversing the Fear Response

In the last Chapter on Wuji Standing we spoke about the position of the chest and shoulders relaxed, and the arms either hanging loosely at the sides or slightly rolled forward, with the palms facing backward. This position of the hands makes a difference. When the hands roll slightly forward around the thighs, this causes a slight rounding of the upper back and shoulders, and a slight hollowing (not collapsing) of the chest. In accordance with classical theory, this position allows the Qi to sink to the Tan Tien. This posture is useful for martial arts purposes to sink the Qi to a lower energy center; as well, it helps with deep relaxation by facilitating the process of letting go in the upper body.

A useful exercise to feel the whole range of Oiling the Hinge to the Door of the Heart is to allow the hands and arms to rotate synchronized with your breathing. Begin with your hands by your sides in a Wuji stance. As you inhale, open your forearms and hands all the way with palms facing forward. Here you will feel your chest and heart open. Then as you exhale, gradually allow your forearms and palms to rotate until your palms are first backward, and then all the way around so that they are facing outward to the sides. This is the position where the heart center is most hollowed or "closed." In this position, the Qi can most easily descend to and fill the belly center (Tan Tien); and you will notice your lower back (Ming Men) fill out slightly. By doing this practice you will "oil the hinge to the door of the heart" facilitating the chest's whole range of movement; and you'll help to prevent the Dowager's hump often associated with humping over in old age.

It should be emphasized that in Qigong practice "closing the door" to a chakra (energy center) does not have a negative connotation. To close a door is to gather the Qi—as when we close the door to our house to recuperate, and gather our life force, after a long day at work. Actually the word, "closing," is a misnomer; the term "closing" means the point of maximum Yin. As in the famous Taoist yin yang symbol, there is a small white dot in the half of the circle that is black, and a small black dot in the part of the circle that is white. So, in the practice of "closing and gathering the energy of the heart," we do not lose a heartfelt relationship to the world even in the most yin, or closed position—there is still a dot of white light. This is not just a conceptual distinction, but a matter of practice, feeling and intention. For a variety of reasons there are times to stop being overly open. Equally important in life is to allow our love to flow out to others, as well as having effective boundaries, saying "no" at appropriate times and not being "co-dependent."[6] Knowing when to say, "no," is a deep form of love of Self and others; it expresses the Integrity of the Sphere of Ourselves. Standing Qigong practice helps us to cultivate the ability to have a well-oiled hinge and appropriately open and close the gates of a chakra. There can be love in opening, as well as in setting boundaries. Hopefully, the bodymind practice of Opening and Closing the Door of the Heart, becomes an embodied metaphor and transfers to our ability to find a balanced stance in our everyday emotional lives.

Rotating the arms, synchronized with the breath, is an initiatory practice to reverse the "fight or flight response" of the sympathetic nervous system. When attacked, we normally breath in, hold our breath and the Qi rises and "freezes." Sighing and exhaling are natural ways that the bodymind lets go of trauma. Practicing the whole exercise of rotating the forearms and hands to the furthest positions of opening and closing, in conjunction with our long-breath, is an ingenious way to deal with the startle reaction and fear involved with the fight or flight response. In conjunction with psychological inner work, this method is a useful part of an integrated treatment approach for anxiety, phobias, fear of confrontation and post traumatic stress. In this practice, we feel the Qi rise, as our palms turn forward, and then activate the relaxation response of the parasympathetic nervous system as we exhale with our palms facing outward to the side. This exhalation, along with the rotation of the arms and hands, helps us to sink the Qi to the Tan Tien, and return to a belly-centered, relaxed place. Since the belly is at the physical center of our body, it helps when we are attacked physically or verbally to "be in our physical center," as compared to having the Qi rise up and be in our defensive, hyper-aroused "heady" reactivity. Later in Section II, the Tai Chi Ruler exercise will be shown as a further practice for reversing the "fight or flight" response.

Standing Meditation

Different Standing Meditation Masters emphasize different variations in the rotation of the hands and forearms—all of which have their own unique advantages. For example, Master Sam Tam favors the latter posture with the palms facing outward to the sides, for some purposes.

Figure 21: Master Sam Tam in Yi Chuan Qigong Standing Meditation Posture

He emphasizes spreading the shoulders out first as the practitioner rotates the shoulders forward, rounds the back, and hollows the chest. The rotation accomplishes two things: (1) for health—it facilitates breathing by creating more room for the lungs, especially the upper lobes, to expand and contract, and (2) for internal martial arts—it aligns the structure of the shoulder girdle and spine for optimal structural integrity necessary to deliver the force (*jing*). Master Tam uses this posture as an intermediary step as part of his whole system of intricate training in Yi Chuan Standing Qigong.

The hand position that I most often use when Standing is one I originally learned from my training in the Yi Chuan system from Masters Cai and Ha, which I adapted to fit with my own understanding and experience:

Hand Position Variations for Opening the Door of the Heart

Assume your basic Wuji stance and allow the hands to be by the sides of the thighs (middle finger is over, but not touching Gallbladder 31). By keeping the hands here, we are right at the center of keeping the door of the heart-center open midway.

Positioning the hands, palms toward the thighs, is the midway position and honors the Taoist idea that "Qi is most easily found at the midway point between yin and yang."

Placing the hands next to this midway point, as compared to rolling slightly forward, keeps the energetic balance a little more up in the heart area. This Gallbladder 31 point is therefore a favored position for those that are depressed, or for those that want to work on keeping more energy on the heart area during practice. For each individual's purpose in practicing and in healing, the position of the hands may change according to the individual's needs on a given occasion. Gallbladder 31 is called the *Wind's Market* in Chinese medicine; it is used for gathering and

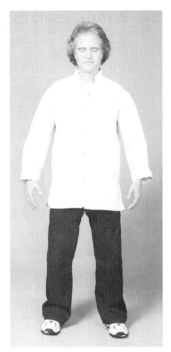

Figure 22: Hand Position Variations for Opening the Door of the Heart

dispersing pathogenic wind and cold, and for transforming dampness. It's been reported to relax the muscles and to help with hip pain and sciatica. Due to my history of hip problems, I find this point very healing. When I "press on it, circle, stop and feel" it feels like I let go of tension in my upper body. I also experience it as an emotional detoxification point that I sometimes touch when I am sitting with patients. Try touching it yourself: circle, stop and feel, and see what you experience.[7]

The midway position of the hands (near GB 31) also facilitates the armpit area to open (called the bird's nest,[8] perhaps to evoke an openness in that area so as not crush an imaginary little bird). We can imagine that there are marbles in the armpits to remind us to keep a little space there, or we can imagine that it is a bird's nest so that the proper openness enters into the armpits and shoulders. When the energy gates of the armpits are opened, the elbows tend to gradually move away from the sides of the body, and the hands move slightly out from the body. Our structure looks as if we are a balloon, with the elbows as the horizontal diameter of the balloon. A slightly rounded contour appears from the shoulders to the elbows and wrists, thus transforming the linear body into a ball. Instead of standing in the military posture, "at attention," with stiff arms by the sides, we focus on opening to the power at our center and allowing that energy to open the sphere of the Self.

We shall have still more to say about how the Yi Chuan helps the body to transform from a line to a sphere in the following chapter on Hidden Keys to Open Gateways of Healing Energy.

Integral Force and Embodied Centeredness

In modern life we often hear people talk about "being centered." In Yi Chuan training, the teacher pushes on the student from many directions to test the centerline of the student, and whether the student can maintain their central equilibrium. Then, when the teacher is not present, this idea of being pushed from any direction helps the student to develop a sense of the sphere. As the power of the posture, and the sense of the ball develops, at further levels of the practice a person can develop *Fajing*, or transforming the physical form into a ball of energy. Once you have developed fajing, when a fellow practitioner pushes against you, they will bounce off of your ball of energy. It is commonplace if you have practiced with an experienced teacher for six months to a year to develop a groundedness so that someone who is heavier and stronger can not push you over, (one key is letting go of "trying" to be rooted). Some use the "integral force" that develops in Yi Chuan for the two-person Taoist method of dual cultivation called "Pushing Hands"—a practice of self-defense. From our viewpoint on the Yi Chuan as a holistic bodymind transformation system, this practice is a metaphor for developing the Sphere of the Self with appropriate boundaries, and the ability to cope with and have fun with the forces we deal with in everyday life.

Standing Meditation: Healing the Healer

The energy that comes from Standing enhances the work of many different kinds of healers, according to students in my classes, and from those who have learned the practice from other Standing Meditation teachers. Acupuncturists feel that by practicing Standing Meditation they can connect with the Qi of the universe; they like to imagine sending it through their bodies when they hold the acupuncture needle. Many massage practitioners report feeling less drained when doing Standing practice during or after, a long day of work laying their hands on others. Nurses and other health professionals report similar benefits when they use Standing to deal with burnout. Psychologists who use these methods similarly report beneficial results.

The Ground of Self-Knowledge, and the Roots of Our Lives

Because this practice is literally a meditation on our stance in life, Standing Meditation serves as the fundamental ground of all Qigong training, as well as a solid ground for psycho-spiritual work. Our body awareness, and awareness of our Selves, increases as we Stand and listen to the signals of our bodies and adjust them accordingly.

Each session of Standing may help you to become aware of how you hold stress. We learn where our Qi is strong, weak or blocked. In time we become aware of the psychological characterological blocks that are held in our bodies—of which we shall have more to say in the next chapter. In Standing we learn to release tension and become students of our bodymind's abilities to heal.

It is said that Qigong Standing practices help form the roots of the tree of our lives…that when we practice diligently, it permeates into all areas of our lives and gives strength and energy to whatever we do. The variations of intention in Standing are infinite. After a while, the practice transcends any particular intention, or our awareness of any particular energy center. We "simply Stand," and that becomes what we are—a Being connecting the earth and the heavens.

Standing Like a Tree: Zhan Zhuang

Zhan Zhuang,[9] or Standing Like a Tree style of meditation, is another name for the Yi Chuan tradition. For those whose stance in life is rooted in modern science,[10] the following scientific research on Zhan Zhuang may be of interest:

> *A study by Yang Sihuan analyzed the EEG patterns of young students, who were 17 to 20 years old who had been practicing "Zhan Zhuang Gong" (Standing Like a Tree) for one year. Thirty-two persons in the Qigong group and thirty-five persons in the control group were involved in this experiment. During a one year period of observation, the subjects of the Qigong group practiced Qigong for 40 minutes every day. There were significant differences between Qigong practitioners and controls in the coherence values between the two occipital regions of the brain. With increasing training periods the coherence went up, seeming to show that there was a dose sensitive relationship.*[11]

Zhan Zhuang Exercise

Figure 23:
YHVH Kabalistic Tree of Life

Zhan Zhuang practice can be done inside a building, using our imagination, or outside. On any day, perhaps on a nice warm one, find a tree that calls you. As you are Standing in the previously mentioned posture with your legs shoulder width apart, knees bent and your hands by your sides, begin to identify with the tree.

Notice your exhalation as it sinks down into your roots. What are you rooted to in your life? Picture your friends, family, loved ones and spiritual traditions as a network of roots beneath you. As you inhale, draw that energy up into your trunk. Picture how you are branching out right now in your life. Your branches reach out for light, and your leaves transform the light into energy. Maybe in time the forces of nature will make your endeavors bear fruit for the earth. Perhaps you'll hear a chirping bird or other sounds that give sound-healing to your branches and the fruit that grows there.

The idea in this practice is that as a tree reaches to the heavens for light and transforms it into energy, so can we. The same force that lets trees grow upward to the heavens and become rooted in the earth, also brings human beings to the upright position, fulfilling our destiny to connect our earthly Selves with the heavenly energy of the cosmos. We become the tree of life that connects heaven and earth, as can be seen in the Kabbalistic picture above, which shows a human being, the secret name of God (the Hebrew letters for God YHVH are hidden in the illustration of this Kabbalistic tree), and the Tree of Life merged into one.

As we Stand, the tree becomes an embodied metaphor for our spiritual development and the obstacles we meet in life. The felt sense in our bodies lets us know if we are inflated and top heavy, or if we are unrooted, we notice our bodies leaning in an unbalanced way to one side or the other. Perhaps our branches are broken due to an injury that occurred when we reached out to another for love, and we were rejected. As we stand and breathe, healing metaphors arise. We may become aware of the "bark" we have that naturally protects us from the assaults of the world; and we discover our natural repair mechanisms. As we inhale and exhale we discover ways to bring balance and harmony to the parts of us that are unbalanced; we let go of the toxins and take in the vital substances around us to aid us in our growth toward the light.

Maybe we too will find the root and the route that led Lao Tzu, author of the Tao Te Ching, in perhaps one of the earliest references to *Zhan Zhuang* to say:

> *Standing alone and unchanging,*
> *One can observe every mystery.*
> *Present at every moment and ceaselessly continuing,*
> *This is the gateway to indescribable marvels.*

Circulating Qi: The Healing Circle that Arises from Stillness

Trees are not rigid, and neither should we be when practicing Standing or Sitting Meditation. The next practice helps to facilitate the fluidity of Being that we seek as we return to our primordial stance in stillness.

After Standing for a period of time and building up your reservoir of Qi, you can begin the practice of circulating Qi. It is important to move gradually into this second phase. This is because our Qi is like a bank account; Standing builds Qi, and circulating spends Qi. Caution must be exercised in spending it too quickly. Besides, it feels so good to spend it when you have a big account, rather than "spending it on credit." (Our government and credit card economy could learn a lot from this Taoist idea.) The importance of moving from stillness comes from the idea that Tai Chi, or the division of the world into the opposites of yin and yang, is preceded by Wuji, stillness. In the Tao Te Ching it says, "From the Tao comes the one, from the one comes the two, from the two comes the five elements and from the five elements come the myriad of things." By first connecting with stillness, our movement is charged with the healing energy that derives from stillness and is more relaxed and graceful.

Experiencing the Circulation of Qi

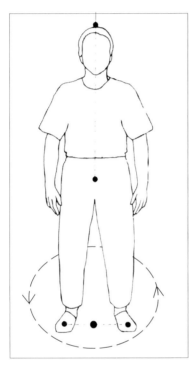

Figure 24:
The Circle that Arises from Stillness.

To experience the circulation of Qi that emanates from stillness, start in your Standing Meditation posture with your weight balanced equally over each foot. Feet are shoulder width apart.

After Standing for three to five minutes, imagine that your spine is like the trunk of a tree or a staff. Slowly shift your weight over the right heel, but only shift the weight 1% so that you are now 51% over your right heel and 49% over your left heel. Then make a circle shifting your weight to the front of your right foot, then to the front of your left foot, and then to the rear. As you are circling you can imagine cutting a hole into the heavens with the staff of your spine—the hole will cut into the earth, below the hui yin point (projected downward between your two feet), and the heavens, above the bai hui point.

Make sure your spine stays erect and does not tilt. Then you can imagine that you are spiraling a snake around the spine that travels from the earth, up to the heavens and back down. After doing this for a short while, return to stillness. The movement should be felt as originating from stillness and returning to it. When you find the stillness in movement, and the movement in stillness, you have experienced two of the gateways to a bliss-full experience of Qi.

A further way to circulate Qi while Standing is to make circles with the movements by shifting your weight slightly from the inside of the feet to the outside; then reverse the circle allowing the movement to go from outside to inside.

The circulation of Qi that emanates from Wuji is central to Taoist methods of healing. It can be used in Sitting Meditation practice to prevent stagnation of Qi by allowing the spine to move very slightly around in a circle. Remember to allow the movement to arise from your stillness rather than "trying" to move. Circulation of Qi helps to prevent rigidity in the Sitting Meditation stance.

This practice of circulation of Qi can aid in massage and bodywork. When there is a tight spot in your body, press it with one finger, circle and stop—feel yourself send love to this spot. Do you experience energy there? Get an acupuncture chart and do the same with a spot on the chart. Become a scientific explorer open to your own truth from what you feel.

Yin/Yang Balancing Exercise

A more advanced healing method to deal with imbalances on either side of the body I call the *yin/yang balancing technique*.[12] For example, if you have tension in your right shoulder, after being with your breath in stillness, touch the knot in that shoulder by placing your left hand and finger on that shoulder and circle your hand, stop and feel. Then, crossing your arms over each other, place your other hand on the opposite shoulder, circle, stop and feel while you are breathing. Press harder on the side that is less tense and softer on the side that is more tense.

You may experience a balancing take place, or possibly the tension shifting from one side to the other. If the tension merely shifts to the opposite side rather than balancing out, you may view it as an experience in knowing that you can move your energy through your touch.

You can then either touch or visualize the bottoms of your feet, and, as you do, imagine sending the blocked energy out through the bottoms of your feet. This can be accomplished through touch, or solely with the direction of your mind's intention (Yi). One of the best intentions is to get in touch with the loving energy of the cosmos that has created such a wondrous world, and imagine focusing that loving energy through your touch.

The Circle of Spirit: Spiraling out to the ends of the Universe[13]

The core idea in the Yi Chuan system is that the intention directs every posture. Depending upon our intention, we can use a posture for self-defense, healing or for spiritual purposes. For spiritual practice try the following method:

*Circle of Spirit
Exercise*

As you are in your Standing Meditation posture as described above, shift your weight 1% so that you are now 51% over you right heel and 49% over your left heel. Then make a circle where you shift your weight to the front of your right foot, then to the front of your left foot and then to the heels. Imagine that the circling is producing a wave that circles out from your body, first a few inches, then a foot then around your immediate surrounding geographic area, then around the city you are in, the state, the country, your continent, then around the earth. Can you feel the peace at your center spreading out to these locations, incorporating them into your field of awareness and spiritual presence?

Next, feel and imagine the circles spreading out around the earth to a circle that incorporates the moon. Then, as you become one with the solar energy, send out energy to the solar system to help life grow and evolve. Feel your energy radiate out in circles to all of the planets, one by one, from Mercury, Venus, Earth, Mars, Jupiter, Saturn, Uranus, Neptune and Pluto. You may even choose to extend your circles out to neighboring galaxies, until the whole universe is your mind.

Finally, reverse the circle so that your weight travels counter-clockwise. Starting with your weight 51% over your left heel, shift it to your front left toes, then over your front right toes, then your back right heel. Circle or spiral your energy back from the ends of the universe, to our solar system's outermost planet Pluto, to the innermost planet Mercury, then to the sun, the

Circle of Spirit
Exercise (continued)

moon, the earth, in reverse order. Meditate on bringing back the depths of peace, love, power... whatever you wish to bring back from the heart of space.

Keep spiraling back with your intention and awareness on bringing this energy back to the earth, to your continent, as you do the involutionary circle back to your present location. Then return to stillness for at least a minute or two, preferably longer, as you feel the movement and the presence of the whole universe in your stillness.

HIDDEN KEYS TO OPEN
GATEWAYS OF HEALING ENERGY

*There must be some primal force,
but it is impossible to locate.
I believe it exists, but cannot see it.
I see its results,
I can even feel it,
but it has no form.*

—Zhuang Zi, *Inner Chapters*, Fourth Century B.C.

The following exercises derive from the basic postures outlined in the previous chapter. It is advisable to do the previous postures before the following ones, because those basic stances help to build our bank accounts of Qi. Once we have stood in them for at least a few minutes, the next postures are useful for further cultivation of Qi.

In the last chapter we discussed how the Yi Chuan is a sophisticated method for transforming the body into a sphere by using the intention to cultivate a readiness to meet a force being applied from many directions. In this sense, the Yi Chuan is a system of "spiritual isometrics"—by meditating upon meeting potential forces, we "develop the muscles of our vital energy." In this section we will find ways of cultivating this awareness through assuming various fixed Standing postures.

Opening Six Energy Gates—
Holding Golden Balls in the Stream of Life and Laying Hands on the Earth

The following exercise is a meditation on using the elements of nature to heal ourselves, First is a meditation on water—from which the Taoists believe comes a key element of the energy of life. Then we use this awareness to meditate on sending healing energy to a particular place on the planet.

Holding Golden Balls in the Stream of Life Exercise

Once again, take your basic Standing stance: feet separated at shoulder width distance, knees bent, pelvis slightly rotated as if you are getting ready to sit down, and hands at your sides. Allow your wrists to rotate so that your palms are facing backward. Then imagine that you are in a slowly moving river on a calm day, and as you breathe in, your hands naturally float up to the surface at shoulder level. As you breathe out, your hands descend down to the area of the stomach and Tan Tien and you hold them there in a fixed posture. At the lowest point of descent, by the waist, the palms are comfortably resting on two imaginary balls. The wrists are just slightly bent, so that the heel of the palm is just barely pressing down. Make sure that the hand is not bent at an angle higher than the wrist, for this is too forced and yang; nor is the wrist higher than the fingers which is too yin. The hands are slightly to the side of the body, so your arms are not tight against the sides and there is space enough for a marble to fit into your armpits.

Figure 25: Dr. Michael Mayer (center) checks Standing Meditation postures of doctoral Psychology students and a medical doctor who are learning how to use the Qigong posture "Holding Golden Balls in the Stream of Life" for healing (California Institute of Integral Studies, 1996).

To enhance the felt sense of this posture, imagine that you are facing upstream (next, imagine facing downstream to create balance) in a slowly moving river; your palms are slightly compressing two balls down into the water with just enough pressure that they are steadied from floating downstream. The energy in your feet sinks down into the stream bed, and your knees bend just so much that you take root and prevent the river from moving you downstream.[1]

Stand in this posture as long as is comfortable—no more than 5 minutes for beginners. If the posture is difficult to maintain, go back to Wuji posture with your hands by the sides. In time, your ability to hold the posture will naturally increase, as will the sense of relaxation if your listen to your body's limits. The gates to ecstasy are not found by forcing yourself to stay in a posture longer than is comfortable.

This posture is the commonly known first posture of Tai Chi called "commencement." As your hands rise and fall, the Qi rises to the heavens and sinks back to the earth. In the Yi Chuan Standing Meditation system this is posture number seven, and is held in stillness. I also sometimes call it "Laying Hands on the Earth," to bring out its healing intent.

Figure 26: Laying Hands on the Earth

To bring out the healing dimension of this posture imagine some part of the earth that is in need of healing. Imagine that you are sending energy there through your hands on your exhalation, and replenishing your Self on the inhalation. (Whether energy can actually be transferred at a distance is a subject of scientific investigation.) However, it has been scientifically documented that high intensity infrasonic emissions can be measured coming from the palms (Lao Gung points) of Qigong masters.[2]

After Standing in stillness for about two minutes, you may feel moved to activate "the Circle that Arises from Stillness" by once again moving your weight from right heel to right toes, then to left toes and left heel. We will now work with opening six energy gates:

In the last chapter, we used the method, "finding the Circle that Arises from Stillness," to circle the staff of the spine and open a gateway into the earth. This circling opens the energy gate of the perineum, located between the anus and genital area. It also opens the energy gate called the *crown chakra,* also called the Thousand-Petalled Lotus, at the top of the head.

Opening the Bubbling Well Points

The third and fourth gateways are found by using the posture "Laying the Hands on the Earth." They are called "the Bubbling Well points" (Kidney 1, in the front, center of both feet). To find these energy centers keep the hands outstretched, palms over two imaginary balls. As you are practicing making "the Circle that Arises from Stillness" bring your awareness to these two energy gates in the center of the feet and notice what happens.

Opening the Energy Gates of the Palms for Healing

The fifth and sixth gateways are called the *lao gung* points (pericardium 8, in the center of the palms). As your hands are outstretched with two imaginary balloons beneath them, and you are circling your weight, see if you can sense the energy circulating in the *lao gung* points. Don't try to force any awareness. Just move from stillness to movement and from movement to stillness. Can you feel the circle of energy when you are in stillness? Can you feel the stillness in your movement? Can you feel the energy circulating in the other four energy centers?

Healing the Earth,
Healing Your Self

Now imagine sending this energy to some place on the earth on your exhalation. By circling, you are massaging the earth. As you are in stillness, the energy still circulates. On the exhalation you can say to yourself, "I send out healing energy and peace to heal the earth," on the inhalation you can say, "I take in healing energy and peace from the earth to heal me (so I can be a transmitter of healing energy)."

Developing the Golden Ball of the Heart and the Sphere of the Self[3]

Developing the Golden Ball of the Heart is useful in developing our heartfelt feelings while we are alone or while we are with another. Scientific research supports the fact that the heart generates electrical and magnetic energy throughout the body. The magnetic field of the heart, measured in femtoteslas, is 5,000 times stronger than that of the brain. The heart's energy impulse travels through the body fluids faster than the nerves, and can create coherence between itself and the brain.[4]

Figure 27: Golden Ball of the Heart Exercise

Start in the Standing Meditation posture, but allow the arms to raise up in front of and facing the heart, as if they are embracing a balloon. Elbows are out to the sides of the body and lower than the wrists—this helps the shoulders to relax. The wrists and forearms are slightly turned out-ward, embodying a posture that looks like holding a ball of liquid that is spilling out from the heart. After the posture has been maintained for a long enough time to build up Qi, you imagine the energy is spilling out and over your outstretched hands to a loved one. The breath coincides with the visualization—as you breath out you imagine giving energy to the world or a loved one, on the inhalation you replenish yourself with the energy around you. Remember to do the long-breath, not forced. After a short

*Golden Ball of the Heart
Exercise continued*

amount of time this visualization becomes much more than that. Can you feel energy flowing out from the heart and the whole body as if you are the sun shining light on the world?

Standing Meditation and the Golden Ball of the Heart Meditation practice becomes a way of developing stability and center. When difficult moments occur in our lives, we practice returning to our ground and our open heart.

The next posture derives from the former and is one of the best for using the Yi Chuan to transform the body into a sphere.

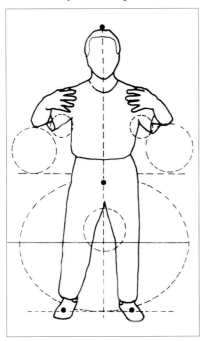

*Figure 28: Transforming the
Body into a Sphere*

In addition to holding a ball, we can imagine that the wrists press forward in front of our hearts into an imaginary ball in front of us; at the same time they get their force by pressing the lower back against an imaginary wall.

This awareness creates a sense of a ball around our circumference, extending around outside of our hands and around the back. This exercise of intention opens the Ming Men, the energy center in the lower back behind the Tan Tien. Eventually we experience the ball not just in our hands, but in our whole upper body. Do not exaggerate the stretching of the ball. By focusing more than just our intention, we could add too much force and tension in our ball.

The next step of the practice is to feel the ball spread through the whole body. This can be facilitated by imagining that the bent legs are holding a ball between them and that there is a hula hoop around the outside of the knees. These images facilitate the spreading of the ball into the lower body.

Gradually, in doing the practice we activate the alchemical transformation of our body from a straight line into a sphere, leading to an altered state of consciousness that is divine.

Had Hermes Trismigistus,[5] the ancient Egyptian Metaphysician, found a similar state of consciousness when he said,

*God is a sphere whose center is everywhere
and whose circumference is nowhere.*

Oiling the Hinge of the Door to the Heart of Space

Some spiritual traditions emphasize the importance of keeping the heart open at all times. In the Yi Chuan tradition, cultivating a well-oiled hinge to the door of the heart is emphasized. This is because each circumstance of life calls for a different degree of openness—sometimes we need to have boundaries. By practicing with the hands outstretched in front of the heart, with about three or four inches in-between, we are at the center point of open and closed, where yin and yang meet. We can imagine holding a ball which is opening and overflowing with energy, or we can visualize a bounded ball containing the heart energy. Thus we use our intention to control the door of the heart chakra. Sometimes we need to replenish the ball of energy by closing the door (no blame) and contain our energy to revitalize ourselves, other times we let our love flow forth.

Figure 29: Opening the Golden Door to the Heart of Space

Another method of *The Ball of the Heart Meditation* practice is to ever-so-slightly open the ball of the heart with your hands as you breathe out, and just barely bend your knees. Close your eyes. As you sink down a little, keep your spine erect. On your inhalation, bring in the ball as if you are gathering energy into your heart and allow the knees to straighten a little without locking them. Imagine the air around you as if it is thick molasses, so your movements can't go quickly. Appreciate the sweetness of that thick, sweet stuff you bring in on your inhalation and give out on your exhalation. Start with bigger circles, then make them smaller and smaller until there is no movement at all. Then feel how the movement is still happening on a cellular level. Do you feel Qi?

In the stillness after stopping all movement, can you feel how each cell of your body opens and closes like your hands did? Since your eyes are closed, you may not be able to sense where the limits of your body ends, and space begins. Inner and outer space have become one, and you have come into alignment with the pulsating breath of space, opening and closing, gathering love and giving love. Can you feel the distinction between your sphere and the larger universal sphere dissolving? If so, you have found "the golden door to the heart of space."

This is one of the best practices for bodymind healing. Once we are in plugged into this reservoir of energy we can explore drawing energy into specific areas of our bodies that are in need of healing, and give energy back to the earth and universe. We can explore the heart of healing. Perhaps a sound like "ha," or a tune or a line from a heartfelt song will add a deeper loving dimension to your experience.

Finding your Stance toward Life and Death

Since the Yi Chuan tradition involves finding our relationship to the elements of creation, it is natural that as we are Standing we may find ourselves embracing our relationship toward the elements of different spiritual traditions. We spoke earlier about the "dissolving practices" which exist in Buddhism, and how Standing Meditation can evoke such states of consciousness. In Tibetan Buddhism, a *Phowa* practice[6] exists whereby the practitioner imagines a deity of their choice sending love and compassion to them from the heavens. This is a practice used for living and dying. The Tibetan Buddhist belief is that dying and the after death state (*bardo realms*) are much like life. Whatever unworked through issues we have in our lives present themselves to us in the after death state; since we don't have a body, the issues may present themselves to us in the form of demonic images. While alive, Tibetan Buddhists practice finding a compassionate relationship toward these issues—the demons of our everyday lives.

One method is to imagine the deity of your choice sending light to you from the heavens. On your inhalation you take in that compassion and on your exhalation you dissolve into the love of the universe.

Standing Meditation postures (the Holding the Golden Ball of the Heart practice in particular) are an ideal way to practice finding your stance toward issues of life and death. As tension arises from holding a posture, you can send compassion to the tension and find a way to let go. When you are dying, having such an attitude and practice can be helpful to relieve pain and tension.

The French Philosopher Michel de Montaigne once said, "Deprive Death of its advantage over you...practice the art of dying." Both the Yi Chuan and Tibetan dying practices can be used to practice the "art of dying." When our issues arise such as envy, anger or a sense of worthlessness, we can practice finding a compassionate stance toward them. Whether we are alive or in an after death bardo state, finding our stance is key.

Maybe as you are standing in the Golden Ball of the Heart exercise with your outstretched hands, you'll imagine the love of the universe coming through your heart, bouncing off of your palms and coming back to your body, and to your life issues. Perhaps you'll find the stance of a Tai Chi warrior toward criticism, allowing it to bounce off your ball; or maybe you'll feel the yielding power to deflect and turn the insult back "just so," with a great bantering phrase. One of the more difficult things in life is when verbally attacked to find a stance of empathy with the pain of the attacker, and to remember, as Rilke said, "Behind every demon is something vulnerable that needs our love." Maybe feelings of overwhelm that once almost blew you over will come to your awareness, and you'll find a stance toward them as if you are a tree with deep roots in the ground, bark that protects you and fruits of kindness and generosity to nourish others.

> *I am reminded of a Buddhist story about a great Boddhisatva who was offered by the Buddha anything he wanted—riches, women or enlightenment. The Boddhisatva said he wanted to go to Hell. In spite of repeated offerings from the Buddha, the Boddhisatva replied that in Hell he would find the most people suffering and in need. When arriving in Hell, he heard the people screaming in a pain almost too much for him to bear; everyone's arms were cut off at the elbow so they could not grasp and eat the fruit that was there. They were writhing in pain from starvation. The Boddhisatva said he wanted to help and would meditate on the issue; the people there laughed at him saying that he would soon see there was no solution to eternal damnation. After a while the Boddhisatva came out of his meditation with an insight. He told the people that they could feed the fruit to each other with their elbows. Following the Boddhisatva's advice, Hell was transformed into heaven by their sharing with one another.*

How can each of us, in life and in death, find our true stance toward the demons and Hell of our everyday lives? What do you want the times of your life to Stand for?

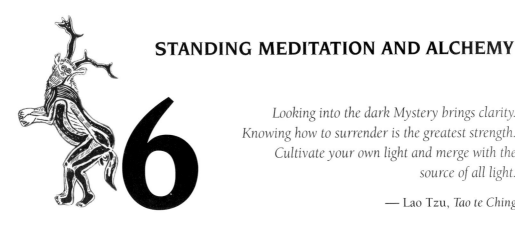

STANDING MEDITATION AND ALCHEMY

Looking into the dark Mystery brings clarity.
Knowing how to surrender is the greatest strength.
Cultivate your own light and merge with the
source of all light.

— Lao Tzu, *Tao te Ching*

In addition to being a method of self-defense, a way of self-healing and a spiritual practice, Standing Meditation practice is a method of alchemical transformation. We have already spoken of how the bodymind can enter into an initiatory process of alchemical transformation when the Qi is activated to clear old characterological energy fixations.

In practicing Wuji and Yi Chuan Standing Meditation one can experience the physical body and the physical world as a sacred treasure house of light condensed into matter. From Standing, and from the movements that follow the Standing, the practitioner can experience the air as if it is like water. That which is taken for granted as "a thing" is transmuted into sacred substance.

Using the Elements of Nature to Amplify the Energy of Our Standing Practices

Are Hot Tubs and Saunas Gateways to the "Elixir of Immortality?"

The esoteric, alchemical dimension of Standing Meditation practice can be activated and enhanced by using the elements of the natural world. Hippocrates, the father of Western Medicine, hypothesized a healing energy, the *vis medicatrix naturae* (the healing power of nature) as the vital force of life. He advised that physicians must identify blocking influences both within the individual and between the individual and the cosmos in order to restore the proper flow of *pneuma* (spirit).

Try Standing in a pool of water on a hot summer day, or in a hot tub on a cooler day and practice Holding the Golden Ball of the Heart Meditation. In this posture, we can experience a letting go and embracing of the world that is so deep it may allow us to feel that we are like the mythic ancient Immortals. It was said they could create planets by feeling the love in their hearts and allowing it to incarnate into form. Can you allow this metaphor to become spiritually real, and feel the peace and beauty of the world that you are creating in your own hands?

A sauna is an ideal place to practice Wuji Standing Meditation. Energy blockages and the encodings of the traumas of life melt away; we experience our bodies dissolve into the air, and then merge with the vast healing resources of space.

Later these sensations come back to us as we are standing in our natural everyday environment. The healing power of the bodymind can recreate these sensations. As "the state dependent memory hypothesis"[1] of modern psychology shows, an altered state can be reproduced by having "an anchor" that helps us return to it. Here, our Wuji Standing posture becomes an anchor that helps us return to "the Sea of Elixir" while alchemically transforming our everyday tensions, and opening us to unfathomable healing resources.

Webster's *Collegiate Dictionary* [2] defines "elixir" as: 1. A substance held capable of changing base metals into gold: philosophers stone; 2. A substance held capable of prolonging life indefinitely. "The Sea of Elixir" is a Taoist term which refers to the practice of focusing on the Tan Tien center beneath the navel and experiencing a merging with universal Qi, thereby changing the substance of one's life energy.

A Final Footnote about Standing, Scuba Diving and Holding the Philosopher's Stone

> *Hidden within is vitality and light.*
> *How does the Master express this truth?*
> *By allowing it to be so.*
>
> —Lao Tzu, *Tao te Ching*

After years of Standing Meditation practice, a feeling developed in my body that my mind could not explain. How could it be that I feel so light, as if like a puppet dangling from the sky, my spine feeling like a string of pearls; yet at the same time I feel heavy, grounded, having substance in a way that my cerebral Self never could experience? It is amazing that my body—that used to be a walking head, broken in the neck, constricted and empty in the heart—can feel like a golden ball, taking in healing energy with the inhalation, and as the ball expands, giving out healing energy on the exhalation.[3]

Was this hypnotic illusion, or was I being initiated into the path of rediscovering the lost golden ball of the Grimm Brothers' fairy tales of *Iron Hans* and the *Frog Princess*? My training as a hypnotherapist says that "objective reality" is co-created by the bodymind's capacity to feel and imagine;[4] and through this capacity, an experience of healing is oftentimes created.

Once I was scuba diving, wearing just that right amount of weight on my belt that allowed me to float freely, fifty feet or so beneath the surface of the water. Like other scuba divers who find this comfortable position of "standing in the water" my arms floated freely with no tension, every joint in my body loosened as I became one with the water from whence we all came. As I breathed in, my lungs inflated like a balloon and I started to rise in the water…five, ten, fifteen feet. Since I was next to an underground mountain, it was as if I was rising up the mountain with the inhalation. As I breathed out and my lungs deflated, I sank down, five, ten, fifteen feet down the mountain.

I remembered the old Taoist texts which reported that the practice of Qigong leads to the experience of becoming lighter as we breathe in, as if we are rising up to the heavens. And, it is said that on our exhalation, a practitioner of Qigong becomes heavy as the Qi becomes compacted, as if sinking down to the bottom of a mountain. This is amazingly similar to the experience of scuba diving; but the early Taoists didn't have scuba diving equipment!

After getting out of the water and lying in bed that night, I experienced a kinesthetic and proprioceptive anomaly of floating up to the ceiling as I inhaled, and my consciousness descending down beneath my body as I exhaled. (This is much like the common experience, after skiing of driving a car down a hill, and feeling as if we are still in motion.) Later, I realized that a similar experience could be had while Standing, through the power of the mind to visualize being in water.

We don't need to scuba dive to raise the spirit and sink the Qi. If we find the correct Wuji Standing position, and imagine that we are in water, on our inhalation we can feel ourselves rising up toward the heavens, and on our exhalation we can feel ourselves coming down to ground us on the earth. The air alchemically transforms into water, and we return to our primordial nature as "beings of light" floating freely in space. We find contentment in being "alight," as Grandmaster Wang Xiangzhai says in the opening quote of Section I.

Perhaps, we are getting a taste of what the early Taoists allude to when they say that the practice of Qigong leads to Wuji (the mother of Qi, the void, the undifferentiated wholeness of life before any opposites exist) or "the elixir of immortality." We are told from the old texts that this state is like experiencing the bliss of returning to the fetal state, young again, floating without concerns in the amniotic fluid of our mothers' womb. In the West this quest for "the elixir" was literalized into a search for an external substance that would make one eternally young. Many early European explorers, such as Ponce de Leon, spent their lives and all of their resources looking for "the fountain of youth."

In the Western esoteric tradition the coming together of the opposites into the experience of the *unos mundos* (one world) is conceptualized in terms of *the philosopher's stone*, the goal of the *opus*. Here, meaning and substance, heaviness and lightness, youthfulness and old age come together into a *mysterium coniunctionis*, a union of opposites. It was the western alchemists' dream to find the philosopher's stone by which "they mean to refer to this one substance, i.e. the water from which everything originates and in which everything is contained." Carl Jung, in his many-year study of alchemy, "calls (this stone) philosophical water, not ordinary water but *aqua mercurialis*."[5]

In western alchemical texts, the metal mercury is spoken of as a key substance used to transform lead into gold, reminding us of the golden Sea of Elixir in Taoist thought. In Greek mythology, the God *Hermes* (Mercury) takes us to the heavens above with his winged sandals and to the realms below in his role as messenger to the underworld—reminding us of the raising of the spirit and sinking of Qi in the Chinese internal healing arts. The parallels between eastern and western esoteric traditions are striking and give an interesting context for conceptualizing our experience of Standing Meditation. But ultimately, each of us defines our own experience.

What Do You Stand For?

Who are we as we are Standing? Depending upon our life stance, we may describe the experience of Standing Mediation as Wuji, *unos mundos* or as a nice feeling of relaxation, a trance state, or an opportunity to work on transforming our characterological and physical blockages.

An ancient alchemist might say that he or she has just experienced the *corpus glorificationis*, the glorious body, freeing the *spiritus mercurius* imprisoned in matter.[6] The scientist wonders and investigates, "What am I feeling when I am Standing this way?" and attempts to measure it quantitatively and qualitatively. The healer wonders, "How can I use this state for healing myself and others?" The spiritually inclined individual may say, "I have just found my ground in Spirit, and am Standing planted in the awesome ground of my divine nature." The mystic says, "I have found the Secret One inside where exists all of the universe, the galaxies and stars." The Buddhist, with a half smile, says, "This is nothing special, I'm 'just standing' here,"—being in the experience of the ordinary. The Hoku master practicing Standing Like a Tree in autumn says, "The dead, dry leaves fall to the Earth, and only what is alive, fresh and strong remains." Kabir, the sufi mystic, calls out from the other side of the grave and gives us his view of the after death state to help us discover our life stance:

> *Whatever we find now, we find then, if we merely live in an apartment now,*
> *that is what we will find when we enter the kingdom of heaven.*

What does our posture say about our life stance? What are we aware of? If we lift our hands into the "Golden Ball of the Heart Meditation" we may find that in each moment we stand in the center of a universe of possibilities, and embrace all of them. Perhaps life is as Grandmaster Wang Xiangzhai said, "When I stand the earth is in my hands, and the universe is in my mind."

What is our stance toward life today, and what will it be tomorrow? As we draw energy from the earth on our inhalation, how will we breathe out the gift of this divine energy to do our life's work? If we can truly Stand holding the earth in our hands, as a loving parent would a child, we will be embracers of planetary consciousness—we will be on the path to finding the place where healing ourselves and healing the planet are one.

On a given day our Standing may lead us to feel like we are one with the universe, or like a stick in the mud. If we feel like a stick in the mud, we must remember that through sinking our roots downward into the muck, through being in the waters of life, and learning to find our balance as the cross-currents pull us, push us, try to uproot us or carry us away from the ground of ourselves—all the while we are in process of growing towards blooming in the air as a lotus.

SECTION II:

BODYMIND HEALING QIGONG:

SELF-HEALING PRACTICES

FOR HEALTH AND LONGEVITY

At the beginning of time, the Gods had just finished their divine work of creating the first humans.
One of the Gods spoke up and said, "Where should we hide the secret of their Self- healing?"

The Earth Goddess said, "Let's hide it the center of the biggest mountain."
"That's no good," replied another. "One day they'll have bulldozers and find it too easily."

"What about hiding it in the depths of the deepest sea?" replied the God of the Sea.
The wise reply came, "They'll have submarines someday, and will find it without any inner work."

A third God suggested, "What about hiding it in the Great Pyramid in a safe up a narrow shaft?"
"Not really any better," replied another.
"Some day they'll have mechanized little vehicles that can just go up the shaft and open the safe."

Then Thoth, the trickster God, spoke up with a wry smile,
"Why don't we just hide the secret of Self-healing inside of their very Selves?
They'll never think of looking there."

And so it was decided.

—Retold and Adapted fom the *Shamanic Oral Archives*
Michael Mayer

Bodymind Healing Qigong™

Overview to Bodymind Healing Qigong (Level 1):

Do you have the patience to wait till your mud settles,
and the water is clear?
Can you remain unmoving til the right action arises by itself?

—Lao-Tzu, *Tao te Ching*

Standing Meditation Qigong is the center-post to a larger system of self-healing methods. The system of exercises that follow have evolved from my practice of various Qigong systems for two decades. Those that practice this system will see that Standing Meditation Qigong is the third set of the Bodymind Healing Qigong initiatory system (BMHQ). The astute student will discover through years of practice that the principle of "stillness in movement, and movement in stillness," with Standing Meditation Qigong at its core, is not a separate set, but a Way of Being woven through the whole ten sets that follow.

Following is the way in which I normally teach my ongoing classes, with the entire ten sets in the order that I, and my students, most prefer to practice them. Normally we practice the entire sequence in a one hour and forty-five minute period, with just a few of the animal movements (See my Bodymind Healing Qigong Video Tape or DVD.). The whole of Hua Tuo's animal frolic set is taught in BMHQ Level II; but I have included some of those movements here to show their role in a Qigong preventative medicine program, and how they illustrate various themes spoken about throughout the book. This is a good place to reiterate the advice given in the prologue to not overdose by doing too many movements at one time. Listen to you own body and be aware of when your Qi bank account is filling from doing the movements and when it is being depleted. Some people like to do just one movement repetitively, or a few movements, for many months.

For those who choose to do the whole set, my advice is, for at least a few months, practice the sets in the order shown here, for they have purposefully developed into this particular sequence. This order optimizes the cultivation and generation of Qi. For example, Tai Chi Ruler gets the Qi flowing so that in the next practice of Standing Meditation you will have already generated energy. After the Standing Meditation, the exercises that follow are meant to purify and disperse the Qi that can stagnate from this Standing practice. Later, once your body gets a sense of why the exercises flow from one set to the other, you may decide to change the order based upon your body's individual needs.

After each of the practices that follow, I elaborate on its bodymind healing purpose so that you can optimize the health and spiritual effects of the exercises by focusing your intention and targeting your practice accordingly. For example, there are exercises for: energizing the body, dispersing stagnant Qi, computer tension in the shoulders, chronic diseases, joint problems, heart, lungs, kidneys, preventing falls amongst the elderly, etc. Please check the index if you are looking for a particular targeted focus, but keep in mind that Chinese philosophy says that isolated focus contradicts the holistic nature of Chinese medicine. If you do practice a single movement, integrate the Standing Meditation into your Moving practice, filling your reservoir of Qi first, before you move. Return to stillness after the movement, noticing your breath throughout.

The Bodymind Healing Qigong initiatory system is best practiced about an hour after eating, or once your food is digested. It is highly beneficial to practice the movements out-of-doors in beautiful surroundings; yet they can be also be done indoors, in a well-ventilated place. During your early practice years, it is beneficial to practice in a quiet environment and at a comfortable temperature. Later these practices can be done anywhere, because you'll be carrying them with you in your cells wherever you are.

Though many people report healing effects of body, mind and spirit from this system of practice, these exercises should not be done as a substitute for treatment from a physician or other appropriate medical professionals.

Some General Principles of Practicing Qigong:

1. **Avoiding Injury**: While practicing, listen to your body's limits and keep returning to stillness, which the Taoists call Wuji. Injuries come from trying to do too much. The Ancient Taoist axiom is that "less is more." Do not over-stretch, or over-practice, but do pay attention to your body's limits. Over time, your body will naturally be able to stretch further and stay in these postures for longer periods of time.

2. **Breath**: Breathe naturally. Over time, your Qigong moving practice will teach you how to naturally "sink and raise your Qi." Begin by checking to see if you are practicing abdominal breathing. Place one hand on your belly, as you breath in your belly goes out; as you breath out the belly comes in. Notice how long the exhalation is, and how long the pause lasts after the exhalation. This "long-breath practice" will eventually become a natural part of your Qigong movements. Your breath will seem to rise to the heavens on the inhalation and sink down deep into the earth with the exhalation. The key to Qigong, and to generating Qi, is in naturally synchronizing this long, unforced breath with your movements.

3. **Posture**: Imagine that the alignment of your spine is as if your are a puppet dangling from the heavens. The upper body is light and the lower body is grounded. The chest is slightly hollowed, and the lower back (*Ming Men*) naturally over time begins to fill out as if it is pressing against a wall behind you. The above postural elements help the Qi to

descend to the belly (Tan Tien), and to the soles of the feet (Kidney 1), the bubbling spring point), and to ascend to the sky above.

4. **Joints:** The joints are not locked in Qigong practice to enable the Qi to flow through them naturally.

5. **Stillness in Movement:** The Taoist classics say, "The stillness that you normally experience is not the true stillness. Only when you find stillness in movement and movement in stillness is 'enlightenment' found." One important difference between Qigong and other exercise systems is the transference of awareness back and forth from stillness to movement. If you practice the following sets with this in mind, you may experience the natural glow of "en-lightened aliveness" emanating from you.

6. **Practice Times:** Do not practice when overly fatigued, hungry or overfed.

THE TEN SETS OF BODYMIND HEALING QIGONG

*I move with the infinite in Nature's power
I hold the fire of the soul,
I hold life and healing.*

—*Rig Veda*

The following are the methods and healing purposes for each movement:

Set 1: Unifying Heaven and Earth: Raising and Lowering Qi with Heavenly Palms

*Heaven was created by an accumulation of Yang
The Earth was created by an accumulation of Yin.
Yang ascends to Heaven; Yin descends to Earth.
Hence the universe represents motion and rest,
controlled by the wisdom of nature.*

—Ilza Veith, *Nei Ching*

Method 1: Raising Qi to the Tan Tien and Back to the Earth

With feet shoulder width apart, begin in a standing position with your knees bent. Your hands are at your sides. Your head reaches toward the heavens and your feet are connected to the earth; your awareness extends out to the horizons around you. Imagine that you are an acupunc-ture needle, giving the earth an acupuncture treatment, which makes it glow with healing energy.

Then rotate palms so that they are facing backward by your sides. The hands then float up to waist level, as if you're standing in a pool of water. As the wrists rise up, they suck the Qi up from the glowing earth beneath your hands. Then allow the hands to lower, pressing the Qi down. This sucking up and pressing down movement is done three times.

Method 2: Press Qi to Kidneys and Circle Around

Then press the palms past the line of your back as far as they can reach comfortably at kidney level. As you twirl your hand around, imagine circulating the Qi around your kidney area.

Bodymind Healing Purpose: This segment of the exercise helps to circulate Qi through the kidney area, which Chinese medicine associates with increasing energy and helping to alleviate fatigue.

Method 3: Raise Qi up the Chakras

Next rotate the palms around and forward, then lift them so that they pass by the ribcage and face your heart. Here, they are holding an imaginary ball, with your middle fingers slightly spread apart, in front of the center of the chest at the nipple-line (CV 17-acupuncture point). Feel the hands bring energy to the heart chakra.

Bodymind Healing Purpose: This segment of the exercise brings the water of the kidney energy to balance the fire of the heart.

Allow your hands to rise to be in front of the third eye, as seen in the picture below.

Method 4: Prayer over Crown Chakra to the Heavens

Then raise your hands above your head and bring them together, as if praying to the heavens.

Method 5: Finding the Heavenly Heart of Space

Then turn the hands around, palms facing forward with pointer fingers and thumbs touching, forming an upside down heart above your head.

Imagine that there is a jet stream of love travelling around the earth, and that you are catching it in this space between your hands.

Method 6: Lowering Qi down the Chakras

Bring your palms together in a Prayer Mudra as your hands come down in front of your third eye, and down to your heart with fingers pointing upward. Secondly, point your palms (still together) fingers forward.

Drawing from the previous posture, Finding the Heavenly Heart of Space, this posture may provide you with a new understanding of the well-known Buddhist mudra of compassion. This Qigong perspective shows how one can draw the energy that vitalizes the heart from the love of the universe.

Method 7: Opening and Gathering Energy into the Center of the Heart

Bring your hands, arms outstretched, in front of your heart about six inches apart. Imagine that you have a ball of healing energy that you are going to give as a present to one who you love, or that you are receiving such a ball from a loved one. As you breathe inward, test whether this is a Qi ball by slightly separating your hands as if trying to pull your hands apart from a sticky ball. As you breathe out, press your hands back together slightly with the heels of your palms pressing inward. Can you feel a force that seems to have an electromagnetic quality, or sensations of tingling or warmth?

Next, as you inhale, separate and expand your palms outward in front of your heart as if you are expanding a balloon that is growing larger; as you exhale allow the ball to contract. Do this movement three times.

Whole Body, Heart-centered Breathing Method: Finally, as you inhale and open your palms, move your weight slightly forward over the balls of your feet. As you exhale and you palms come toward each other, move your weight back toward your heels. This activates a whole body, heart-centered way of breathing.

Bodymind Healing Purpose: This particular movement, Opening and Gathering Energy into the Center of the Heart, is one of the best ways for beginners to experience "Qi," and the ball of Qi that is a fundamental center-post of Qigong healing. The unforced intention of opening and gathering energy into the energy gate of the heart cultivates self-healing abilities. The Whole Body, Heart-centered Breathing Method is great for love and life. For example, try this exercise when feeling emotionally drained, chronically weak, or empty in the heart chakra, after a break-up with a loved one, or to strengthen the spine (middle thoracic vertebras) behind the heart area. Experiment with this exercise in conjunction with other psychological, bodymind healing, and medical approaches.

Method 8: Opening and Gathering Energy into the Center of the Tan Tien

Method: After the hands meet in front of the heart for the third time in the last exercise, point the fingers downward, and lower the hands, palms together, to the navel (Tan Tien). Again, point the fingers forward, palms together. Slowly inhale as you expand an imaginary ball outward; exhale as the ball contracts. Open and close three times. Hands come back together in front on the Tan Tien.

Whole Body, Belly-Centered Breathing Method: As in the Whole Body, Heart-centered Breathing Method above, as you inhale, open your palms in front your belly, out to the sides, and move your weight slightly forward over the balls of your feet. As you exhale, your palms come toward each other and you move your weight back toward your heels. As you are rocking backward, slightly stretch your lower back (Ming Men), imagining that you are pressing it against an imaginary wall. This activates a whole body, belly-centered way of breathing.

Bodymind Healing Purpose: This particular movement, Opening and Gathering energy into the Center of the Tan Tien, along with the Whole Body, Belly-centered Breathing Method is useful for self-empowerment and for preventing lower back problems. For treatment of lower back problems try using this method in conjunction with treatment by other health professionals, and listening to your body.

Close Set 1 by opening the hands back to your sides in your Standing Meditation posture. Then open your hands to the side and bring them around in front of the heart to begin Set 2—Tai Chi Ruler.

Bodymind Healing Purpose: The set, Unifying Heaven and Earth: Raising and Lowering Qi with Heavenly Palms, is a set unto itself. A human being is a place for the forces of heaven and earth to meet. Heaven is light and yang, like the radiant sun, with its ability to create life and energy; earth is heaven's denser, yin partner in creating the beautiful life forms of the world of nature. When we acknowledge and make sacred this joining in us, we hold in our hands a gentle power that can guide these forces to play in us, heal us and do their work in accordance with the Way of things.

This set facilitates the joining of heaven and earth. The movements help you draw energy up from the earth, into the kidneys, circulate the Qi around the kidneys, then raise it up to the heart, third eye, and above the head. When the palms meet, you gather heavenly Qi, and as the palms form an upside down Heart Mudra; they gather the energy of the heart of space. The heavenly Qi comes down through the chakras one at a time, then the ball of Qi expands and contracts bringing the heart chakra and Tan Tien into balance. A complete healing circle is made by raising and lowering the Qi to open and balance the chakras. Repeat twice during each practice session, or as many times as feels right.

Set 2: Tai Chi Ruler

The three treasures of vitality, energy, and spirit
experience a daily flourishing of life, and fill the whole body
so that the great medicine can be expected to be produced naturally.

—Chuang Tsu

Method: Place the right foot slightly in front of the left. The left foot is at a 45-degree angle and your left toe is aligned with the middle of the right foot. Keep a fist's distance between the extended backward line of the right foot and the left heel.

Slowly rock backward onto your left foot, and inhale while your left knee bends and your right toes raise off the ground. Next, breathe out as you rock forward while your back, left heel rises naturally up off the ground. Repeat until you feel the sensation of filling and emptying your forward and rear foot, in turn. Your weight, when forward, should be over your right foot, knee bent. When your weight is on your left, back foot, your bent knee approaches being over the front your foot. Be careful not to extend your forward knee beyond your front toes.

Next, integrate hand movements. Place your hands about 6-8 inches apart, palms facing each other as if you have a ball between your hands. Your hands should be far enough apart so that the upper arms allow space for imaginary balls to fit in the armpits. As you rock forward, allow the hands to come down to the Tan Tien area (three finger's width distance below the navel). As you rock backward, the hands rise up toward the shoulders.

After at least 12 repetitions on one side, switch which leg is forward and repeat the movement to insure balance between the right and left sides of the body.

Rolling the Ball of Life

Method: Roll the Tai Chi ball by turning one palm upward (as shown) as the weight shifts into the forward leg, back heel raises. As you shift your weight backwards with front toe rising, imagine yourself pouring water/energy from the palm down hand, and leg beneath it, to the palm up hand and the leg beneath it. The circles of movement from the hand and leg to the opposite leg can be extended into a figure eight. Envision energy or water to bubbling up from the earth through the bottom of the foot (Kidney 1). As the palm rises, your weight shifts, and the breath comes in, bringing air up through the kidneys. Then as your weight shifts, the breath comes out, your backward hand is palm down, and the energy/water flows back to the earth through the opposite leg.

Bodymind Healing Purpose: Rocking is a primordial way of going into trance and creating an altered state of consciousness. It brings us back to being rocked by our mothers, or the universal mother, activating an alchemical process of transformation through *regressus ad uterum* (regression back to the womb).

In addition, Tai Chi Ruler is used for feeling "the pulse of life energy" in our bodies. This natural expansion and contraction, letting go and taking in (yin and yang), happens with every breath. Some people like to experience this by adding a phrase on the inhalation such as, "I'm taking in the fresh," and on the exhalation, "I'm letting out the stale." At first, a person may experience vibration or warmth in the hands. Allow this feeling to gradually spread to the elbows and shoulders, then throughout the body. Eventually you may feel the movement on a cellular level and become aware of the cells of the body expanding and contracting, taking in and letting go. This pulsation is actually more primordial than even the breath—modern researchers such as Ernest Rossi have rediscovered this Taoist key to healing and call it "ultradian rhythms." He and others use it for bodymind healing and hypno-therapeutic inductions for healing.

In Qigong self-healing, repetition is a key. Try practicing this exercise for two minutes or more, directing your intention and long-breath to a body part, and imagine that your body's tension is in the circle of the Tai Chi Ruler movement. Notice what happens. Tai Chi Ruler practice is particularly beneficial for upper body blocks such as shoulder and neck tension.

As the hands rise up in the first Tai Chi Ruler exercise, the lower back slightly pushes back. This is a method for reversing the fear response in the body. If someone comes to attack or push on you and you respond with fear, your upper body will retreat backwards and your energy will break at the midsection of your body (Tan Tien and Ming Men). Tai Chi Ruler is an ingenious way to circumvent the fear response and the breaking of the Qi by following the rising of the energy up as you inhale, and bringing the hands in as the lower back (Ming Men) presses slightly outward. Then you sink your Qi (to the Tan Tien) as you breathe out. It is a useful adjunct to psychotherapy treatment for victims of abuse for re-empowerment, and for finding your center in times of fragmentation or feeling scattered from the stresses of daily life.

Tai Chi Ruler, according to Ken Cohen's *The Way of Qigong*, is attributed to the tenth-century Taoist recluse, Chen Xi-yi whose name means "beyond sound and sight" or "unfathomable." It is a Taoist Alchemy practice which can be used to transform and balance the fire and water elements and touch on unfathomable experiences. The hands rise up enticing the fire in the body to rise; as the hands go down the Qi sinks, and makes contact with the descending waters of the bodymind. In Chinese medicine, longevity and the prevention of disease are seen, in part, to be based on balancing the elements of fire and water. As you do your first Tai Chi Ruler exercise, allow the ball of Qi to rise and fall. Imagine that you are bringing the fire and waters within you into balance.

Eczema and psoriasis, are examples of diseases of excess fire. Edema, bloating, excess tiredness, fatigue and stagnation of Qi in general are examples of excess water. As you do the first Tai Chi Ruler exercise, the fires of the body become activated, which helps to increase energy and burn off unwanted toxins. But, this can dehydrate the body fluids, as is true in all exercise. In Taoist alchemy, the saliva is swallowed along with the exhalation, and the downward movement of the hands, to balance the rising fire of Qigong practice. A key to this balance is setting your intention so that the relaxation response of the parasympathetic nervous system is balanced with the fight or flight activation response of the sympathetic nervous system. Qigong is the ideal exercise in this respect for creating what the Chinese call "*sung*," or relaxed alertness. It is partly for this reason that Qigong is an excellent longevity technique to balance energy generation and relaxation.

The second Tai Chi Ruler exercise, Rolling the Ball of Life, is an excellent practice for keeping the Kidney Qi (the water principle) in balance. Chinese medicine believes that the kidneys are a key component of creating and dispersing the vital energy of the body. Rolling the Ball of Life is a particularly well-suited exercise for circulating energy through the kidneys. Try experimenting with this Self-healing method in conjunction with your other health practices for preventing renal failure syndromes, chronic depleted energy, fatigue, low immune function, and lower back pain stemming from weakness.

Spiritual Purpose: Imagine yourself as an initiate in Chen Xi-yi's Jade Spring Temple at the foot of Mount Hua, using this movement system to arise in the morning to awaken your healing relationship to the universe. While practicing, imagine you have the power to heal the world in your hands. Many people enjoy doing this exercise before Standing Meditation to generate Qi. Don't underestimate this movement's power. Regardless of whether it's true that Chen Xi-yi's bones glowed red after he died as the monks of his temple say, you can imagine the movement's power going so deep it energizes your bones.

Set 3: Wuji Qigong

Yet the timeless in you is aware of life's timelessness,
And knows that yesterday is but today's memory,
and tomorrow is today's dream.
And that which sings and contemplates in you
is still dwelling within the bounds of that moment
which scattered the stars into space.

—Kahil Gibran

This is the most important "non-movement of Qigong," also called *Zhan Zhuang* (Standing like a Tree), or "the million dollar secret" of Qigong. It involves doing "no-thing." As was discussed earlier, recent scientific research has shown that *Zhan Zhuang Qigong* training increased the coherence of EEGs between the two frontal regions, between two occipital regions and between left and right temporal areas of the brain.

Method: Keep both feet parallel, pointing straightforward, between a hip and shoulder width apart. The knees are unlocked, approaching being over the toes, and slightly expanding towards the outside, as if holding a helium balloon between them. The pelvis is slightly turned forward as if you are getting ready to sit down on a stool. The lower back is slightly pushed out so that the lumbar curve begins to disappear allowing the back to approach being straight in the location of the Ming Men—the area of the lower back behind the Tan Tien. The chest and shoulders are relaxed, causing a slight rounding of the upper back. The arms hang loosely at the sides. The tongue is touching the top of the palate just behind the teeth to connect the *Jen Mei* channel down the front of the body and the *Tu Mei* channel up the back.

The eyes can either be open in a soft gaze, half open, closed and looking straight ahead, or open and looking down the secret *Taoist plumb line* along the line-of-sight of the nose. This "plumb line" can be found by focusing on a deep thought or feeling, and then noticing where your eyes drop naturally. Each position of the eyes activates a different intention (*Yi*). As you begin to feel the pleasant, energetic sensations brought on by this exercise, maybe a half smile will emerge from deep within you.

Notice the natural flow of the breath. Pay attention to how long and deep your breath is without trying to force it to be calm. See if you're breathing with the Long-breath Method, which, as we discussed in Section I, is like you are pressing on a tire with a slight hole in it; a "short breath," on the other hand, is like a blowout in a flat tire. Be aware of any sensations or thoughts that emerge during the practice.

Bodymind Healing Purpose: Stillness is the most powerful way of bringing out the psychological material that blocks the rivers of our Qi. Unlike the normal addictive patterns of activity to which we all succumb in Western civilization, in Standing Meditation we can't move away from our ingrained patterns because in stillness our blockages captivate our attention.

By being with our Selves we initiate a pattern of alchemical transformation which over time dissolves chronic body blockages. However, during the process tingling, vibrating, shaking, and even intense sudden involuntary jumping may occur as blocks in the rivers of Qi shake loose. Don't be alarmed, just breathe through it, or take a break and come back to the practice when you are ready. Occasionally a feeling of numbness in the hands, feet, one side of the body, or even the whole body may emerge. Aching may occur in various parts of the body, particularly in the areas of old injuries. Varying sensations of temperature are common including warmth, sweating or coldness. A sense of asymmetry often arises in various parts of the body. For example, one hand or leg may feel higher or longer than the other. All of these are signs of the activation of Qi healing old areas of blockage. As the light of the sun gradually melts ice in a river, so may the warmth of our loving energy, in time, melt away our blocked areas.

Spiritual Purpose: This is a key method for experiencing the golden energy of the *Sea of Elixir*—an experience of dissolving into a sea of cosmic bliss, spoken of in *The Secret of the Golden Flower*.[1] Through posture and practice we learn to re-align ourselves with the healing energies of the cosmos. Use this exercise to open the energy gates of the bodymind so that the physical body is transformed into an energy body that is one with the Tao.

In the Western alchemical traditions, as well, the importance of dissolving into the void is given primary importance. In one text it says, "Until all be made water, perform no operation," which fits well with the Taoist axiom that one should practice *Wuji* methods before Moving. The transformative purpose of the dissolving stage of alchemy is put well in the *Rosarium Philosophorum*, "The *solutio* has a two-fold effect: it causes one form to disappear and a new regenerated form to emerge." And if we want to change something about our life stance, Western Alchemy and Eastern Wuji practices join in believing that "Substances can not be transformed unless they are first reduced to *Prima Materia* (their first matter)."[2]

As was seen in Section I, Wuji Standing Meditation can be practiced in the form called *Zhan Zhuang* (Standing like a Tree) to shape-shift, and absorb the symbolic attributes of a tree. As you Stand you may develop further harmony with nature and its powers as you use your imagination to absorb and send energy back to trees. Notice your inhalation as you draw in imaginary energy from your roots beneath the ground. Imagine that your spine is like a tree trunk as the energy comes up to the top of your head, called the *bai hui* point, at the crown. As you exhale, imagine the energy coming down the front of your body, your tongue lightly touches the palette behind your teeth, then you follow your breath back down to your roots. Feel the way your spine makes a connection between the heavens above and the earth below. After a number of breaths, imagine yourself as a tree with deep roots, branches reaching out for the light, and transforming that light into energy as you imagine giving your fruit to others.

Holding Golden Balls in the Stream of Life

Imagine that you are facing upstream in a slowly moving river; your palms are slightly compressing two balls down into the water with just enough pressure so that they are steadied from floating downstream. The energy in your feet sinks down into the streambed, and your knees bend just so much that you take root and prevent the river from moving you downstream. Then practice this exercise as if you are facing downstream.

Laying Hands on the Earth

One variation to bring out the healing intention of Holding Golden Balls in the Stream of Life is to focus on some part of the earth that is in need of healing. Imagine that you are sending energy there through your hands on the exhalation and replenishing yourself on the inhalation.

Developing the Golden Ball of the Heart

There are infinite ways to discover your true Being,
But love holds the brightest torch.
If you follow it, you will be guided beyond
the limits of age and death.
Come out of the circle of time,
and find yourself in the circle of love.

—Deepak Chopra
Ageless Body, Timeless Mind

Start in the Standing Meditation posture, but allow the arms to rise up in front of and facing the heart as if they are embracing a balloon. Elbows are out to the side of the body and lower than the wrists. This helps the shoulders to relax. The hands are slightly turned outward, embodying a posture that looks as if you are holding a ball of liquid that is spilling out from the heart. After the posture has been maintained for a long enough time to build up Qi, you imagine the energy is spilling out over your outstretched hands to a loved one.

The breath coincides with the visualization—as you breathe out, you imagine giving energy to the world or a loved one, as you breathe in, you replenish yourself with the energy around you. Remember to practice Long-breath, not forced. After a short amount of time this visualization becomes much more. Can you feel energy flowing out from the heart and the whole body as if you are the sun shining light on the world?

Holding Three Balls in Front of the Heart

Method: Next, imagine that you are holding two balls filled with helium so that you are using just enough pressure to stop them from floating off into space. Then imagine that another ball is placed between the two balls you are holding. You want to apply just enough pressure to stop the third ball from falling and floating off into space. Imagine that your heart energy is placed into the third ball. Use the balanced yang energy in your right hand, and yin in your left hand to balance the energy of your heart. The hands can also be placed, palms down, as the second picture shows. Tap into the energy of Wuji stillness. Don't forget to breathe naturally.

Bodymind Healing Purpose: To build the reservoir of balanced Qi for hypertension and hypotension, heart chakra blockages, emotional wounding to the heart, chronic emptiness, and hollowness of the heart chakra. Many benefit from practicing Eugene Gendlin's "Focusing" process[3] while practicing this posture. Try using "Focusing" to discover the "felt meaning" of your emotional blocks, and to experience the "felt shift "that occurs when the felt meaning of those blocks emerge.

Holding Three Balls in Front of the Belly

As in the previous posture, imagine that you are holding three balls filled with helium. Imagine that your heart energy is placed into the third ball. Use the balanced energy of the yang ball in your right hand, and the yin energy of your left hand to balance the energy of your internal organs. Tap into the energy of Wuji stillness. Don't forget to breathe naturally.

Bodymind Healing Purpose: Use this posture to meditate on balancing the organs in the Tan Tien area (stomach, intestines, etc.). Obviously other factors need to be brought into balance as well, such as diet, exercise, etc. This Standing Meditation focuses on changing habits that are creating imbalances in this area of the body including diet, emotional factors, etc. For example, one of my patients got in touch with his "carbohydrate addiction," and found the stance to go on a low carbohydrate Atkins diet. He subsequently lost ten pounds in a few weeks and has kept off this weight to date.

Circulating Qi: The Healing Circle that Arises from Stillness

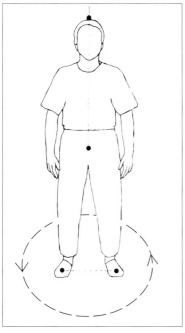

Figure 30

Trees are not rigid, nor should you be when practicing Standing or Sitting Meditation. The next practice helps to facilitate fluidity of Being as you move from your primordial stance in stillness. After Standing for a period of time in the place where you've built your reservoir of Qi, you can begin the practice of circulating Qi. It is important to not rush into this second phase.

To experience the circulation of Qi that emanates from stillness, start in your Standing Meditation posture with weight balanced equally over each foot. Feet are shoulder width apart.

After Standing for three to five minutes, imagine that your spine is like the trunk of a tree, or a staff. Slowly shift your weight over the right heel, but only shift the weight 1% so that you are now 51% over you right heel and 49% over your left heel. Then make a circle where you shift your weight to the front of your right foot, then to the front of your left foot and then to the rear. As you are circling, imagine cutting a hole into the heavens with the staff of your spine—the staff will cut into the earth below the *hui yin* point (projected downward between your two feet) and into the heavens above the *bai hui* point.

Make sure your spine stays erect and does not tilt. Imagine a snake spiraling around your spine and traveling from the earth, up to the heavens, then back down.

After doing this for a short while, return to stillness. The movement should be experienced as originating from stillness and returning to it. When you find the stillness in movement, and the movement in stillness, you have experienced one of the qualities of Qi.

Bodymind Healing Purpose: The circulation of Qi that emanates from Wuji is central to Taoist methods of healing; it parallels the key symbol of ancient holistic Western medicine—the staff of Aesclepius. This exercise can be used in Sitting Meditation practice to prevent stagnation of Qi by allowing the spine to move very slightly around in a circle. Remember to allow the movement to arise from your stillness rather than "trying" to move. Circulation of Qi helps prevent rigidity in the Sitting Meditation stance. This practice of circulation of Qi can aid in massage and body work.

Exploring Acupressure Self-Touch with the Circle that Arises from Stillness

When there is a tight spot in your body, press it with one finger, circle and stop and feel. Send love to this spot. Do you experience energy there? Get an acupuncture chart and do the same with a spot on the chart. Become a scientific explorer, open up to your own truth, guided by what you feel.

The "One Hand Near, One Hand Far" Method: Balance your Energy Field for Health

The recent flowering of the Standing Meditation healing tradition in the West is enhanced by the gift of Dr. Zhi Gang Sha's "One Hand Near, One Hand Far" method.[4] He is a lineage holder of the Zhi Neng (pronounced *ju nung*) healing tradition, which translates as "intelligence and capabilities of the mind." His system of healing combines Standing Meditation, hand postures, sound and visualizations. The theoretical basis for his method is that energy in the body naturally moves from high to low intensity fields, and it uses the aforementioned elements to facilitate such movement of energy. In a case of excess energy, the patient puts one hand close to the area of excess and their other hand further away from their body in order to move the excess away from the area of high intensity. In cases of deficiency, the patient places one hand further away from the deficient area of the body and the other hand closer to another body part to bring the energy from the high intensity, strong area to the low intensity, deficient area. For example, for high systolic and high diastolic hypertension, the near hand is placed over the crown of the head or facing the forehead, and the far away hand is by the lower abdomen. The patient visualizes light flowing from the head to the lower abdomen as he or she repeats the sound *yi* (for the head) and *jiu* (for the abdomen).

Dr. Sha uses many hand postures and sounds for a wide variety of other conditions. Group ritual, where a whole group chants together, amplifies the placebo effect, and perhaps may increase the healing dimensions of "the energy field" itself. Many anecdotal reports exist of the healing effects of his methods.[5]

The sounds Dr. Sha uses for different parts of the body are:

Body Part	Chinese Word	English Pronunciation
Head	yi	ee
Heart	ar	arh
Chest	san	san
Esophagus	si	su
Stomach, spleen	wu	woo
Ribs	liu	lu (like ewe)
Liver	chi	chee
Navel	ba	bah
Lower abdomen	jiu	jo (like Joe)
Anus	shi	shir
Limbs, hands feet, legs	shiyi	shiree

The sounds Dr. Sha uses for different organs are:

Organ	Healing Sound
Liver	Jiao
Heart	Zhi
Spleen	Gong
Lungs	Shang
Kidneys	Yu

Try experimenting with Dr. Sha's ideas and sounds and adapt them to your own inclinations. Dr. Sha, in his group healings, likes to use chants that honor the power of the universe to heal. For example, while in Standing postures, Dr. Sha has the group do variations on the following chant and ritual:

> *Dear mind, body, soul of…(the problematic body part).… I love you, you have some blocks. Help yourself. Come back to balance. Then the group chants over and over, "God's light, God's light…" over and over. Then the group chants repetitively, "Be well, be well. Heal, heal. Thank you. Thank you."*

As you are doing the above ritual in your Standing Meditation posture feel free to call on the healers of all ages, an element of nature, your own representation of God or a healing deity, for example, Jesus, Buddha, Wakantaka, Kuan Yin, Mohammed, Krishna, Isis, Aesclepius or YHVH (the nameless Jehovah).

Though Dr. Sha uses the energy of group ritual and the sound of chanting this can easily be adapted to a Self-Healing ritual. Try it on your own in conjunction with complementary care by your chosen team of health professionals.

Set 4: Exercises after Standing to Disperse Stagnant Qi

Method 1: Electromagnetic Cleansing of Skin

Begin with hands at your side. While breathing in, raise your hands to the side until they are outstretched over your head. As your palms face the top of your head, stop and breathe nice Long-breaths. Imagine that your right hand is reflecting the energy of the sun, and the left hand is reflecting the energy of the moon to the crown of your head. The top of your head is like a flower ready to bloom. Like a flower can't be rushed to bloom, neither can you be.

First cycle—Cleansing the Skin: Next, imagine that the right and left hands are charged like electromagnets with a Yang (right hand) and Yin (left hand) polarity. Imagine that any stagnant energy remaining on your skin after standing is like iron filings. Very slowly and while you're breathing, allow your hands to gradually descend and pick up these iron filings through magnetic attraction. When you reach the bottom, with your hands by your sides, turn off the electric magnet by letting go for a few long-breaths. Imagine that the iron filings are turning into molten lava and seeping back to the iron at the core of the earth.

Second cycle—Cleansing the Internal Organs: Breathe in slowly as you raise your hands above your head. As you breathe out, the hands lower gradually. Repeat as above, but this time imagine that the electromagnetic Yang and Yin polar energies are attracting stagnant Qi from the internal organs and healing them.

Third cycle—Cleansing the Bone Marrow: Repeat as above, but this time imagine that you are cleansing the bone marrow. Again, at the end of your cycle of hands raising and lowering, imagine the iron filings are returning to the earth. Take a few long-breaths and feel how the stagnant Qi leaves on the exhalation and fresh Qi comes in on the inhalation.

Bodymind Healing Purpose: According to modern Physics, human beings are condensed light. When the light of the universe condenses in our body and runs into our emotional and physical blockages, it is like a river where log-jams block free flow. Standing Meditation makes us aware of, and constellates, these places of stagnant Qi. Dissolving and dispersing stagnant Qi exercises can break up the log-jams, and allow the river of life to move again, to evaporate into water vapor and to transform into space. In time, with awareness, we return to our source as the Beings of light we are.

Method 2: Massaging and Tapping

Method: Another step in dispersing stagnant Qi is to look at your hands, notice if you see or feel anything different about them (such as if they are splotchy with red coloring, a sign of Qi, or if they are warmer than usual). Then, rub your hands together to generate Qi, and next, lightly massage your body wherever it needs attention. Go down the outside of the legs and up the inside. Try lightly tapping on your body; then, stop and feel the energy as you are in stillness.

Method 3: Horse Tapping Feet

Method: After Standing Meditation, simply tap your toes against the ground as if you are knocking off some dirt. Then circle the ankle. Master Sam Tam advises to touch the toe to the ground to allow for a fuller rotation of your ankle.

Bodymind Healing Purpose: Helps to disperse the stagnant Qi in the feet, which may accumulate after Standing. By rotating the ankles, circulation is enhanced there.

Shamanic/Spiritual Purpose: Many Qigong movements come from early humans watching and learning from their animal brethren. After Standing Meditation, we follow the teachings of horses who also stand for long periods of time and tap their hooves on the earth to disperse stagnant Qi.

Method 4: Horse Whipping Tail

Method: With the arms loose, turn the pelvis from the waist and allow that movement to swing the arms so that the hands go over the shoulders and whip as far as they extend naturally over the trapezius muscle. Like a horse whipping a fly on its back with its tail...no effort.

Bodymind Healing Purpose: Helps to loosen pent up energy and tension in the shoulders. We often carry the burdens of "civilized" life in the shoulders.

Spiritual Purpose: This move teaches us how to let go (Wu Wei, effortless effort), as a child instinctively knows how to let go. Watch how easily children can do this movement compared to how it feels for us to do this after a day at the office with intense, intellectual activity. And yet, we can be like a child again with a swing of the arms.

Method 5: Tapping around the Belly Clock

Allow your fists to close, but not too tightly (called soft fists). Start with both fists on each side of the belly and tap to your own drum beat, not too hard, not too soft. Tap around your whole belly in a clockwise circle to increase circulation.

Bodymind Healing Purpose: This exercise helps increase the circulation in the digestive tract. Try it for stagnant Qi in the belly area. Try using this for constipation and excess weight due to a sedentary lifestyle. In addition, examine dietary factors with a nutrition consultant and/or your medical doctor.

Method 6: Wild Goose Taps its Chest—The Way to Say Hello and Goodbye

Method: Make your hands look like a bird's beak. With the beak, tap points on your chest. Try tapping on the point, Lung 1, which is on the line midway between the collarbone and the armpit, right where your shoulder joint meets your body in a little hollow. This exercise is best done out-of-doors. As you tap on your chest, imagine bringing in the healing power of nature into your chest; as your hands go out, open the bird's beak and feel as if you are giving back to nature.

It is important at the end of this sequence to open both hands completely, and imagine giving the heart's energy to nature or a loved one. Or, as seen in the last picture in this sequence, place one hand on the heart and the fingers of the other hand opens. Some people like to add a mantra along with the movement, such as, "I give to life (as the hands open and you breathe out); I receive the healing I need from life (as the hands tap the chest and you breathe in)."

Bodymind Healing Purpose: Experiment with tapping on these points for bronchial congestion and blocked energy in the chest. Tap on the points shown in the picture where the shoulder joint meets the body (Lung 1), for issues involving grief and letting go, and for increasing the Qi of the lungs. Use your doctor, psychologist, and acupuncturist's complementary care.

Spiritual Purpose: I have adapted the last movement in this sequence, which I call *Wild Goose says Hello and Goodbye*, into my favorite greeting. Try tapping your heart and extending your "wild goose beak hand" to someone who you are especially pleased to meet. I also like to use this movement to say "good-bye" to someone with whom I have had a meaningful encounter. Try tapping your heart and opening your "goose beak hand" after being with someone who you appreciate. It is a way of leaving a Qi-full piece of your heart in gratitude to someone who has touched your heart in your meeting.

Set 5: Five Element Internal Organ Healing

Wood: Opening the Shoulder Well, to Release Muscular Tension from the Gall Bladder Meridian

Method: Stand with your feet shoulder width apart, knees slightly bent, pelvis slightly tucked in. Cross both hands, with right over the left, in front of the heart, at a comfortable distance from the body, and as if you are holding a ball. Then open them downward to the sides of the body, then up over the head. Interlock the fingers, pushing the hands, palms facing out and upward to the heavens. Look up and back at the small pinkie fingers. Keep your awareness on your line-of-sight up to the pinkies. You'll feel this movement opening an important acupoint, Gall Bladder 21, located about one to two inches from the base of the neck, on the midline between the neck and shoulders, anterior to the trapezius muscle.

Bodymind Healing Purpose: Opens one of the key energy gates where tension is held from excess intellectual activity, office work, too much time on the computer and carrying emotional burdens. This helps to realign one aspect of the earth energy ruled by the gall bladder, which Chinese medicine believes has to do with decision-making and self-assertion. This point (GB 21) has been called Shoulder Well, because a reservoir of healing energy resides there if only we can take the civilized cover off of it and tap into its deep healing resources.

Spiritual Purpose: Opens the door to the higher chakras, which tend to be locked at the shoulders due to our holding on to the "civilized" tensions and burdens of life."

Fire: Buddha Opens the Heart to the Heavens

Method: As in the last exercise, assume your Standing position. Cross the hands in front of the heart, wrists touching, then open them down and to the sides, then up over the head. After interlocking the fingers, palms facing out and up, open the hands so that the two middle fingers point at each other. Open the hands while making the sound "ah" three times as you exhale.

Bodymind Healing Purpose: This posture opens the emotional center of the heart, located at CV 17, about four finger's width above the bottom of the breastbone. It induces the feeling of joy.

Spiritual Purpose: We often see statues of the Buddha in this *mudra*, (divine gesture). It opens one of the key energy gates to connect with the heart energy of the universe; it opens a door to the "heart of space."

Earth: Raising Qi to the Heavens and Sinking Qi to the Earth, to Balance the Stomach Meridian

Earth: Raising Qi (continued)

Method: Allow the hands, palms up, to rise up, first to the belly (Tan Tien), and then, with palms down, to come back down to the earth. Synchronize the inhalation and the raising of the heels with your hand movements. Next allow the heels and the hands to rise (palms up) to the heart, then with palms down, return to the earth. Finally, allow the hands to rise up, palms up, to the sky, then with palms down, return to the earth. An additional component is to imagine the energy rising up through the bottom of the feet (Kidney 1) up the sides of the body (Yin and Yang Chiao Mo called the Great Bridge Channel) then going back down through the bottoms of the feet.

Bodymind Healing Purpose: This is one of the most basic Qigong exercises. It can be used to either energize, or ground the body's energy. For times of low energy, focus your intention on the raising up motion and on the inhalation. Focus on the exhalation, and the movement of the Qi down the central and lateral channels of the body, for stress reduction or hypertension, particularly in times of excess anger when our coping skills are limited. (These can be cases that Chinese medicine calls "Stagnant Liver Qi" or "Liver Fire Rising"). Variations on this posture go back to Hua Tuo's Bear Animal Frolic, and were used as a medical prescription in the First Century A.D. This exercise is useful for energizing and grounding the body's natural sense of power coming from the earth.

Earth: Crane Stands on One Leg, for Balance

Method: Begin with your right foot facing forward, the heel of your left foot is one fist apart from the right foot, and at a 45-degree angle. Allow the hands to rise up to the shoulders with the wrists leading, as if sucking up two balls from the ground. As the wrists rise, breathe in and allow the knee to rise along with them until it's parallel to the ground at the pelvis level. As the hands come down, turn the right foot outward 45 degrees, bend the knee, let your weight sink down and breathe out as the hands come down to the Tan Tien. Repeat the cycle on the other side. Try using the sound "haw" subvocally to ground the earth energy on the exhalation.

For the first few weeks of practicing this exercise, you may prefer to go gradually and not raise the foot any higher than with the toe touching the ground. After a few weeks, or when sufficient strength develops, gradually raise the foot up. The Taoist method of training is to progress slowly to avoid injury or strain. At the most advanced level, as you breathe in with the knee raised, allow the body to raise by extending the back leg, which is on the ground. As you breathe out, the body lowers as you bend your back leg. This is excellent strength training if done gradually and while staying in tune with your body's needs.

Bodymind Healing Purpose: Over 30% of people aged 65 or over experience at least one fall per year and 15% of those falls result in serious injuries. Falls are the sixth largest cause of death among seniors and contribute to a general health decline even when they're not the direct cause of death. The Journal of the American Medical Association (May 3, 1995) reports that exercises like this one, stemming from Tai Chi/Qigong, have been shown to be more beneficial than exercises from other systems for decreasing falls amongst the elderly. This practice strengthens the legs and helps with balance.

Spiritual Purpose: An earth energy imbalance can be related to over-thinking, worry, obsessiveness and anxiety. This exercise helps to raise the spirit (as the hands and breath comes up), and sink the Qi (as the hands and breath comes down). The movement helps us to be a meeting place for the peaceful and vital forces of Heaven and Earth. It thereby grounds us and can heal excesses of intellectual activity. "Walking in balance on the earth" will no longer be just a figure of speech.

Metal: Opening the Bow, for the Lungs

Method: Begin with your feet pointing forward at shoulder width apart. Turn the right foot 135 degrees around from facing center so that the right knee is over the toes. Your weight is 60% forward, and you are facing backward, 180 degrees from front centerline Place the left thumb into the point (Lung 1) in the center crease of the line of the shoulder, equidistant between the clavicle and the armpit. Press your thumb inward toward the body, make a circle, and notice whether you feel any energetic sensations. Place the right hand outstretched 180 degrees, elbow is slightly bent, and the right pointer finger is straight up while the three fingers next to it are bent into a "dragon's palm." After circling a number of times, stop and breathe into your lung points and your lungs with your hand still outstretched, for at least four exhalations. Can you feel the circulation of the Lung Meridian Qi in the stillness after the movement? Do the same posture on the other side, with left foot turned and left palm extended.

As you gaze out and over your thumb, which is the end of the lung meridian, and at your Lung 1 point in the shoulder crease, imagine that you are shooting an arrow from your body outward. It can be an arrow of love, an arrow representing something that you'd like to let go of, or you can use the posture to direct energy towards some element of nature or object of focus. Don't feel inhibited to turn on music you like and twist and gyrate your whole body and thumb, clearing out your lung meridian.

Bodymind Healing Purpose: The lungs, in Chinese medicine, are connected emotionally to grief and sadness. This posture is also good for letting go of stale air with the exhalation and bringing in the fresh on the inhalation. Try this movement for bronchial congestion along with other health care.

Spiritual Purpose: The lungs are considered to be the organ for letting go and non-attachment. As you do this exercise, feel what you want to let go of in your life as you say the sound "ah" (as differentiated from "ha" for the heart), others like to say "shhh "or "sha." This posture is also good for developing intentionality, called "Yi" in Chinese, as you aim the arrow of your Lung Meridian.

Water: Energizing the Kidneys

Method: Stand with your feet shoulder width apart, knees slightly bent, pelvis slightly tucked in. Reach your right hand around your back to your left kidney and rub in a circular direction with the soft area between your thumb and pointer finger knuckle (acupoint Large Intestine 4, called Hoku). At the same time, stretch your left hand across your body at kidney level. After rubbing for at least 18 circles, stop and feel your kidneys with your hand still outstretched for at least 4 exhalations. Can you feel the circulation of the kidney's Qi in the stillness after the movement? Reverse positions so that your left hand goes around the back to the right kidney and rubs, while the right hand crosses over the body. The sound is either *chir-ee* to energize the kidneys, or *whooh*, as in a soft, yet deep sigh, letting go of fear.

Bodymind Healing Purpose: The Taoists and Chinese medicine tells us that the kidneys are the source of life energy. By rubbing around the kidney area, called the Sea of Vitality, we help to increase our body's energy, and work with the process of healing constitutional deficiencies. Practice it in the wintertime to warm the kidneys. Try it for emotional issues having to do with fear and insecurity. Use the exercise in conjunction with your treatment by other health professionals.

Spiritual Purpose: This exercise activates the Sea of Vitality and builds our awareness of the energy of life that is our source of power. By practicing this exercise, we learn to appreciate our position in this world as "energetic Beings."

Wood: Releasing Toxins and Stagnant Qi from the Liver

Method: Begin with both feet parallel, pointing forward, between hip and shoulder width apart. Place your right hand slightly out from the body and at the level of your heart; the fingers should be straight up, yet outstretched as if around a ball. Place your left hand, with fingers pointed downward, at the level of your liver. Turn to the left from your centerline, as if you were pressing on a long balloon. The hands slowly squeeze together as if stale or toxic energy is being released from a small hole in the balloon while you make the sound "sssss."Others use the sound "*huh*" or "*shuuu*" for the Liver. Reverse the posture by turning to the right around your centerline, as the left hand is in the upper posture by your heart and the right hand is below.

Bodymind Healing Purpose: This posture is for meditating on eliminating toxins from the body in general, and from the liver in particular. Try it the day after a night of partying or when you sense your body is getting toxic.

The negative emotion of the liver has to do with hostility, frustration, or anger, all of which this posture helps to release. For emotional healing while doing this exercise, first imagine an area of your life where you are feeling anger. You can release it out of the balloon, and transform your feeling into self-assertion and power. Try this practice along with Hua Tuo's Bear Animal Frolic for liver related issues in conjunction with other health treatment.

Spiritual Purpose: As your negative energy is released into the environment, you can imagine turning it into fertilizer that is adding nutrients to the earth.

Set 6: Exercises for Transforming the Muscles, Ligaments, and Tendons

Spinal Stretch: Yi Jin Jing

Method: Begin with the feet at shoulder width apart, hands by your side. Allow the hands, palms up, to rise by your sides and over the top of your head as you inhale. As you exhale, allow the hands to come down, tracing two separate lines down the two lateral channels of the body. (In Chinese medicine this exercise balances the Great Bridge Channel, or *Yang and Yin Chiao Mo*, which balances and bridges the yin and yang meridians). Still on the exhalation, allow the whole upper body and head to lower toward the ground until the hands are dangling close to the ground, with the head hanging loose. Take a few breaths into and out of the lower back, feeling the deep expansion and contraction in that area as you slightly rise up from, and back to, the ground. Then raise your back up gradually, as if you are stacking the vertebrae one on top of the other. Feel each vertebra open and stack on top of the one below it. You may feel a rush of energy climbing up your back to the top of your head, which is the Central Channel (Jen Mo and Tu Mo), of the spine opening up.

When you are standing again, continue to inhale as you stretch the fists back, palms up, until the fists are at the side of the chest with the elbows in their furthest back position. (This empowers the heart chakra.)

112   Secrets to Living Younger Longer

Then, as if releasing an elastic band, breathe out as the palms come out facing forward, so that the arms are as if they are embracing a ball with the outer arms facing in toward your body. The two middle fingers point toward each other. This movement is useful for forming boundaries and creating protective Qi (Wei Qi).

Next, as you inhale, allow the middle fingers to touch the thumbs as the other fingers group around them in the shape of a Crane's Beak

As you inhale allow the Crane's Beak to rise up, the rounded wrist leading the way, while at the same time rising up on your toes. Finally, on the exhalation, the hands come back down the two lateral channels with the hands ending up at your sides.

Bodymind Healing Purpose: In the Sixth Century A.D., Boddhidharma, a Buddhist monk, came to the Shaolin temple in China. When he witnessed the monks getting sick from long hours spent in Sitting postures, he transmitted a healing system to reverse these effects. From this period of time he developed the *Yi Jin Jing* exercises to heal the muscles, tendons, and bone marrow. You'll notice that the spine is stretched in complementary opposing directions to increase its flexibility. As you bend over, the spine bows, and as you rise up and stretch the fists back, the spine is torqued in the opposite direction. Likewise, you can feel the opposite stretches of the spine as the hands in the Crane's Beak position pull up, and the rubber band of the spine releases as you bring the hands back down.

The bending down portion of this exercise should not be practiced if you have any severe injury in your lower vertebrae due to the deep stretching of the lower back. Likewise, the exercise could have adverse effects in the case of a recent concussion, due to the position of your head being down with the blood rushing to it.

Spiritual Purpose: From the earliest of times in the West, the staff of Hermes and Aesclepius, with the snake winding around it, and the Kundalini dragon in the East, symbolized the movement of the snake energy coming from the ground, up the spine and out the top of the head. The opening of the spine allows the human being to assume his or her birthright as the animal who stands fully erect, connecting heaven and earth through the staff of the spine.

The Taoist development of the spine (particularly when practiced in conjunction with Microcosmic Orbit Breathing) emphasizes circling the energy up and down the spine as opposed to raising it straight up. This enables the practitioner to avoid some serious health problems, such as Kundalini psychosis, that can come from raising the energy up the spine in a linear, forced way.

Abductor Stretch

Method: Begin standing with the feet approximately two shoulder widths apart, or as far apart as is comfortable so the knees can comfortably go over them. With spine erect, shift the weight from side to side over each foot. If this is too difficult, for the first few weeks of practice place your hands on your knees to protect them from straining. After a few weeks, or when your body is ready, gradually bend over all the way to the ground.

As you shift to the right, place your hands on the ground on the right side as your weight shifts over your right knee. Turning your neck, look up to the left. Stay aware of your knees, making sure there is no excess strain, and keep both feet solidly on the ground. With your hands still on the ground, walk your hands, one over the other, until your weight is over the left knee. Your neck turns to the right. Repeat as necessary.

Bodymind Healing Purpose: Stretches the abductors on the inside of the legs, and connects the opening of the pelvic floor to the releasing of the neck. As is well-known for cranial-sacral work, the pelvis and neck are connected. The Taoists also knew that the neck and pelvic zones were both energy passage zones between major parts of the body—head and trunk, and upper body and legs, respectively. Use this practice to help heal imbalances and create strength and flexibility for musculo-skeletal issues in the neck and pelvis.

This exercise is a variation of one of the famous Qigong exercise systems, called "The Eight Pieces of Brocade," developed by Marshal Yueh Fei in the twelfth century to improve the health of his soldiers.

Spiritual Purpose: Opens the energy gates to these significant zones of the body and helps create a better connection to the earth. It also opens the Sea of Vitality, bringing energy into the kidneys and legs.

Set 7: Ancient Animal Qigong

Whoever can guide his breath like the dragon,
pull it in and circulate it like the tiger,
stretch like the bear or swallow it like the tortoise,
who moreover can fly like the swallow,
coil like the snake, stretch like the bird...
he will live a long life.

—Ge Hong (283–343 A.D.)
Baopuzi, *Book of the Master who Embraces Simplicity*

Introduction to the Shamanic Tradition of Animal Movements

A Native American fisherman, in the times of old, paddled his kayak into an unknown bay. As he walked, exploring this untouched new territory, he heard uproarious laughter and cautiously followed the sound until it led him to the mouth of a cave. After carefully creeping through a great cavern, he saw gathered around a great roaring fire animals of all varieties, large and small. They were playing a game that made them laugh from the depths of their different souls. The game was "shape-shifting," in which they embodied the postures of different forms and their bodies changed into those forms. The fisherman was in awe as the animals turned into human form and the human beings turned into animal forms. [6]

This story, told in Chapter 1, is told again here to repeat our essential theme. Movement has been used as a tool from ancient times to transform consciousness and to heal. Animal movements may be the oldest forms of Qigong used for this purpose.

One of the ways that animals survive in the wild—with extremes of temperature and enduring other traumas—is by the way they move. Early shamans studied their movements and learned that every different animal had secrets to teach about generating energy and healing different parts of the body. They used this knowledge to heal themselves and their tribe.

As discussed earlier, scholarly evidence shows that the animal movements were used by shamans in the Zhou dynasty (1028-221 B.C.). During a New Year's ritual known as the Great Exorcism (Da No), a shaman danced through the village, followed by a procession of villagers wearing masks of the zodiacal animals to drive out pestilence and demons. In the King Ma tomb, (168 B.C.), at Mawangdui in one of the coffins, a piece of silk was found, called the *Daoyin tu*, which showed 44 figures representing nearly all the major categories of modern Qigong, including breathing, stances and movement. Among the captions, under some of the figures are the names of animals including hawk, wolf, crane, dragon, cat, and bear. The captions name specific medical disorders such as kidney disease, flatulence, painful knees, and anxiety.[7]

Following is a set of animal movements that you may practice as part of your transformational journey to shape-shift into the instinctual Ways of Being that may be needed in your life. The exercises that follow begin with movements gleaned from various Qigong systems, which incorporate the primordial knowledge encoded in animal movements. First are some movements representing the Snake, the Praying Mantis, the Dragon and the Wild Goose. Then some animal movements are chosen to represent the Five Animal Frolics of famous Third Century A.D. physician Hua Tuo (110-207 A.D.). He was the first Taoist physician who synthesized earlier Taoist methods into a five-animal form: bear, crane, monkey, tiger, and deer. Two of my Animal Frolics teachers, Ken Cohen and Dr. Alex Feng, like to repeat Hua Tuo's famous statement which emphasizes that movement is important to health, "Door hinges don't become worm-infested, running water doesn't become fetid."

The exercises are not direct representations of the intricate full systems of Qigong from which they are derived. There are obviously substantial omissions. The movements are chosen to represent this book's intention of combining breadth and depth, to the extent possible here, in acquainting the reader with a few gems from the treasure house of the Qigong Animal Forms. Each one of Hua Tuo's Animal Frolics has many movements, and here you will see just a few movements representing each animal. (In Bodymind Healing Qigong Level 2, the whole of Hua Tuo's Animal Frolic Form is taught, which includes between five and eight movements per animal. Likewise, Wild Goose Qigong is a very extensive system and here only one movement is chosen to represent it.) Our purpose is to inspire the reader with an appreciation for the secrets that animals possess to facilitate our healing as human beings. As does a book synopsis invite the reader to read further, so it is my hope that the postures chosen here will entice the reader to practice and imbibe these primordial Ways of Being, and find a deeper harmony with the Ways of Nature, and the healing path of the Tao. Please investigate further with teachers in your geographical area.

As you follow the path of the lost Native American fisherman in the above story, you can use these movements in the cave of your everyday life to shape-shift into the form needed for your healing. Some of my students who are shy have benefited from practicing the Tiger; those who are excessively serious have lightened up from the humorous antics of Monkey Qigong; and those with blocked pelvic and sexual energy have benefited from the Dragon as part of their inner work. At the Health Medicine Institute, in conjunction with the medical team with whom I work, the Crane movements have been helpful to quite a few patients. Combined with guided imagery and other Qigong exercises, including Walking Meditation, the Crane movements have played a significant healing role with patients recovering from "failed back surgery syndrome." As well, these methods have helped patients who have hip disorders, and movement disorders involving balance and difficulty walking. In intermediate level Bodymind Healing Qigong training, students are given a particular animal or elemental form (fire, earth, metal, water, wood) to practice what fits with their constitutional or health needs.

As you practice these movements over your lifetime, as the Native American fisherman did, if you sit before the fire of your intention, you may find yourself shape-shifting from one state of consciousness to another, depending upon what your higher Self needs. By assuming these postures and doing these movements, you may become aligned with the creator of those archetypal energy potentials inherent in life.

The Spirit of the Practice of the Animal Movements

If we are here for any good purpose at all,
other than collating texts, running rivers, and learning the stars,
I suspect it is to entertain the rest of nature.
A gang of sexy primate clowns.
All the little critters, creep in close to listen
when human beings are in a good mood…
{and they watch when human beings make some good moves}.

—Adapted from Gary Snyder
The Practice of the Wild

"This we know—the earth does not belong to man,
Man belongs to the earth.
All things are connected like the blood that unites one family.
Whatever befalls the earth befalls the sons of the earth.
Man did not weave the web of life; he is merely a strand of it.
Whatever he does to the web he does to himself."

—Chief Seattle[8]

The two quotes above represent two different stances to take in relationship to the Animal Movements…the humorous and respectful. Gary Snyder would say, "Have fun when you are practicing the animal forms." Chief Seattle might advise that when you are doing the following animal movements to keep in mind, and in heart, your gratefulness for the wider universe of elements and for our animal brethren of which we are a part. In Chinese there is a single word for HeartMind, (*Xin*, pronounced *shin*). May you find your HeartMind as you practice these moves.

Find the State of Being that you need to create as you practice the following movements. Most importantly, don't just do the form, invest yourself with the spirit of the animal you are practicing.

Shedding Snakeskin from the Legs: Dionysus meets Chinese Shamanism

Method: As you are rising up from the previous posture, from the last set, Transforming the Muscles Ligaments and Bones Marrow, called Abductor Stretch, turn 45 degrees to the right from your centerline. With your hands and fingers outstretched, pull back toward your Tan Tien (three fingers below the belly button). Imagine that your fingers are connected to elastic bands so that it is a bit hard to pull them from the ground. Then allow the elastic bands to pull your upper body and your hands back, almost to the ground, while your body is still 45 degrees to the right. Next, while bent over, turn to the left and repeat, pulling up and relaxing back down. Repeat as many times as desired. As you inhale and exhale, feel which muscles are tightening and loosening. As your hands are coming down an inch or so from your legs, imagine that you are scraping off, or shedding snakeskin from the legs.

Bodymind Healing Purpose: The psoas muscle is one of the deepest muscles in the body. It extends from the thigh, through the pelvic floor and then attaches to the spine near the last rib at vertebra T12, and the lumber vertebrae beginning at Lumbar 1. The excessive tightening of the psoas muscle is the beginning of many postural misalignments, including (the apparent "shrinking," or stooping over, of many elderly people. The psoas muscle is related to the health of the kidneys.

By imagining yourself cleansing snakeskin from the legs and moving the hands all the way up to the kidney, the sense of clearing can be accentuated. In conjunction with treatment by other health professionals, try this movement for skin disorders, for general clearing of stress from the body, and for general reactivation of the vital energy of the body when stressed.

Spiritual Purpose: Opening the Kidney Qi helps to strengthen the vital energy of the body for spiritual and energetic work, and for healing yourself and others. Interestingly enough, just as the Chinese developed exercises to help this part of the body, so in Greece we hear that Dionysus (the Greek symbol for vital energy) was born from Zeus's thigh, where the insertion point is for the psoas muscle.

The shamanic imagery of shedding the snakeskin helps to activate the shedding of stagnant energy, and vitalize the kidney and the yin meridians along the inside of the legs. In the Temple of Aesclepius, the first known holistic healing center in the West, the snake was revered for its energy medicine properties. The Aesclepian symbol of the snake around a staff was co-opted as the central symbol of Western medicine; over time, its association with energy healing was eliminated.

Moving a Snake through the Joints

Method: Keep your legs a bit further apart than in other movements in Bodymind Healing Qigong, but listen to your body's limits. As you shift to the right side, your right palm faces out next to the right thigh and the back of the left hand slides up your thigh. Then shift your weight back to the left side as your left palm faces up by your left leg; the back of your right palm slides up the right side of your leg. This exercise is paired with the following exercise:

Dipping your Hands into the Waters of Life

Method: After Moving a Snake through your Joints, bend forward as your palms face upward; then bend backwards (not too far, listen to your body's limits) as your palms face up. First do this exercise by your hips, and then by your shoulder joints, as shown in the accompanying illustrations.

The next step of this two-part movement is to tune into your own body and feel where the spiral of life is needed to help clear areas of chronic blockage.

Then do the exercise at half-speed, then at a quarter-speed, then, do it so slowly that it is barely happening. Then stop all movement and see if you can feel the energy still moving.

In the *Tao te Ching* it says,

"The stillness that we normally feel is not the true stillness. Only when you find stillness in movement and movement in stillness is Enlightenment found."

Imagine that you can feel the spiraling of the double helix of your DNA energizing your cells. This age-old Taoist exercise can initiate you into primordial healing, by activating a spiraling energy at a cellular level. Recent research has confirmed that DNA indeed vibrates. Imagine the photons of light at the cellular level spreading out through the body. Feel the place where stillness and movement meet as lovers. As you place your tongue in the hollow of the roof of your mouth, allow Yin and Yang and stillness and movement to meet as lovers within your own body.

Bodymind Healing Purpose: This two-movement sequence is excellent for developing what the Chinese internal Martial artists call *sung*, or relaxed alertness. Activating the spiral of life with these movements interspersed with stillness is helpful for joint diseases, and is a complementary treatment for hip blockages and shoulder blockages, for the prevention of chronic diseases and for immobility of the hip and shoulder joints. After checking with your doctor or other medical health professionals, try these two exercises for any chronic disease that is related to stagnant energy, including muscular blocks from overexertion or from a sedentary lifestyle. Listen to your body. Do not overexert; and pace the movement to your own needs, emphasizing the stillness or the movement as needed. This movement, and in particular the stillness, is excellent for filling the reservoir of your energy field (Wuji).

Grasping the Ox's Tail

Method: This exercise is also done in a larger stance, with the feet wider than shoulder width apart. Turn your body around 180 degrees so that the right foot is forward and on one side of an imaginary line, and the left, rear foot is one fist distance to the other side of the line. With the right foot forward and the knee approaching being over the toes, inhale and lift the left hand into a Crane's Beak with your elbow slightly bent.

The thumb is touching the middle finger and the other fingers are wrapped around it, as if you are grasping an ox's tail. The left wrist is in the highest position at shoulder level.

The right hand is reaching behind the right hip as if grasping an ox's tail, the fingers are in a crane's beak grasping upward. Then reverse sides, so that the left leg is forward and the right wrist is up at shoulder level. After a month of practice, turn the body inward toward the centerline 5-10 degrees to give a stretch to the psoas.

Bodymind Healing Purpose: This practice stretches the hamstrings and quadriceps on the thighs. Good for leg strengthening.

Spiritual Purpose: If you stay with your breath for a while, the position is like standing Yoga. It gives a good stretch while opening the energy of these large muscles of the body to boost your experience of oneness with the universe.

Giving the Earth an Acupuncture Treatment

Method: From Grasping the Ox's Tail, take your fingers, which were pointing down, and point them forward. Focus on something in nature that is parallel with a part of your body that is in need of healing. Imagine sending energy from your heart to your outstretched fingers and to that place in nature. Then imagine that tree, flower or mountain bringing healing energy back to your body.

Praying Mantis Holds Two Acupuncture Needles

Method: Continue, as in the last posture, Giving the Earth an Acupuncture Treatment, but raise both hands in front of your body. Find two points in your body that your intuition guides you to bring into balance, and choose two spots in front of you in nature with which to "shape-shift." For example, one of my students had a blockage in the right shoulder area. In this posture, she focused on the hillside in front of her and saw two trees there. She "became the two trees" and felt her shoulder pain release after envisioning the sinking of her Qi into the roots of the two trees. She reported feeling the energy of the roots of the two trees helping to ground and balance the "uptight energy" in her two shoulders.

Bodymind Healing Purpose: These two exercises, Giving the Earth an Acupuncture Treatment and Praying Mantis Holds Two Acupuncture Needles, are useful for entering into an altered state and focusing intention on parts of the body in need of healing. They are particularly useful for left/right imbalances due to the stresses of modern life. The focus on nature opens the practitioner to a shamanic pathway of exchanging energies with nature. It is an initiatory practice into the primordial healing relationship that shamans had with nature in the animistic age of *participation mystique* with the earth. As always, natural long-breath is a key to opening the door to the healing life force of the universe.

Dragon

Method: As in the posture above, begin with your feet wider than shoulder width apart, turn the body 180 degrees to the right so that one foot is on each side of an imaginary line about one fist width away from this line. Next, turn the right, front foot so that the toe is outstretched 45 degrees (no more, or you can damage the knees). Your right knee should be close to being over your right toes. The hands are pushing out into the inside of an imaginary balloon. The left, forward hand is on the front centerline at shoulder level with the fingers pointed outward to the right.

The right hand outstretched behind you is slightly below hip level. Your head is turned to the right and looking back at your rear, right toes through the part of your hand between the thumb and forefinger (called the *Tiger's Mouth*). Breathe into this posture for about four exhalations and feel what is happening energetically. Then reverse sides so that you are turning to the left, with the left foot turned 45 degrees, the right hand forward and left hand backward, pressing out on the imaginary balloon.

After a few months of practicing moving from one side to another, you may discover how the movement activates a dragon-like energy that winds up and around the spine. This movement can be practiced in high, medium and low stances. Move gradually, over a lifetime of practice, to lower stances, honoring the principle of moving gradually and listening to the body. If you are practicing the lowest posture, stay aware of your knees to avoid injury.

Bodymind Healing Purpose: This is the deepest stretch of all postures in the Bodymind Healing Qigong system, and it opens the musculature in the pelvic area. It connects the entire body in such a way to maximize the combination of stretching and energetic movement of the energy around the spine. Experiment with this posture for sexual energy blockages, inhibitions in your ability to assert yourself in the world, low energy, and chronic fatigue.

Spiritual Purpose: The snake or dragon energy is seen, in many traditions, as "the booster rocket" that enables the initiate to move to spiritual heights. It is a cross-cultural archetype seen in the *Kundalini* of the Hindus, the snake of the Cabalistic tradition, in Delphine, the dragon of Greek mythology, and in the dragon of the *shamankas* in early China. Here in this Taoist animal form practice, when you move from one side to the other, the initiate experiences the raising of spirit and the sinking of the Qi in such a way that it spirals around the spine. Try not to lose your balance as the energy rises.

Different from spiritual traditions that focus on raising the energy upward in a unidirectional manner, and thereby sometimes contributing to manic, inflated, or even psychotic energetic phenomenon, here in this Taoist movement, there is a balance of up and down, forward and backward. This maintains a nice balance because of the form of the posture and movement.

Perhaps while doing this posture you may meet, within yourself, the dragon lady of the Lo River, who the Third Century poet Ts'ao Chih described as "twisting and turning like a roving dragon…who has shining pearls that make her torso radiant."

Wild Goose: Wild Goose Searches for Food

Method: Begin by crossing the hands, breathing in, and stepping out—as in the Crane Walking movement. Then bend down, keeping the spine as straight as possible, as your hands come down in front of your outstretched leg, and you begin to breath out. Then separate the hands and finish the exhalation. Practice this on both sides. Gradually go lower while listening to your body's ability to stretch.

Bodymind Healing Purpose: It is difficult to choose one movement out of this extensive, intricate Qigong system. And yet a book on Qigong healing would be incomplete without acknowledgement of the Wild Goose system. Once before, a Wild Goose posture was shown at the end of the Dispersing Stagnant Qi set. The Wild Goose Taps its Chest exercise was shown as a method to help invigorate the Lung Qi, and to say a Qi-full hello and good-bye. The movement Wild Goose Searches for Food is particularly good for opening the lower back and energizing the kidneys. Experiment with using this movement for low energy, fatigue, sexual impotency and infertility. One patient, a month after knee surgery, found it helpful for alleviating knee pain. If you try this yourself for knee problems, consult with your orthopedic doctor. Do this movement with your injured knee forward, not in the rear bent position.

Hua Tuo's Five Animal Frolics—Selected Movements

In the following selected movements of Hua Tuo's Animal Frolics, those familiar with Chinese medicine will notice that the movements go through the creation cycle of the elements. The Bear for Wood (Liver, Gallbladder), Crane for Fire (Heart, Small Intestine), Monkey for Earth (Stomach, Spleen), Tiger for Metal (Lungs, Large Intestine) and Deer for Water (Kidney, Bladder). Many students find that there is wisdom in practicing them in this order.

The creation cycle of Chinese medicine has a thousand years of wisdom about the creation of energy, which can be found in many Chinese textbooks.[9] Wood fuels fire, which turns to ash (Earth), which gives birth to Metal, on which water coalesces. In practicing Animal Frolics Qigong, each student may come up with their own story line stemming from their practice. For example, the Bear gets the powerful energy to come up from the earth, which then opens the soaring heart (Crane); then we have fun and play with the energy of life (Monkey). Once we have a heartfelt and playful attitude toward life we are ready to activate our ferocity as we stalk the earth for what we need to nourish us (Tiger). Then we can gracefully spring through the forests of life as we listen and look out gently on the world (Deer); all the while our upward-pointing horns connect us to the cosmic purpose of our meanderings. Deep meaning emerges from each student's practice depending upon what needs to be brought back into balance.

As Westerners, we should be careful about defining the animals in narrow terms—saying that one animal is for one element or purpose. Each animal is related to many elements and is part of a family who exists as an integrated whole. On the other hand, Chinese doctors do, at times, prescribe a given animal or animal movement to strengthen an organ or issue that is out of balance. Likewise, in the section that follows I will give some traditional associations of elements, organs, sounds, gaze, colors, seasons, directions and health benefits for each animal. It is important not to be rigid about thinking these are the only way to view the animals' healing qualities. Different Masters with whom I have studied, associate different qualities to different animals. The key is in the *Yi;* what is most important in activating the animals healing powers is our intention not our categorical thinking.

The Bear

Bear Breathing—Bear Claw

   Method: Begin with your feet shoulder width apart and make your hands into bear claws, palms up, next to your belly. As you slowly, yet powerfully, inhale, your hands rise to the heart. Then turn your claws over, palms down, pressing down to the belly (Tan Tien) as you exhale and slightly round your lower back (Ming Men). The claws rise up and go down three times.

Bear Rocking and Bear Walking

Bear Rocking and Bear Walking (continued)

Method: Then, slowly turn your shoulders and swing your arms from side to side three times while synchronizing your movements with your deep, unforced breath. As your arms swing back bring your awareness to the bottom of your spine. After the third swing, when your claws come to the left side, lift your left leg up with the left toes touching the ground. Step forward with your left leg at a 45-degree angle in the bow and arrow stance as shown, and swing your left arm out as you step forward. Swing both arms back and forth three times; each time your hand is in the furthest back position, look backwards (not shown). Then step the right leg out 45 degrees and repeat the movement.

Bear Pouncing

Method: After stepping to the right in the Bear Walking exercise, bring your bear claws up to your chest. While stepping to the left 45 degrees, pounce down to the left and lift your right leg up in back of you—hold for a count of three. Reverse the movement to the other side, turning 180 degrees each time. Repeat this movement three times.

Bear Pushes the Tree

Method: As you come out of the Bear Pouncing posture, step 180 degrees to the left with your bear claws at chest level. Push forward in an upward angle. Then pull your palms back, palms down. Feel the force coming from the ground, through your foot and up through your waist. Repeat three times.

Tai Chi practitioners will notice the similarity between Bear Pushes the Tree and the movement in Tai Chi called "Push," which adds to the hypothesis that some Tai Chi movements have origins in the shamanic tradition of Healing Animal Movements.

Bodymind Healing Purposes of the Bear movements: The Bear in Hua Tuo's system represents the wood element. When practicing the Bear, meditate on your soft strength. The Bear has heavy, sunken energy representing stability, security and grounded power. Though seemingly clumsy, the Bear is full of spirit and fast with power and grounded agility. The Bear's gaze is confident, as if looking at a foe. Bear Qigong is used to clear away *stagnant Liver Qi*, and balance *excess Liver Fire* and *Liver Wind* which can result from excess stress or out of balance anger. When we eat overly greasy food, or the stresses of life accumulate and we don't cope appropriately, the Qi can stagnate, and the fires of the body build up and rise. Excess heat can produce internal wind that attacks the liver. Symptoms can range from blurred vision, insomnia, irritability and a heart that is not calm. Stroke is often caused by internal wind according to Traditional Chinese Medicine. Bear movements are used primarily to soothe the function of the liver, and also the Qi, blood, emotions and the functions of the stomach, spleen, kidney, tendons, eyes and gall bladder. Bear movements are also particularly beneficial for strengthening the Tan Tien and Ming Men.

Bear Element: Wood
Bear Primary Organ: Liver
Bear Sound: *Xu*, pronounced *Shhhhu*
Bear Color: Green
Bear season: Spring
Bear Direction: East

Bear Claw and Bear Breathing activates one of the eight extra "Strange Flow" meridians called the *Penetrating Channel* (Chang Mo). This channel is also called "the sea of the twelve meridians" which reveals its primal power for generating life energy and restoring depleted energy. According to Taoist Yoga, the Governing Vessel, Conception Vessel and the Penetrating Channel are the three great psychic channels connecting the vital centers from the root to the crown. From them radiates the minor channels by means of which cosmic energy is transmitted through the body. Qigong breath and movement practices help to activate, clear and balance these channels.

Bear Rocking and Walking is good for getting the energy to move around the *Belt Channel* (Tai Mo), which is good for regulating the functions of the abdominal region and preventing and healing hip blockages. The Belt Channel is the only horizontal channel, and it regulates and equalizes all of the meridians which flow through the back, front and sides of the torso.[10]

Bear Pouncing can be practiced while imagining you are taking energy up the inside of the leg (up the Liver Meridian). When your back foot is raised in Bear Pouncing, focus on strengthening the liver. In Chapter 1 the hypothesis was suggested that the origins of acupuncture and the Chinese meridian system may lie in the movements of the earlier shamanic masters of the animal *daoyin* practices. Regardless of the truth of this hypothesis, while practicing the Bear Pouncing posture, and the other Bear movements, perhaps you will find some healing for Liver issues in your life having to do with anger, depression, self-assertion and detoxification.

Finally, when you practice **Bear Pushes the Tree**, feel the strength coming up from your back leg. Imagine expelling toxins from your liver (Liver 14, on the right side of the body), and imagine recharging and balancing the functions of your liver as you draw the claws back in.

The Crane

Crane Walking

Method: First step out at a 45-degree angle and cross your arms in front of the heart. As your hands rise up, and your leg rises up, keep your toe still touching the ground. Synchronize the movement with your breath, repeat on right and left side at least four times.

Crane Flying

Method: Take another step, as in Crane Walking; but this time on the inhalation, lift your knee along with your arm, so that the knee is parallel to your hip. Then, as you breathe out, allow the hands to descend as if lowering them in water. Repeat as above.

Crane Opens the Heart

Method: As above, begin this *nata* (spiritual set of movements) by crossing the hands as you take a step out 45 degrees, breath in, then spread the hands out, palms facing outward as you exhale. Repeat on each side.

Crane Opens the Door to the Heavens

Method: **Crane Opens the Door to the Heavens** has two movements: **Crane Offers a Gift from the Heart** and **Crane Soaring.** Bring the hands in front of the heart, as if you are a "Crane Offering a Gift from your Heart" to someone you love, or to the universe itself, while you step out 45 degrees and inhale. Then as you step out, bring the backs of your hands together. As you exhale, scoop the air out and around your sides (as if it is water), scooping around your sides and heart area.

Some people like to stop this movement with the palms facing together (shoulder width apart) in the back with your chest pushed forward. Shake your hands as if your wings are fluttering, as if you are a Crane Soaring.

Others like to make this into a circling meditation to all four directions. For this latter method, continue to circle and twist your hands around your sides in the Offering a Gift from your Heart posture to the Crane Soaring posture. This exercise is a shamanic practice for opening to the four directions of the surrounding universe, and for opening the heart to each direction. End the sequence by bringing the hands back together in the first Offering the Gift of the Heart posture, and then bring the hands back down to your sides.

Bodymind Healing Purposes of the Crane movements: The Crane in Hua Tuo's system represents the fire element. The Crane exercises affect the function of the Heart, Small Intestine, Pericardium and Triple Warmer Meridians. It is associated with the heart chakra and with passion and love. Its spirit emphasizes lightness and freedom. It combines stillness, elegance and immovability—being steady, composed and poised when it perches on a tree branch. In soaring, it is like the tip of a flame of fire almost as if it is disappearing into space. The Crane is associated with longevity, perhaps because of its strength in making such long journeys in its yearly migrations; and it flies so high it seems like it is a messenger from the heavens. The Crane's gaze is spiritually alert as if looking out at endless sky.

Crane Element: Fire
Crane Primary Organ: Heart
Crane Sound: *Ha*
Crane Color: Red
Crane Season: Summer
Crane Direction: South

The first two exercises, **Crane Walking** and **Crane Flying** are both useful practice for the elderly who want to prevent falls. Falls amongst the elderly are the sixth leading cause of death in the United States, with 30% of people aged 65 or more experiencing at least one fall per year, and 15% of those falls resulting in serious injuries. Falls in 1984 cost senior citizens $3.7 billion per year.[11] The exercise is also useful for strengthening the lungs, and energizing and relaxing the body.

For patients recovering from surgery, where movement and ease of walking is limited, it is helpful to just use Crane Walking before trying Crane Flying. In our Health Medicine Clinic, I have seen people who are suffering from sport injuries and people who have a difficult time walking, both benefit from the slow synchronization of breath and movement of Crane Walking. Practice it on the left and right, in conjunction with treatment by your doctor or physical therapist.

The last two exercises, **Crane Opens the Heart and Crane Opens the Door to the Heavens** are useful for opening the energy of the heart, for depression, emotional wounding after a breakup of a significant relationship, or grief over a loss of a loved one. The healing energy of these postures brings us to an experience of love of the world (*anima mundi*), after the loss of a loved one (*anima personalis*). This exercise is useful as a complementary exercise, along with psychotherapy, for healing grief. Try using the Crane Sound *Ha* along with the movement to amplify its healing effects.

The shaking of the arms in **Crane Soaring** is helpful for releasing shoulder tension. The visualization in Crane Soaring is to make the shake go from the outside of your arms and your pinky finger to the depression in your jaw (mandibular joint, Small Intestine 19) when you open your mouth. This opens the line of the Small Intestine Meridian, which is the yang counterpart, the husband, to the yin Heart Meridian. As you are fluttering your arms (wings) imagine that you are separating the pure from the impure in your heart which is one of the functions of the Small Intestine Meridian, according to Dr. Alex Feng.

In the first Chapter of this book, we suggested the hypothesis that some of the earliest Chinese doctors and shamanic healers knew the connection between animal movements and healing. Below we see a drawing from a stone relief of Pien Chhio, the eminent Chinese physician who practiced his healing methods during the 6th to 4th century BC, represented as a bird giving treatment to a patient.

Figure 31: Ornitho-Android Figure: Close-up, Treating One Kneeling Patient

When you practice the Crane movements have you joined the Chinese physicians like Pien Chhio and Hua Tuo, and the *gandarvas*, the human-headed avian inhabitants of the Indian Vedas who were supposed to be good physicians? Have you found some healing for your heart, some love and joy as you enroll into the curriculum of the Crane? How can you pass on your lightness of being, your pure heart, to others for their healing?

The Monkey

Commencement

Method: Step out with your legs spread shoulder width apart. Put your two monkey hands next to your sides as shown. Your hands are hooked with the thumb and four fingers held together. Index and thumb are pushed together and the rest of the fingers gather around these two. Your body makes three hooks—at the fingers, wrists and elbows.

Monkey Picks Fruit

Method: With feet shoulder width apart, step to the left and look to the right with the left hand hooked at shoulder height. Pull your hand in as though picking fruit. Your right hand is at waist level, left foot is up on your toe, and your weight is on your right leg. Do the same thing on both sides, moving from left to right or around in a circular pattern. Look right and then left with your eyes wide open. Monkey breath involves inhaling through the nose and the cracks of the teeth, and exhaling through the mouth only. Click your teeth, and really imagine that you are scanning the environment playfully, but with an awareness of the possibility of predators coming out from the environment around you.

Bodymind Healing Purpose: The Monkey represents the Earth element, and the functions of the organs of the Stomach and Spleen in Chinese medicine. The Monkey is quick, but has stillness within. Its survival depends on both alertness and stillness. The many and varied movements involved in the **Monkey Picks Fruit** exercise (eyes open wide, teeth clicking, breathing through mouth, teeth and nose) often makes us laugh and brings us in touch with our own rigidities. It brings out the earthy fun side of ourselves, healing the parts of us that are overly adapted to being civilized.

Monkey Element: Earth
Monkey Primary Organ: Stomach/Spleen
Monkey Sound: *Huh*
Monkey Color: Yellow
Monkey Season: Long summer
Monkey Direction: Central

The Tiger

Tiger Walking

Method: This first Walking Meditation exercise pictured here comes from *Yi Chuan Qigong*; it is an excellent preparation for the following Hua Tuo Tiger Frolic. Begin by breathing in and out with feet parallel. Then, slowly shift the weight to the right side as you inhale, while the left leg comes in toward the right. As the leg moves out, take a crescent moon step outward on the exhalation as the hands claw out like a tiger. Breathe in as the hands come back in to the Tan Tien area. The key to this exercise's healing effects is to have the lower back area (Ming Men) spread out as the hands claw forward. Imagine pushing the lower back out gently against a wall, without collapsing the chest. When you move, imagine bringing the energy up your tail and into your spine. There is a pause after each move—the tiger returning to stillness. Practice this as a Walking Meditation, walking with left foot forward, then the right. Find an intention of stalking so that you can pause, and be totally still at any point in your stepping, so you won't be heard or seen by your prey.

Buddhist Mindful Meditation practitioners like to adapt this movement into mindful Walking Meditation practice. As you step out, and your tiger claws stretch out, expand your lower back (Ming Men), breathe out, and shift your weight slowly into your forward foot. Say to yourself, "I give to the earth." As your back foot comes in to join your other foot, your tiger claws come in, and as you breath in, say, "I take energy from the earth to heal myself and all sentient beings." The physical structural elements of the Animal Frolic add Qi to the Buddhist's intentionality.

Tiger Pawing, Grabbing and Searching

Method: Hua Tuo's Tiger set has a three-movement sequence called, **Tiger Pawing, Grabbing and Searching** (pictured above). From the last Yi Chuan movement, bring your right hand back, scooping imaginary water as your right hip opens; then bring your right hand forward in front of your right lung (acupoint Lung 1) into a claw. Simultaneously with the movement of your right paw, the left paw sweeps in front of your belly and brushes across your knee until it rests on an imaginary ball by your left knee—as in the first picture below. Tai Chi practitioners will note the similarity between this movement and Brush Knee Forward, adding to the hypothesis that Tai Chi has some of its origins in Shamanic Animal Movements.

Next, for the second part of this sequence, pull your right claw back, as if tearing, until the right claw is next to your knee. In the second picture below you will see the two hands next to the two knees. In the third and final part of this sequence, look to the right as you turn your hip to the right and slightly squeeze in your anus, imagining it is like a tail. As you turn three times to the left and right, your individual claws tear separately in rhythm at a level between your hip and knee, synchronizing with the direction that your eyes are searching in a horizontal plane around you. Then turn three more times looking down coyly as you search the ground area around you. Practice this on both sides, with the right and left legs forward; as always, synchronize the movement with your breath. It is as if you are a Tiger Grabbing and Searching.

Bodymind Healing Purposes of the Tiger Movements: In Hua Tuo's system, the Tiger represents the Metal element and primarily the lungs, and also the kidneys, and spine (Governing Vessel). The spirit of the Tiger is dignity and power; its stillness is like the quiet of a moonlit night. The roar of the tiger shows strength of the lung and kidneys. The spirit of the gaze is piercing with controlled wildness, so you don't frighten away that which you want to devour in your life. Try using this exercise for strengthening the body in general, strengthening the lungs and specifically for strengthening the lower back, bones and spine. Also use this movement for cases of prolapse of organs that have deficient Qi. Chinese medicine uses the metaphor of a straw that has liquid in it that you trap. The air suctioned by your finger at the top of the straw stops the liquid from spilling out. The Lung Meridian activates the Qi that keeps the organs filled so they can hold their vital force.

Tiger Element: Metal
Tiger Primary Organ: Lungs
Tiger Sound: *Si, Sa, Ah, Shh*
Tiger Color: White
Tiger Season: Fall
Tiger Direction: West

When practicing **Tiger Pawing** with one hand up in the Brush Knee Forward posture, the lungs and kidneys are activated. The **Tiger Grabbing and Searching** part of the sequence, particularly as your tiger eyes search high and low, is an ingenious way to connect the lungs and kidneys because of the ways the gaze of your eyes and the turning movement move through those areas of your body. The turning movement in Tiger Searching also exercises the spine, opens the hips and can be particularly beneficial for relief of neck and shoulder tension.

On an emotional level the lung relates to grief and letting go. Use the Tiger movement to rebuild strength after a period of mourning the death of a loved one. The loss of hair after the loss of a loved one, according to Chinese medicine, can be because of the weakened connection between the Lung and Kidney Qi. Likewise for cases of asthma, the Tiger is a valuable part of your integrated health treatment.

The Deer

Deer Looks Backward

Method: Begin by stepping out as you breathe out. If the right foot is forward, the right palm faces down and is more forward than the left palm, which is also facing down. Look over the back leg and imagine that you are drawing energy up through the coccyx. Continue on each side.

Then become a Deer Turning by turning to the side into a scissor-step. In the low posture your knee is touching your calf. (For the first months of practice it is better to be in a higher posture than the one shown here to avoid knee injury.) Bring your fingers up into the Deer Horn mudra shown with two fingers pointing upward, either the pointer and middle fingers or the thumb and pinky (as shown).

Happy Deer

Method: Another way of beginning the Deer Frolic is called the Happy Deer; three fingers point upwards with thumbs pointing to your temples. Adding to this way of beginning, turn your body 45 degrees to the side, and make the two steps of Happy Deer into a walking meditation. There are a variety of hand mudras that are used for the deer. #1. As shown in the previous set of pictures, your hands can touch your head with your pointer and middle fingers pointing up to the heavens (called the *sword mudra*). #2. You can use your thumb and index finger pointing upward and touching your ear lobes or temples. #3, Some favor using three fingers upward (the thumb, pointer finger and pinky) and keeping the thumbs slightly distant from touching the temples. This is to open the Lao Gung points and purify the sexual energy and connect the libido to the spirit.

The final sequence of the Deer has three moves: **Deer Double Ears, Deer Hooves Draw Inward, Deer Rutting and Butting.** Begin by stepping out at a 45 degree angle with your hands shaped like deer hooves. Then draw your hooves back inward to your Tan Tien. Finally, give yourself a nice stretch as one arm goes above your head like a deer in rutting season, when libido is high, butting another deer with your horn. You can imagine a deer using its lower horn to block another attacking deer's horns, and bringing its upper horns around to strike, or "count coup," touching the other deer to let it know it better not be aggressive. Feel the energy coming up from the ground through the pelvis, giving your hips and pelvis a nice stretch. Do the practice by moving 45 degrees to the right and left sides. Do the threefold sequence three times to each side. Practitioners of the long form of Tai Chi will notice here another example of Tai Chi's origins in the Animal Frolics. Deer Double Ears is very similar to "Double Wind Fills the Ears" of Tai Chi; and Deer Rutting and Butting is very similar to "Taming the Tiger" of the third cross-hands section of Yang style Tai Chi.

Bodymind Healing Purposes of the Deer Movements: In Hua Tuo's system the Deer represents the water element and the kidneys. So, use this movement as part of your integrated health care along with your doctor's advice, dietary considerations and drinking plenty of water to prevent and treat renal failure syndromes. For increasing vitality combine this movement with the Water/Kidney exercise in BMHQ Set 5: Healing the Internal Organs. The Deer's healing powers activate the brain, the spine (along with the Conception and Governing Vessels) and the joints and tendons. Shamans teach that the Deer sleeps with its hooves tucked into its perineum to circulate, and not dissipate, its Qi. The Deer represents freedom of movement, a relaxed and flexible mind and body, innocence, spontaneity and the feeling that the whole world is green grass for you to roam freely alone or with your herd. Though most think that the Deer is yin due to its gentle appearance and its connection to the kidney and water principle, in Chinese medicine the deer is often said to be pure yang. Perhaps this is because it draws from nature's stillness to burst forth like a child with unbounded, leaping energy.

Deer Element: Water
Deer Primary Organ: Kidneys
Deer Sound: *whooh,* making a wind-like sound which is good for expelling fear, or Chir-eee—the *chir* activates the kidneys and the *eee* opens the head and upper chakras.
Deer Color: Blue or Black
Deer Season: Winter
Deer Direction: North

The first Deer posture, **Deer Looks Backward**, is for bringing energy into the prostate gland for men, and into the ovaries for women. The second part of this exercise, **Deer Turning**, is for opening the crown chakra to the heavens, for those who are depressed, or for those who want to open their higher energy centers. Experiment with the different hand mudras to see what your experience is. For example, touching your ears with your thumbs and raising your fingers up may help to open your radar to listen to the deeper meanings contained in people's words and sounds. As well, touching the ears may help you to become attuned to the sounds of nature, purify sexual energy and to connect your libido to the spirituality of life. Keeping two fingers up may open the dualistic thinking of your mind to the oneness of nature and the universe. Be careful when doing the low scissor-step shown here. For most people, it takes many months to go low and to build up the strength and flexibility of your knee ligaments. Listen to your body to avoid straining the knee ligaments. One reason for lowering yourself is to draw from the deeper essence of nature's energy, and the deeper essence of your energy (Jing), to transform it into Qi and then raise it to become spirit (Shen).

In **Happy Deer**, where three fingers are pointing up above the head, the Lao Gung points (Pericardium 8, the Palace of Labor) are opened; these points are known in Chinese medicine for physical, mental and spiritual revitalization. Regardless of which of the three hand mudras you prefer in **Deer Turning**, when practicing your scissor-step, be aware of the connection between the bottoms of your feet (Kidney 1) and your horns pointing upward. Feel your vitality, alertness, innocence and openness to life restored.

The **Deer Double Ears** practice, coupled with **Deer Hooves Draw Inward** is useful for bringing the energy from your Tan Tien or kidneys to your ears. In moving your deer hooves up, imagine that you are going to fill another person or your own ears with words of healing. The ears are connected to the kidneys in Chinese medicine. So, when you are feeling depleted and lost in the bramble bushes of life, use this practice for restoring vitality by opening your symbolic ears to listen to your true voice calling from the primordial woodlands; and then follow your true Path.

The whole sequence **Deer Double Ears, Deer Hooves Draw Inward and Deer Rutting and Butting** gives an excellent stretch to the hip area. In the prologue of this book I told the story of my vision quest experience with a deer kissing my eyes. Native Americans believe that when an animal visits in a dream or in a vision that it has a special gift, which sometimes takes a lifetime to fully understand. I had a hernia operation when I was young; physical therapy was not a common treatment in those days. So, my muscles atrophied around the surgery and led to an energy blockage in my hip which was correlated with neck problems for years. The last part of the threefold sequence, **Deer Rutting and Butting** is one of the best exercises I have discovered for healing my hip and neck imbalances. How amazing that after all these years the gift of the Deer is still coming to me in terms of this healing practice; and what a treasure it is that I can share it with others who suffer from hip and neck imbalances. In Chinese medicine this exercise is also said to open the *Yang Linking Vessel* (Yang Chang Mo, also called the Great Bridge Channel).[12] Traditionally, these two Strange Flow linking vessels (*Yang and Yin Chaio Mo*), which go up the back and down the front of the body, are said to be keys in balancing energy, and are used for hyper or hypotension. How interesting that without knowing about the association of the Deer Rutting movement with healing hypertension, I spent the better part of a year researching and writing articles on Qigong and hypertension, and specialized in developing an integrated treatment approach to hypertension. The Deer again?

What in your life right now is being influenced by your Medicine Animal, or is in need of its healing power?

Set 8: Spiritual Qigong

Confucius instructed: First, set your HeartMind on the One,
Then listen, not with your ear, nor even with your HeartMind.
Listen with your Qi,
The very essence of your ultimate self.
The ear can only hear.
The HeartMind is typically entangled in evaluation.
The Qi is completely open and receptive to every subtle level of being.

—Chuang Tzu, *Inner Chapters*, Fourth Century B.C.

Beating the Heavenly Drum and Opening the Eyes to the Beauty of the World

Method: Find a nice quite place to practice. Begin with at least a minute of Wuji Standing Meditation. Then place the palms of the hands over the ears rather tightly, but not forcefully, so that the ears are sealed as much as possible from outside noise. Your fingers are on the part of the head where the skull meets the neck muscles, a place that the Taoist's call *the jade pillow*. Take at least seven slow exhalations while tapping your ring, middle and pointer fingers in repetitive order on this area, beating the heavenly drum.

Then with your hands still over your ears, on the next exhalation bow downward so that your head is by or below your knees. Continue to tap on your jade pillow. Stay in this downward position for seven breaths.

Then *slowly* rise up one vertebra at a time. When you come to standing, slowly take your hands away from your ears, keep them about six inches away from your ears and listen.

In cases of severe spinal injury, disk degeneration or concussion, omit the bending down portion of this exercise.

To close the set, allow the hands to come around from your last posture, crossing in front of your chest. Keep your eyes closed for seven breaths; then open the hands (in Tiger's Mouth position) in front of the eyes and outward, as if you are a child opening your eyes in wonder at the universe.

The movement, Opening your Eyes to the Beauty of the World, came to me one day as I was practicing Beating the Heavenly Drum. Perhaps you too will develop a movement of your own, stemming from your practice, that will add to the timeless lineage and tradition of Qigong.

Hold this Standing Meditation posture, Opening your Eyes to the Beauty of the World, for about seven breaths; the hands are outstretched, palms point out, at eye level. Then, focus on connecting with an object in nature. While meditating upon that object, open your eyes and heart. Imagine that you are taking in the healing power of that object. For example, if it is a tree, take in its groundedness and its ability to branch out or bear fruit. How would your life be different if you were like that tree? Take it in, on your inhalation, and give back to the object on your exhalation.

Bodymind/Spirit Healing Purpose: Unlike other spiritual traditions that emphasize opening the chakras, the Taoist tradition emphasizes having access to the opening and closing of the energy gates to the body, i.e. metaphorically speaking, having a flexible, oiled hinge. In the postures above we seal the ears and eyes and then open them. The closing of these sensory gates helps to gather Qi there, and the opening of them helps us to appreciate the world as it is, as an arena of marvels, full of wonder, awe and mystery. Ah, what bliss to be alive!

Set 9: Walking Meditation: Yi Chuan Qigong

The Next Step on your Path:
Walking Meditation

After many years of study of philosophical subjects, Malik Dinar wanted to travel in search of knowledge. So he searched for the Hidden Teacher that he had read so much about in his years of seeking. Walking out of his house with only a few dates for provision, he came upon a dervish named Fatih plodding along the dusty road. He asked the dervish if he could walk with him, and if the dervish could help him to find his Hidden Teacher.

"Can I help you? Can you help me?" said the dervish in a joking manner. "The Hidden Teacher is in a man's self. How he finds him depends upon what use he makes of experience." They came to a tree, which was creaking and swaying, and the dervish stopped, proclaiming that the tree was saying, "Something is hurting me, please stop awhile and take it out of my side so that I may find peace."

"I am in too much of a hurry to meet the Teacher I'm to find down the road" said Dinar, "and besides, how can a tree talk anyway?" So they went on their way. After a few miles the dervish said, "I thought that I smelt honey. Perhaps a wild bee's hive had been built in the tree and that was the source of its pain." Dinar then wanted to go back so that they could collect the honey, eat some and sell the rest for the journey.

When they arrived back at the tree, they saw other travelers collecting an enormous amount of honey. "What luck we have had," these men said, "This is enough honey to feed a city." A depressed Dinar and the dervish went on their way again. Soon they came to a mountain where they heard a humming. The dervish, Fatih, put his ear to the ground. Then he said, "Below us there are millions of ants who are crying out for help. They say they are excavating, but have come across strange rocks which bar their progress, and they are pleading for help from us to dig them away."

"Ants and rocks are not our business, brother," said Dinar, "I have more important things to do because I am seeking my Teacher." When they stopped for the night, Dinar noticed that he had lost his knife and thought that he must have lost it near the anthill. The next morning they retraced their steps, and when they arrived at the anthill, they couldn't find Dinar's knife, but instead found a group of people, covered in mud, resting beside a pile of gold coins. "These," said the people, "are a hidden hoard which we have just dug up. We were on the road when a frail old dervish called to us; 'Dig at this spot and you will find that which is rocks to some, but gold to others.'"

One of the men remarked, "The dervish with you looks strangely like the one we saw yesterday." "All dervishes look very much alike," said Fatih. Dinar and Fatih continued their travels and came to a beautiful riverbank. As they sat waiting for the ferry, a fish rose to the surface and mouthed at them. "This fish," said the dervish, "is saying, 'Catch me and give me the herb right there on the bank next to you. Then I will be able to find relief and bring it up. Travelers have mercy!'"

At that moment the ferryboat appeared and Dinar, impatient to get ahead, pushed the dervish into it. On the other side of the bank the next morning, the ferryman appeared to them while they were drinking tea. He kissed the dervish's hand in deep appreciation. The ferryman explained that last night when he saw them on the opposite bank he resolved to make one more trip, even though they looked poor, for the 'baraka'—the blessing of helping the travelers. When he was about to put away his boat after dropping them off he saw the fish which had thrown itself on the bank. It was trying to swallow a piece of plant. The ferryman put the plant into its mouth and the fish threw up a stone and flopped back into the water. The stone was a huge and flawless diamond of incalculable value and brilliance.

"You are a devil!" shouted the infuriated Dinar to the dervish Fatih. "You knew about all three treasures by means of some hidden perception, yet you did not tell me at the time. Is that true companionship? Formerly, my ill luck was strong enough, but without you, I wouldn't even have known of the possibilities hidden in trees, anthills and fish—of all things!"

No sooner had he said these words than he felt as though a mighty wind was sweeping through his very soul. And then he knew that the very reverse of what he said was the truth. The dervish touched Dinar lightly on the shoulder and smiled. "Now brother, you will find that you can learn by experience. I am he who is at the command of the Hidden Teacher."

When Dinar dared to look up, he saw his Teacher walking down the road with a small band of travelers who were arguing about the perils of the journey ahead of them. Malik Dinar became one of the early classical masters, a companion and exemplar of The Man who Arrived.

The Story of Malik Dinar
—Idries Shah, *Tales of the Dervishes*

The tale of Malik Dinar captures the essence of Taoist practices. As Malik Dinar did, we often walk, rushing down the road, to find the next thing of interest in life. By doing so, we miss the treasure that is hidden in the present moment. We miss the sweetness, the gold and the brilliant gems hidden right beneath our feet, which we can discover if we walk in a more present manner —as humans, *being*.

Walking Meditation Practice: The Sacred Walk

> *If I had the Buddha's eye and could see through everything,*
> *I could discern the marks of worry and sorrow*
> *you leave in your footprints after you pass,*
> *like the scientist who can detect tiny living beings*
> *in a drip of pond water with a microscope.*
> *Walk so that your footprints bear only the marks*
> *of peaceful joy and complete freedom.*
> *To do this, you have to learn to let go*
> *—let go of your sorrows, let go of your worries.*
> *That is the secret of walking meditation.*

—Thich Nhat Hahn
A Guide to Walking Meditation[13]

After Standing Meditation, the next step on the path of becoming an initiate into this tradition, is re-learning how to walk. Since the aim of Taoist initiation is to return to the origin of things and to find our primordial awareness, a secure base must first be achieved in our Standing posture. In order to find Qi, we need to find stillness in our steps. Wuji Standing provides the base from which we walk. It introduces us to an energy field from which we draw our Qi. Usually when we walk, we are walking to get somewhere, our steps are compulsive, and we lose our stillness. Our bodies carry the metaphor of modern life, where we are constantly being pulled forward by life, instead of being allowed to move at our own pace. Our anxiety and our fears of not arriving on time are walking instead of our peaceful Selves.

In the Taoist tradition, Walking is the next step on the path to cultivating our connection to the spirit of the universe. It challenges us to stay connected to our reservoir of peacefulness that is to be found when our inner waters are deep and still. The beautiful thing about the Taoist form of practice is that we will immediately experience when our connection to this stillness is broken. As in other forms of meditation, we find stillness in the cave of our fixed posture; maybe even a feeling of bliss will emerge. But what happens when we move around in the world? Walking Meditation gives us a chance to experience our connection with our root, and to cultivate the experience of bringing it with us. In the Taoist classics this is called *Reeling Silk* because if we do the Walking correctly, it is as if we are drawing silk threads from a spool or cocoon of Qi, and the energetic connection remains unbroken on each step.

My *Yi Chuan* Walking Meditation teachers joke, saying, "People usually don't walk, they fall forward." By slowing down our steps, we can learn to walk mindfully. In doing so, we feel our steps, and metaphorically, we don't rush into life. We appreciate the act of stepping into the world, carrying our unbroken sphere of intention to life.

The following is a practice for Walking Meditation, which comes from the *Yi Chuan* tradition[14] to help us contact our Primordial Self.

And Enoch walked with the Source of Powers.

—*Book of Genesis*, 6:9

With the Source of Powers did Noah walk.

—*Book of Genesis*, 17:1

1. The beginning stance. Start by standing with your legs shoulder width apart, knees slightly bent, the buttocks slightly turned in as if you are getting ready to sit down. The area in your lower back (Ming Men) is filled by this rotation of the pelvis. Your head and tailbone form a centerline, as you imagine that you are being held like a puppet by the sky.

2. Preparation, balance and leg strengthening. Slowly shift your weight from one leg to the other. First your weight is 50%–50%. Then, very gradually shift the weight back and forth from right and left until you can support 100% of your weight on each leg as the other leg slowly comes in to join it.

3. Crescent moon step: Walking like a cat. While supporting all weight on one leg, move the other leg forward and feel how far out is a comfortable step—not too big. Very slowly and gradually put down your weight, experiencing it go 5%, 10%, etc. until the weight is 100% over that foot. The spirit in your walking is like a stalking cat, as if your safety and next meal depended upon the way you moved. Don't be limited by the metaphor of a stalking cat. Try walking like a turtle; and maybe you'll find its path to long life. A further metaphor to help your Yi Chuan walking is to imagine that you have sandpaper under your shoes and you are sanding a deck as you walk.

4. The breath. As you walk and your foot comes in to join the other leg, slowly inhale. As you draw a crescent moon with your foot, stepping forward and out, step down and slowly exhale.

5. The hand movements. First, just keep your hands by your sides. Then, slowly lift them up on the inhalation, feeling the Qi building with the movement; and gradually lower them a bit on the exhalation. It's as if you have a balloon under your hands. On the inhalation the ball rises; on the exhalation, let go of the ball, returning it to the earth. Your walking becomes a metaphor for receiving universal energy and returning it to the earth. You may imagine that the energy you are giving to the earth, if it is filled with tension, is a gift, like fertilizer, that helps living things on the earth grow.

6. Advanced hand movements. More advanced practices involve following the guidelines above and using other hand movements. Power Stalking is done with the hands placed two finger's width below the navel (Tan Tien), and spread apart as if they are resting on two imaginary balls floating on water close to waist level. The wrists are positioned as if they are just barely beginning to press the imaginary balls down into the water. This walking position is the Walking Meditation version of the earlier standing posture, Laying Hands on the Earth.

The second part of Power Stalking is to allow the wrists to rise up as you inhale; the wrists go back down as you exhale and step down. "Power" here refers to allowing the power of the earth to rise up to the belly (Tan Tien), and then to sink down through the bottoms of the feet (Kidney 1) as your hands press down.

Walking with Heart and Mindfulness

We are like sleepwalkers, not knowing what we are doing or where we are heading. Whether human beings can wake up or not depends on whether we can take conscientious and mindful steps. That is why the future of human beings, as well as the future of all life on this earth, depends on your steps.

—Thich Nhat Hahn
A Guide to Walking Meditation

Mindful Heart Chakra Walking is done like Power Stalking, but the hands are embracing in front of the heart (at CV 15) with the middle fingers a few inches apart, right in front of the point midway between the nipples. Elbows are slightly lower. This posture is best experienced by imagining that the hands are gathering a honey-like liquid, and are simultaneously letting this liquid spill out over the tops of the arms. Make your walking *Mindful*.[15] As your foot comes to join the other foot in the middle of the crescent, the breath comes in, and your embracing hands slightly lower, bringing in healing energy into the Tan Tien. As your foot goes out, your breath goes out, and your arms rise. Then imagine sending love out through your heart to a person you care about, or to humanity. While inhaling, think or say, "I receive," while exhaling, say or think, "I give." Direct your intention and purpose to the trees around you, to those you love, to humanity as a whole, or to wherever your heart calls. Qi is found on the boundary line between yin and yang, and here we can experience this Qi as we give and receive.

It has been said that walking is one of the best and most natural forms of exercise. With walking, there is not as much danger of over-stressing the joints as there is in the more forceful action of running. The right/left cross-crawl motion, that is so healing to the body, comes naturally when we walk, as the right arm rises and the left foot steps forward. It reminds the bodymind of the translateral crossing movement that we first used as crawling babies.

Those with difficulty walking, or those who are recovering from sports injuries, joint diseases or chronic movement disorders such as Parkinson or Multiple Sclerosis, have reported benefiting from doing the Walking exercises with a chair next to them for added support. The important thing here is to use the chair to get used to the slow shifting of weight from 50/50, to the gradual addition of more weight on each leg.

An ancient dictum says, "Healing comes from returning to the origin of things." Since the origin of Walking is Standing, the practitioner develops strength and Qi by first Standing, and slowly shifting from side to side in synchronization with the breath. Then gradually, one begins to use crescent moon steps outward and shift the weight into the forward leg. Inhale as the leg comes in to join the front leg; exhale, as the weight is put into the forward leg.

But beyond the bodily exercise that we sedentary modern beings certainly need, exercising our spiritual selves is equally important. Walking Meditation practice exercises our spirit. It can be practiced in our homes, or out in nature during the day or at night. There is beauty in doing the practice in a natural environment; but wherever we are, Walking is a way to practice carrying our stance in stillness, and peace to the world.

The Yi Chuan tradition involves developing "intention," and this intention varies depending upon our purpose in practice. Another purpose of the practice Yi Chuan, and Walking Meditation is as a method of self-defense. We will explore how Yi Chuan can be practiced in this way at the end of the Tai Chi section.

Set 10: Yang Style Tai Chi Chuan
First Cross Hands

Tai Chi, The Supreme Ultimate, the immense absolute,
is the expression of the Great Harmony
—the balance and mutual support of Yin and Yang.
Whether boxing with your shadow
or engaging in the complexity of life and things,
the Supreme Ultimate within and around you secures the potential for harmony and ease in
every moment of the eternal present.

—Wu Wei, legendary Qi Master
Quoted by Roger Janke in *The Healing Promise of Qi*

I'm happy to have the opportunity to share with you an approach to Tai Chi Chuan that comes from the Yang lineage, through Yang Sau Chung, which I learned from Sifu Fong Ha. I have added to it my experience and understanding which comes from over 20 years of practicing and teaching Tai Chi Chuan along with other Eastern and Western healing arts including acupressure, cross-cultural healing and hypnosis. My emphasis is on the healing meanings of each movement. Though there is much research on the healing effects of Tai Chi and Qigong, one must be careful not to substitute the practice of these movements for necessary medical attention. One should be aware that a normal part of practicing these arts is that they activate an alchemical healing process whereby old blockages, physical or emotional, can emerge in order to be worked through at a deeper level. As part of this healing process you may discover through your practice ways to Self-heal. Facilitation by teachers of the tradition may help in this process, or you may choose to go to an appropriate medical professional.

Many people ask, "What is the difference between Tai Chi and Qigong?" Tai Chi is the most well-known system of Qigong. Some people say that Tai Chi is an internal martial art and has nothing to do with healing. The viewpoint found in this book is that Tai Chi is part of the ancient holistic lineage that contains four purposes: #1. Internal martial art–self defense #2. Health and longevity #3. Self-transformation #4. Spiritual unfoldment. The discerning student will notice the similarities between the earlier Qigong movements gleaned from different systems of Qigong. For example, notice the similarity between the Qigong Wood/Liver posture in the Healing the Internal Organs section and the shoulder stroke movement of Tai Chi. The Crane's Beak that is used in external Qigong healing, and is seen in the earlier Wild Goose Taps its Chest to extract negative Qi from the body, is found in the Tai Chi movement Single Whip. As you practice the Tai Chi set, allow the intention to be focused on all four of the above purposes and you will enter into its holistic initiatory process.

Below is a description of the movements. Here, in Bodymind Healing Qigong Level 1, we practice the first third of the 108-movement Long-form Yang style Tai Chi set to establish the basic principles of Tai Chi. In Level 2 and 3 training, the whole 108-movement set is learned on both the left and right sides along with six two-person sets including *San Shou*. San Shou combines the whole set of Tai Chi movements into a beautiful two-person set. These are some of the greatest treasures, which I received from my Sifu, Master Fong Ha.

Remember that the purpose of every movement includes healing, self-defense and spiritual awakening. Ultimately the purpose of each movement is to transform the mind and body into an energy body that is one with the Tao. When we tune into each posture as a method to heal the bodymind, our own inner wisdom leads us to the deeper secrets of movement as mudra—a divine healing gesture.

Some General Principles for Tai Chi Practice

Tai Chi creates an altered state of consciousness. If you were in a group of people whose eyes were closed and you wanted to explain what the room was like, you would say there is a chair in front of you, a picture to the right and so on. Eventually the people would get a sense of the space; but to really get it they would need to open their eyes and see it for themselves. Similarly in Tai Chi practice, there is a space to enter—some of the elements of that space are as follows. Eventually you will experience this space for yourself as boundaries dissolve and you become one with your surroundings.

Posture: Imagine that you are a puppet dangling from a star in the heavens—this opens the crown of the head (Bai Hui). At the same time, imagine that you are carrying a book on the top of your head. The chin is slightly tucked in and the chest is slightly hollowed, which is achieved by slightly rounding the shoulders. The lower back (Ming Men) will naturally begin to fill out by slightly tucking in the tailbone—it helps to imagine that you are pressing it against a wall behind you. Relax the shoulders and sink the elbows. All of these postural elements will help to maintain an erect posture that may give you the sense of your spine being like a string of pearls. If you don't try to force the above postural elements and they evolve this way naturally, the experience will be a light and uplifted feeling and, at the same time, a feeling of being grounded and rooted in the earth. Joints are not locked. Move as if you are a puppet held by the heavens. The chest is relaxed, not puffed out. The lower back will extend naturally with various movements as if it is pressing out against an imaginary wall. It is best to have a Tai Chi teacher to show you this. Be careful that your knees don't extend over your toes. For more on the posture, see the illustrations that follow.

Each Posture is a Stance and a Movement: Each movement is a Standing Meditation posture and a Moving practice. To get the best results, practice each movement as a Standing Meditation and then as a Moving Meditation.

Synchronize Breath and Movement: Breathe naturally. My teachers would not give specific instructions because they wanted me to discover how to synchronize natural breath and movement. You may find that as your hands move forward your breath goes out, and as your hands come in, you breathe in. As your hands rise the breath comes in, as the hands come down the breath comes out. Every movement in the Tai Chi set is actually two movements; your weight shifts backward and forward like a wave. Exhale as your weight goes forward, and inhale as your weight shifts back. This fundamental aspect of Tai Chi is called "filling and emptying."

Reeling Silk: Each movement of the Tai Chi set is practiced with movements that are smooth and continuous. It is as if you are reeling silk from a cocoon. The silk is attached to various parts of your body and to the environment around you. Be careful not to break the imaginary silk threads. Another metaphor may help. You may begin to feel as if you are moving through a substance like water. This is part of Taoist initiatory system, which alchemically transforms the sense of the space around the practitioner. This practice is like shamanic shape-shifting of air into water. Over time, many practitioners report that their overall body sense is transformed into being light yet heavy.

Harmonize the Upper and the Lower: This is sometime referred to as the six harmonies as the wrist and the ankles, the elbows and the knees, and the shoulders and the wrists move in synchronized harmony.

Mind is concentrated yet Tranquil: Concepts that seem to be opposites are unified in Tai Chi practice. That is why it is said that Tai Chi is the embodiment of Taoist philosophy. As is true of many Eastern practices, the thoughts which preoccupy our everyday lives move into the background with the shift of our attention to our breath and movements. A new center of awareness is found, which is the flow of the universe through the practitioner. A deeper level of thought arises from the deep currents beneath the surface of our everyday thinking.

Relaxed yet Energized, with Non-forced Intention: In the West we have no word that combines the two qualities of being relaxed and energized. Tai Chi helps to cultivate *sung*, like a cat totally at ease yet ready to pounce. Tai Chi develops an intention that is natural and comfortable.

Step like a Stalking Cat: When you take a step in Tai Chi, the spirit in your walking is like a cat; with each step you are stalking, yet relaxed, as if your safety and next meal depended upon your way of putting your foot down. By taking your steps this way you will "maximize air time," building strength in the legs and cultivating deeper abilities to sink your Qi. I enjoy practicing single movements of Tai Chi in the woods at night. For example, as I practice Brush Knee Forward in the dark, I imagine that my life depends on not making noise while stepping on a broken branch, or falling into an unseen hole. When you practice your movements, imagine that you are in a place where your life depends on how you put your Tai Chi foot down. Synchronize your footsteps with Long-breath.

Transforming Yourself from a Line into a Ball of Energy: The postural elements spoken of earlier, such as allowing the lower back to press back against an imaginary wall (opening the Ming Men), are part of the alchemical process of transforming yourself from a line into a ball. Earlier we spoke of this in terms of the Western Grimm's fairy tale, *Iron Hans*, where the king's son is in search of his lost Golden Ball.

In Tai Chi Push Hands, discussed at the end of this chapter, another way to develop this ball is learned. In preparation for this practice imagine that when you are practicing alone, another person is lightly pushing on your body; then later, when you are doing Push Hands with another, imagine that you are practicing alone. This, in time, develops your ability to bounce another person off of your sphere (*Fajing*) if they try to push you. It is best not to try to develop this ability until after at least 6 months to a year of practice. First, the practitioner needs to develop relaxed, smooth movements to develop the golden sphere, or else the sphere will lack the necessary flexibility and substance. A qualified teacher can take you to the next step to develop *Fajing*.

The Shamanic Origins of Tai Chi

The Imagination is a function or faculty
that gives one access to an intermediary world
between the realm of unfathomable and hidden mystery
and the world of sensible and gross forms.

—Isabella Robinet
Taoist Meditation

Regarding the origins of Tai Chi, there is much scholarship from researchers such as Doug Wile.[16] In this scholarly research, various pieces of the origins are put into place. For example, it has been said that Tai Chi began as a martial art at the time of the Ming Dynasty in the 16th century, when General Chi Chi Kuang synthesized 16 different martial art forms into a 32-posture form for troop training.

The most common legend is that Chang San-Feng (1391-1459), a Taoist during the Sung Dynasty, went to Wu Tang Mountain to study and meditate on "The Way." He saw a magpie fighting with a snake and watched the movements of the snake yielding and spiraling to avoid the bird's attacks. The bird could not bite the snake. Tai Chi's circular movements, representing tranquility in motion, were developed from his observance of the forces of nature, of Yin and Yang combining. They were further refined by the Taoist monks at Wu Tang Mountain and by others through the ages. Then they were passed on to the Chen, Yang, and Wu families.

Now let's allow our intuition to do some inner research and travel back to still earlier times. In accordance with the thesis of this book, the origins of stillness and movement used for holistic purposes go back to primordial times.

Sit somewhere out in nature and allow your mind to create a picture of primordial times in ancient China, or anywhere in nature. Surrounding you are mountains, valleys, rivers and other natural elements. Now take a leap further in your imagination…

Once upon a time, there were many "primitive" tribes living in old China. At the top of one of the mountains, near the place where the tigers wandered, lived a shaman. Over the years, and through studying the movements of the Tiger, he learned how to tame the wild beast with various movements. In addition, he learned how to heal parts of his body and others' due to the strength it took to deal with and even to ride the tiger (… in much the same way that our modern day cowboys develop great strength to tame wild horses). The Tiger Master learned to develop, stretch and heal the sinews, muscles and even his lower back.

Another shaman similarly studied the way of the Snake. He learned how to keep his joints flexible by imitating the energetic spiraling movements of the Snake. The Rooster Master was seen much of the time standing on one leg, and had great balance. The Deer Master in the local forest developed grace by imitating the Deer, and learned how to energize his sexual vitality and prostate gland.

The Crane Master, after many years of study, learned how to imitate the movement of the Crane's beak. One day, the Crane Master saw a Pelican bite her own chest while taking her flesh in her beak and feeding her offspring. The Master got the idea to imitate the bird's beak to extract pain and toxic Qi from her fellow tribesman. Another Master who lived on a plateau nearby was a Rain Master. It was said he could move the clouds by a secret movement called Cloud Hands. When his fellow tribesmen were emotionally distraught, they would come to him to clear their sadness, grief and other troubling emotions. Finally, The Shamanic Star Master was often seen at night practicing Gathering Starlight; his talent was bringing light to the darkness of peoples' lives. He said it was important for people to slow down and reflect. Those that copied his movement called it Grasping the Bird's Tail; they said that this movement could even slow down a bird, and could prevent it from taking off. (Some say that two of the ancestor's of the Cloud Hand and Gathering Starlight Shamans married and traveled to the Middle East where they taught these movements to one of the ancestors of Sigmund Freud.)

At each solstice and equinox these Masters would meet on a hilltop to exchange gifts and knowledge. (It is said that this was the origin of our modern conferences.) At one of these Solstice gatherings, the Crane Master, known for having great vision and the important qualities of being emotional and empathetic, spoke up. He asked, "What happens if the Mongolians attack our region and all of these great arts are lost?" The Tiger Master scoffed saying, "Our skills are so great that even if these new metal balls (bullets) were shot at us, our ability to move whilst holding the great ball of life, and our strength will overcome the invaders." The Crane Master's viewpoint won the day, when he said, "Why don't we, just to be safe, have each animal master take a few of his movements, combine them with the Master's of the other Ancient ways, and develop them into a set? Each of us can contribute a few movements."

*This imaginal story arose from a meditation
on an isolated mountain top
after practicing Tai Chi,
one fine summer day*

—Michael Mayer

We are lucky that the mythic Crane Master's viewpoint led to the saving of this sacred set of movements, for indeed the Mongolians did invade. The ancient way of the Animal Masters, and the way of the masters of the other forces of nature were lost, but elements of them were saved in an abbreviated set.

This set is now called Tai Chi Chuan. It is the supreme and ultimate method of combining Yin and Yang (Tai Chi), and holding the powers of the elemental forces of the universe with a sacred grasp in your hand (Chuan). Those who wish to do scholarship to prove the validity of this tale may instead choose to practice the art of Tai Chi as if this story is true, and imagine the set transporting you back to those times. You may then find those primordial ways of moving that incorporate self-defense, healing and spiritual unfoldment.

It is common to hear teachers of Tai Chi say, "practice as if you are dangling like a puppet from the heavens." This is usually seen to be a way to align posture to maximize Qi flow. However, there is a deeper, shamanic meaning to this stance, as well, to be uncovered. We explained in the glossary that the Chinese character for "chi" in Tai Chi is not Qi, meaning life energy. The I Ching states that the Chinese term "chi" means a ridgepole in a house. This is usually elaborated upon by saying that it is the place where Yin and Yang meet at the roof of a house, or the sunny and shady side of a mountain. Thus, in this interpretation, Tai Chi is about finding the meeting places of opposites where Yin and Yang meet. A shamanic meaning of "chi" is discovered if we take the idea that the ridgepole is not merely the horizontal ridgepole of a house, but in its oldest meaning was the vertical celestial pole, according to the scholar Joseph Needham. The Pole Star remains stationary while all the constellations revolve around it. An interesting parallel is that in the Roman mysteries of Mithras, the initiate was told that he was becoming one with the central axis of the earth that led to the North Star. Even the sun was seen to be revolving around this axis. The "investiture ceremony" filled the initiate with a sense of centeredness, and alignment with the heavenly axis. The Mithraic mysteries add a depth of understanding when we hear that in China, the "chi" in the I Ching is a pole connected to the "heavenly root." By imagining that the crown of our head is connected with the North Star, and the world is circling around us, we can experience becoming the heavenly root of the Celestial Pole, connecting heaven and earth. This fits with the cross-cultural spiritual notion of the initiate becoming aligned with the *axis mundi*, the axis of the world around which the archetypal forces of the universe, including Yin, Yang and the five elements, play out their cosmic creative dance. Whether in the universe, in our house or in our bodies, alignment with heavenly purpose and grounding this in our everyday lives is a key aspect of shamanic healing, or creating a "centre of the world" where sacred space can be created. Imagination creates reality. Try practicing Tai Chi with the intention of aligning yourself with the Axis Mundi, and see how it affects your movements and your life…. It couldn't hurt![17]

Tai Chi Chuan Long Form, First Cross Hands

Is Tai Chi Chuan Practice the reason for your longevity?
Not directly. Tai Chi Chuan helps cultivate a relaxed spirit.
Having a relaxed spirit is the secret of longevity.

—Interview with 105-year-old Tai Chi Chuan Master Wu Tu Nan,
Quoted by Ken Cohen in *The Way of Qigong*

0 Position: Wuji Standing

Method: Keep feet parallel, between hip and shoulder width apart, toes pointing forward. Align the body's centerline in accordance with the saying, "Three points in a straight line." This means (a) the midpoint of the line, which connects the two Bubbling Well acupuncture points of the feet, (b) the *hui yin point*, or perineum, located between the anus and genitals, and (c) the *ba hui point* on the crown of the head. The knees are bent and unlocked, almost directly over the toes, and slightly opening toward the outside as if holding a balloon between them. The abdomen is slightly sucked in, and the lower back is slightly pushed out so that the lumbar curve begins to disappear. The back is straight in the area of the Ming Men, which is the area of the lower back behind the Tan Tien.

The chest and shoulders are relaxed, causing a slight rounding of the upper back. The arms hang loosely at the side. The tongue is touching the top of the palate just behind the teeth to connect the *Jen Mei* channel down the front of the body and the *Tu Mei* channel up the back. The eyes can either be open in a soft gaze, half open, or can be closed and "looking" straight ahead. The lips are gently touching each other; a half smile might feel natural.

Bodymind Healing Purpose: Called "the million dollar secret of Tai Chi and Qigong," this is a powerful method for self-healing and empowerment. It activates the alchemical forces of Qi to transmute chronic blockages. It creates a trance state that may feel like you've found the *Sea of Elixir*, the name for a state of oceanic bliss that comes from Taoist alchemy practice that was associated with healing and immortality.[18]

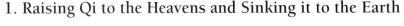

1. Raising Qi to the Heavens and Sinking it to the Earth

Method: Allow your wrists to float up to your shoulders and then come back down to the belly (Tan Tien) as if they are rising and falling in warm water.

Bodymind Healing Purpose: Balances the left and right Central Channels of the body, activates points in the center of the palms *(Lao Gung),* and teaches effortless effort *(Wu Wei).* Notice the similarity to the Yi Chuan Qigong Standing posture, Holding Golden Balls in the Waters of Life.

2. Taoist Immortal Creates a Heavenly Rainbow

Method: Weight moves to the right then left, as hands circle and paint a rainbow along with the body movement to the left. Your body ends up being turned 45 degrees to the left with hands in front of heart, embracing a ball which is given to you as a gift from the heavens.

Ancient legends tell of Rain Master Shamans' powers to influence the weather by prayer and finding harmony with the heavens. Imagine that you are such a shaman and that by cultivating a sacred attitude that you can create a heavenly rainbow. Practice this movement repetitively, reversing the direction of the circle of your hands. What things in your life, what people in your life, would you like to connect with a heavenly rainbow?

Bodymind Healing Purpose: Balances the belly (Tan Tien) and heart centers. Opens the heart to one of the four directions. Creates sacred space and a heavenly rainbow.

3. Grasping the Bird's Tail (Single Ward off)

Method: Turn to the right and pivot your right foot at a 45-degree angle as your hands form a ball with your right hand palm down (by Lung 1), left palm turned upward by your right hip. Step the left foot out 2 1/2 feet, while the rear, right foot is at 45-degree angle. Left hand is in front of Lung 1; the right hand pulls back to Tan Tien with the palm down. Imagine that your left hand is under a bird's neck and the other hand is petting the bird down to its tail so gently, and with so much caring, that it will not fly away.

Bodymind Healing Purpose: Activates the cross-balance of pelvis and shoulders, wrists and Ming Men. It begins to transform the shape of the body from a line to a ball. It was said that Chang San Feng, the legendary founder of Tai Chi, developed such magnetic adhesiveness from his Qi cultivation that a bird could not take off from his hand—this movement invokes the gentleness, power and magnetic Qi exhibited by him.

4. Transition to Double Ward Off; To Increase Vital Energy (Kidney Qi)

Method: Turn to right, and open the right foot 45 degrees so it is facing the direction you are now going towards. Shift the weight into the right foot as your right palm turns face up and your left palm turns over face down, as if you are pouring water from right to left. Then shift the weight back again to the left foot as the right palm turns over and the left palm turns up. Now imagine that you are pouring energy from one side to the other.

Try experimenting with this movement as a single, repetitive exercise. Visualize yourself moving energy from the earth, bubbling up through the bottoms of the feet (Kidney 1), up through the legs, through each kidney, and then back to the ground.

Bodymind Healing Purpose: Chinese medicine associates the Kidney Qi with vitality. In conjunction with treatment by your other health professionals, practice this movement for fatigue, sexual impotency, lower back problems, insomnia and stress related disorders.

4.A. Double Ward Off

Method: Turn to the right, holding an imaginary ball. Your left foot turns out 45 degrees. Then step forward 2 1/2 feet with your right leg. Your right palm faces toward acupuncture point Lung 1, your left palm faces outward in front of your left Lung 1.

Bodymind Healing Purpose: This movement balances the lung channel and opens the heart and lungs to absorb the healing energies of the environment.

5. Roll Back

Method: First roll back by moving right palm down; your left palm face up as the weight moves over your left leg. Then bring your hands down together as the weight shifts to left and the left knee and hip opens 45 degrees. Be careful not to overextend your knee past the side of your foot.

Bodymind Healing Purpose: This movement helps to let go of held excess energy. It opens the hip and knee joints and is beneficial for healing the Kidney Qi. It is the most important movement for learning how to yield—a key element of activating the parasympathetic nervous system and learning how to avoid unnecessary confrontation in life. This is a key movement for stress reduction. Try it as a repetitive sequence with Press and Push when you're holding onto tension after a long day at work to relax, and re-empower yourself.

6. Press

Method: Place left hand on right wrist as left knee closes to being back over the toe, the hip turns back to face forward and weight moves forward.

Bodymind Healing Purpose: Touching the inside of the arm with loving intention calms the Heart and Pericardium Meridian. Develops protective Qi (*Wei Qi*). When done together, Roll Back and Press are a good practice for opening the hip joint (*Kwa*), and can be an effective part of arthritis prevention in the hip. Touching the point three fingers width from the wrist (Pericardium 6) is useful for treating insomnia.

7. Push

Method: Move like a wave—down and in, as weight shifts back. Then push out in an upward slanting direction as you move your weight forward.

Bodymind Healing Purpose: This exercise empowers and activates Yang energy. This movement teaches how to keep Yang energy in balance with Yin, how to not overextend into excess Yang, nor collapse into excess Yin. As your weight goes forward, make sure your knee doesn't extend over your forward toe. The sequence Roll Back, Press and Push is often practiced as a repetitive sequence on left and right sides of the body. It is useful for letting go of and grounding energy, and then allowing energy to rise up from the ground, through your Self, and to the environment.

This movement, Push, may be derived from Hua Tuo's Bear Animal Frolic, which is used for cleansing, balancing and strengthening the liver and Liver Qi. (For illustrations see the Animal Form section of this book.) Try visualizing taking energy from the ground, moving it up the inside of the leg through the liver, and then pushing from the area outside of the ribs below the nipple (Liver 14). Those who are familiar with the Chinese medical tradition will recognize this as "tracing the Liver Meridian." Experiment with this exercise and repeat as needed for excess anger, hypertension, after food poisoning, after eating a meal with excess toxins, or for general purging the body from toxins. Integrate this practice with support from other appropriate health professionals.

8. Pa Gua Fish

Method: Move straight back while your left hand comes back further than the right. Your right foot makes a "T" with the left foot. First move to the left with your weight over the outside of the left leg (as shown below). Keep your left hand on top—your hands are like fish scales. Then repeat the same posture, turning back to the right side with weight over the right leg, with right hand on top.

Bodymind Healing Purpose: Strengthens the bodymind in relationship to external forces. It activates the yang meridians on the outside of the legs. It is a way to practice the developing of boundaries and guarding the four directions.

9. Single Whip

Method: Your outstretched left hand is in front of Lung 1, your right hand makes a Crane's Beak. When you move your Crane's Beak out, do it slowly as if extracting a silk thread from your Lung 1 point.

Bodymind Healing Purpose: Opens the lungs and upper body. It cultivates the ability to absorb and discharge energy from the hands. The Crane's Beak is used in traditional Chinese medicine clinics by external Qigong practitioners to extract disease. Notice the similarity between this movement and the Bodymind Healing Qigong (BMHQ) Metal practice for the lungs. The Taiji practitioner of Single Whip can add to the healing effects of the movement by stretching the Lung Meridian along the lines of the BMHQ practice outlined earlier.

10. Playing the Guitar: (Lifting hands)

Method: Turn your body at a 90-degree angle with the right hand more forward than the left, right foot touching the ground with heel only. Practice this movement as a Walking Meditation on both sides. As the foot turns 45 degrees, move your weight over that foot and allow the hands to come down to the belly. As the foot rises, the hands rise up and you embrace an imaginary ball in front of your heart.

Bodymind Healing Purpose: Balances the heart and belly (Tan Tien) centers. It cleanses the belly area and helps to bring energy to the heart. When the front toe rises, the Ming Men center in the lower back opens. This helps with lower back problems and empowers the kidneys.

11. Shoulder Stroke

Method: Your left hand is palm out by the shoulder while the right hand circles down to protect the genitals.

Bodymind Healing Purpose: This exercise is a good meditation on healing the liver (notice the similarity between this Tai Chi movement and the Bodymind Healing Qigong Wood practice for the liver). Imagine squeezing out emotional or food toxins from the liver while focusing your intention below your ribs on the right side of your body.

12. White Crane Spreads Wings

Method: Position your right hand by your third eye, left hand by Tan Tien. Left leg is forward and the left toe touches the ground.

Bodymind Healing Purpose: This exercise helps to open and balance the third eye and Tan Tien. Try using it as a repetitive Walking Meditation on left and ride sides for balancing power and spiritual energies. It is also useful for stretching the lateral channels of the body, for imbalances on right and left sides of the body, or for imbalances between your spiritual and everyday self. The ancient roots of the bird postures go back to the Hermetic mystery tradition. Hermes' sacred bird, the Ibis, has one foot in the waters of life, and his head above the waters— a useful metaphor and practice for being *in* the waters of life, yet not *of* them.

13. Brush Knee Forward

Method: From White Crane Spread Wings, first do one Roll Back to the right side of your body, right palm faces up next to your hip, left palm faces down. Then Brush Knee Forward by bringing your left hand, palm down, over your left knee as if you are snaking your hand through water. At the end of the movement your right palm faces out in front of Lung 1 and your left hand holds a ball with the palm facing downward at the Tan Tien as shown in the picture above. Then do one Playing the Guitar, then three Brush Knees, then one Playing the Guitar, then one Brush Knee (not shown).

Bodymind Healing Purpose: This posture helps clear the Tan Tien and empower the yang energies. After some consistent, repetitive practice, you may find the Aesclepian snake, and understand why the Greek Aesclepian symbol of the snake winding around a staff was chosen to be the symbol of Western medicine. The secret is in moving your bottom hand in front of your belly with a snake-like motion. The Taoist monk inside of you might say that this helps to open the Sea of Elixir—one of the keys to longevity, according to Taoist alchemy.

A variation on this movement is to repetitively practice Brush Knee Forward as a Walking Meditation and make your hands into a Tiger's Claw—your claw comes out in Brush Knee Forward, then you claw back to your knee as if tearing at something. Then look backwards to the left and right with your intention toward your tail. You are now doing *Tiger Pawing,* a movement that comes from Hua Tuo's Tiger Animal Frolics, which preceded Tai Chi by thousands of years; it may be the derivation of Brush Knee Forward. When you practice Brush Knee with the spirit of the Tiger, you'll discover how the movement activates the Lung, Spine and Kidney Qi. It was used by Hua Tuo to strengthen and heal these parts of the body as it is by some Chinese doctors today.

14. Step Forward and Punch

14. Step Forward and Punch (continued)

Method: Your right fist moves toward left as your palm and weight shifts to the left. Then Whip Punch as your right Dragon Foot steps forward. Pull the bow back with both Dragon Feet pointed outward at 45-degree angles (as shown in the first picture below). Then step the left foot forward as your right hand becomes an arrow moving through your left hand's half circle.

Bodymind Healing Purpose: This exercise demonstrates why Tai Chi is called "chuan" (the fist). In this movement you can find Taoist healing secrets of the fist. For example, imagine grasping the five elements into a whole as you make your fist. By only squeezing the fist at the end of the movement, as if like milking a cow's udder, you'll find a non-forced way of making a fist. *Dragon foot* refers to when the foot is turned to a 45-degree angle, as shown in the picture. Turning the foot this way, with the knee bent, opens the pelvic energy (*kua*). This type of movement, when done properly, is useful in preventing arthritis of the hip. As with all postures, practice this on both left and right sides to prevent imbalances.

15. Taking Snakeskin off the Elbow

Method: Your left wrist passes under your right elbow (as shown below). Then push forward as in Movement #7 (see Push on page 162).

Bodymind Healing Purpose: Try this for feeling Qi and dispersing stagnant Qi in your arms and wrists. Practice this movement interspersed with stillness Qigong and visualization practices for repetitive stress-related injuries and carpal tunnel syndrome.

16. Embrace the Tiger, Return to the Mountain

Method: Shift your weight to the right, then left, and place your feet together. Your right wrist is in front of the left wrist (as illustrated). Be aware of how the Ming Men extends slightly out in back as if you are embracing a ball in front of you. Then your hands go down and back up, embracing the heavens and returning down to the Tan Tien (as illustrated).

Bodymind Healing Purpose: This movement helps transform the body from a line into a ball. It empowers the lower back (Ming Men); and by touching the inside of the wrist to the outside, it balances the yin and yang energies of the body.

Additional Tai Chi Movements for Health and Longevity

*If I want to live longer I must learn Tai Chi
and accomplish it both physically and mentally.
To accomplish it mentally is much more difficult.*

—T.T. Liang, 102-year-old Tai Chi Master
Quoted from *"Steal my Art"*

Two other movements are added here. Both are taken from Bodymind Qigong Level 2. They are part of the second section of the Tai Chi sequence and are a good illustration of the use of Tai Chi as a method of bodymind healing.

Cloud Hands: For Clearing the Heart

Method: Begin in a Standing Meditation position, holding the Qi ball, while noticing your breath. Then imagine that you are in an ancient mythical land where you can move the clouds. As you turn to the left, your body turns 45 degrees and your hands move as if they can magnetically hold and move the clouds from your heart. As your left footsteps to the left side, shift your weight to the left the right foot joins your left, shoulder width apart. At the end of the movement, you flick your hands slightly as if letting go of the clouds.

Bodymind Healing Purpose: Cloud Hands is a way to cleanse the heart of emotional issues. Visualize events of your everyday life or past traumas and experience putting them in a cloud. As you turn, you flick them away. Experiment with this movement for prevention of heart disease, hypertension, clearing trauma, and even for stomach problems involving anxiety, work-related stress, insomnia, and for preventive medicine in general. Integrate this exercise into your life as a complement to your consultation with your doctor, psychologist, or other health professional.

Golden Rooster Stands on One Leg: For Enhancing Balance

Method: Golden Rooster can be practiced as a Walking Meditation. As you breathe in, the leg rises up to waist level. As you breathe out, the hands come down, preparing for the next movement. Practice it on both sides, raising first one knee, stepping, and then raising the other knee. Keep the back knee joint unlocked, and be careful to not go too low because that can put undue stress on the knee. Beginners can start by keeping the forward leg on the ground, or practicing with a chair next to them for support, as shown earlier in the Crane sequence.

Bodymind Healing Purpose: This movement comes from the second set of Tai Chi Chuan. According to a 1995 article in The Journal of the American Medical Association, Tai Chi is the best exercise system to prevent falls amongst the elderly. Movements like Golden Rooster are excellent for creating balance and increasing strength in the legs.

The Tai Chi and Yi Chuan Two-Person, Joining Hands, Self-development Method: The Practice of the Golden Ball

Looking into the dark Mystery brings clarity
Knowing how to surrender is the greatest strength.
Cultivate your own light
And merge with the source of all light.
This is the practice of eternity.

—Lao Tzu, *Tao te Ching* #52

The two-person training method that I have had the blessing to be initiated into is a combination of Tai Chi and Yi Chuan. You will now see how the principles of *Yi*, *Tai Chi* and *Chuan* are cultivated in these two-person practices, and how such practices play an important role in testing our ability to be in touch with the elements of creation. A clarification of terms in the context of two-person practices may help: *Yi* means cultivating intention, *Tai Chi* means cultivating the ability to move from Yin to Yang, yielding and coming forth as appropriate, and the word *Chuan* (fist, five fingers), as we have said earlier, esoterically means cultivating the five elements of creation (fire, earth, metal, water and wood) so that they are in our grasp. Letting go of the grasp of the elements and surrendering to emptiness (*Wuji Qigong*) is the greatest strength.

It is important to remember that in Chinese practices, Western distinctions can be artificial. Therefore in the following sections, even though we will isolate the elements as they apply to various practices, in actuality, all elements must blend together in a unified whole for our practice to be effective.

One practice, called *Shili* (practicing strength), is a way to test the earth and wood elements of the practitioner and to cultivate integration. If a student is ungrounded (Earth), the teacher may suggest an exercise we saw earlier like the Standing Meditation Zhang Zhuang practice of Standing Like a Tree. In this exercise we focus on our Long-breath and sink our Qi; while our teacher pushes on us from many angles, we see if we can maintain our sense of rootedness.

Shili can also be practiced as a Walking Meditation. For example, Person A can assume the Developing the Golden Ball of the Heart posture with their palms facing toward their own body; Person B puts their hands, palm down, on Person A's forearms. Both people walk together maintaining contact. Whoever is out of balance feels unstable while walking or gets knocked off center (not shown).

The practice of Tai Chi Push Hands, or Joining Hands, is one of the most popular ways to test the practitioner's ability to embody various Taoist principles and to grasp the power of the elements.[19] When practicing alone, we imagine practicing with another to cultivate our ability to embody the different elements of creation; when doing Push Hands with another, we practice reactivating the elements of our solo practice, and we see if we can find the relaxed state we found when alone.

Figures 32–34: Master Fong Ha doing Joining Hands practice with author.

In the pictures above we see the Tai Chi movements Push and Roll Back. Two practitioners "join hands" with each other and move back and forth to test the ability to yield and divert the force of an attacker. Person A becomes yang with a dot of yin as he pushes forward, palm facing toward the other's centerline; Person B is yin with a dot of yang, and with the back of one hand forward, he yields and adheres to the Push of Person A. Then Person B turns 45 degrees and reverses the circle becoming the "yang" partner.

If a student is overconfident, pushy or reaching for more than their root allows, they learn the lesson of the Earth and Wood Elements. A tree that overreaches its root system becomes weak and is easily toppled. Likewise, Tai Chi Push Hands tests our ability to yield like Water. This is an embodiment of Taoist philosophy and Wu Wei, or effortless effort. In this practice there is "a following" that takes place. Each person learns to not fight against an oncoming force. If we "try to push another" we quickly learn that this puts us at a disadvantage of becoming unstable—an important Taoist lesson about the value of yielding when attacked. Our ability to ground is tested in Tai Chi Push Hands; as we are pulled or pushed, we are tested in whether we can maintain our balance and central equilibrium under pressure. In the pictures above you see me trying to "push" my Sifu Fong Ha; he adeptly turns at a 45-degree angle deflecting my force. In the third picture, he disrupts my central equilibrium by Rolling Back.

The Fire Element is activated as the practitioner expands his or her ball of Qi and bounces the other person off if they are aggressive. If you can find a state of non-attachment when being bounced, you may find the treasure chest of gold within (Metal). It's like the game of rock, paper, scissors that we played as children where one element faces the other to "test its metal."

In practicing Yi Chuan and Tai Chi we cultivate "intention" by shape-shifting into various elements of creation. We practice becoming a ball of energy and rolling when appropriate with the oncoming force. Whether we have become the ball is not a concept, it is a felt experience tested in the practice. When the practitioner transforms him or herself into a ball of energy, the attacker will bounce off (as pictured below as I Push at Master Ha). This is called *Fajing*, the explosive power of the sphere of Qi.

Figure 35: Sifu Fong Ha bouncing the author with fajing.

The Chinese character *Jing* in ther term *Fajing* means force or physical power. In English this character is spelled the same as a different Chinese character, *Jing* which means "essential energy," one of the three great treasures in classical Taoist thought. This latter term can refer to "sperm, the energy of nature or the energy that comes from our ancestors. The former character, Jing, in the internal martial arts traditions similarly has many different meanings for types of force or physical power. The many terms show the subtleties and intricacies of he practice, and are difficult for the uninitiated and for those of us who are not Chinese scholars, including myself, to fully grasp. Nonetheless in hearing about the principles, doors can open to refining our practice.

For example, in addition to the explosive power of the ball of Qi in the Yi Chuan and Xing Yi traditions (*Fajing*) the way the power is manifested is differentiated. When substantial and obvious power is manifested in the discharge it is called *Mingjing*. To develop this substantial power practitioners practice with a rubber ball, leather ball and iron ball. Drilling and spiraling energy is called *Luoshunjing* and is seen in Chen style Tai Chi and in the movement, Moving Snakes through the Joints, in Bodymind Healing Qigong. A subtle part of the Yi Chuan tradition is to use hidden or insubstantial force (*Anjing*) by issuing a discharge with Yi or Qi and a minimum of substance. In the Yi Chaun tradition, mysterious force (*Huajing*) is cultivated by a practice whereby first the student yields to their fellow practitioner's push and makes a big circle backwards and forward to discharge him or her; next he or she makes smaller and smaller circles in their discharge until finally it as if no circle of force at all can be perceived in the discharge. A unique part of the Yi Chuan tradition, which Wang Xiangzhai contributed, is the power of the ball of energy to discharge in all directions (*Hun yun li*). This is the type of development practice that we spoke of earlier in Section I, "Are you a Pushover?" Here your fellow practitioner pushes on you from all directions; and you see if you can maintain your central equilibrium as you begin to cultivate your sphere.

It is not our focus here to go into the distinctions between different schools, and which traditions use various types of Jing; nor is it relevant to our purpose to describe what type of practices are used by each of my teachers, Masters Cai, Ha and Tam. Their respective levels of mastery are best experienced by their own words and touch. Our purpose is to establish that here, a world away from the Western origins of the Golden Ball myth, exists a sophisticated tradition to work on cultivating our spheres of energy.

One of the elements of Tai Chi and Yi Chuan Push Hands training, is the ability to use "no force" while pushing another, that is emptying, or appearing to empty, one's sphere of energy. This is an embodiment of Taoist philosophy and Wu Wei, or effortless effort. It is part of the skill of yielding. "No-force" can have at least two separate meanings: #1. Wu Wei, the effortless effort, and yielding commonly practiced in Tai Chi Push Hands spoken about above, #2 The minimal amount of force necessary to discharge or uproot your fellow practitioners by shifting from the use of strength to the use of Qi and intention.

Another Jing, *Kongjing*, (in Mandarin: also called *Hungjing* in Cantonese)is the practice of discharging another without touch, which is often called "empty force." Some people mystify the practice of Kongjing, non-touching Push Hands, by talking about it as if the force of the Master could blow a person around like the wind.

According to Master Ha,[21] notions of "distant external force,"[22] or "external emission," in this context are a misnomer. In actuality what the lay person sees when watching a Master discharge a practitioner from a distance is "intentional awareness" and "awareness of intention." What is called Kungjing, or empty force, is the most refined outgrowth of *Tingjing*, or listening energy, which involves the cultivation of sensitivity to, and moving with, another person's sphere of energy.[23]

"Dual cultivation," and awareness training, whether touching or not touching, requires a level of skill from both practitioners. In addition to listening ability, the person discharged needs to have the ability to fill his Ming Men and have developed integration so his ball of Qi can receive the explosive force of the other. "Integration of the ball of Qi" here means having the hollow of one's back (Ming Men) filled and connected to the point of contact on the hand. Without integration, the student could be hit, or tumble backwards from the "rubber banding" of the force coming back at him. The practice involves the student cultivating "integral force" so that when discharged, he will land back on the ground intact, maintaining the cohesiveness of the ball of Qi

As one's sophistication grows, their ability to do "no-thing," and use as little force as necessary to repel an attacker (Person A), grows. This degree of emptiness is difficult to cultivate and requires the master of the art (Person B) to empty himself of fear, or trying or strength. When attacked, Person B is thus able to yield, disrupting the central equilibrium of the attacker evoking a startle reflex. To the aggressor, it feels like falling into a trap of emptiness. Then, the adept of the art follows and adheres with Qi to the retreating force of the attacker, as the attacker pushes off the expanding sphere of Person B. Using as little force as necessary, the adept of the art thereby uproots and discharges Person A. Below we see me bounce into the air as Master Tam uses no apparent force to uproot me.

Figure 36: After I strike at Master Tam, he yields maintaining his central equilibrium as I lose mine. He follows my spiraling force until I fall into the trap of emptiness.

Figure 37: Master Tam yields, not using any apparent force of his own, as I begin to recoil backwards.

Figure 38: Notice the blurriness of the picture of me, showing the speed at which I am recoiling backwards, and Master Tam's stillness.

Figure 39: I am beginning to be uprooted by Master Tam's use of my force to discharge me; and I push off his expanding sphere to maintain the cohesiveness of my sphere.

Figure 40: My bouncing off of his sphere of energy sends me flying with both feet off the ground. My Ming Men is filled to prevent the disintegration of my sphere.

Figure 41: I begin to land.

Figure 42: I land with a fair degree of cohesiveness of my Qi Ball, after an experience that felt like being shot out of a cannon. It is not unusual to end up 10 to 15 feet from the point of discharge by the master of the art.

In my conception of Tai Chi and Yi Chuan Joining Hands, and Fajing practice we have a way to practice becoming like the Golden Ball of the alchemists where opposites meet and become transmuted. The attacker experiences his strength defeated by emptiness, aggression changes to gentleness and density transforms to lightness. Tension is taught by Relaxation. Fragmentation learns to embody Integration. Trying too hard becomes transformed by Letting Go. Here is a practice for bringing together in ourselves the elements of creation into a functioning wholeness that is light and yet has substance. We practice shape-shifting into a ball. And even when we are the one who is bounced, the lesson that we learn about trying to defeat another is fun, and brings a golden smile to our face in the learning. Is this not lead becoming gold?

Have we here found "the lost Golden Ball" of the Western mythology? The Golden Ball is an archetypal symbol of the collective unconscious. As a symbol, it is important not to literalize the Golden Ball to limit its expansive meanings; on the other hand we should not shrink from attempting to embody its energy. The word "symbol" comes from the Greek word *symbolon* which was originally a broken stick used in a trading agreement. To mark the transfer of ownership of an object from one person to another, a stick was broken in half to symbolize the sale. Just as these sticks were reminders of a greater unity, symbols today help reconnect us with something larger than ourselves.

Here in the Eastern Practice of Tai Chi and Yi Chuan Joining Hands we have a practice to re-store a unity, an integration, to broken parts of ourselves. In dissolving our energy blockages, and transforming our Pushing into Joining Hands, we join hands with our partner in our joint endeavor to become in harmony with the elements of creation, and the larger sphere of universal Qi.

As for my own development, with the help of my teachers I am growing very slowly like a tree under the light of their tutelage. Not being a martial artist, my primary purpose in learning the Push Hands methods is to explore and develop this part of the root system of the *Chuan Fa*, for the sake of "healing," in the broadest sense of the word, as outlined in this book. The practices help us to further open the energy pathways (meridians) for our healing, and they have the potential to generalize to help to change our life stances and ways of moving with others. They are a method to develop a "well-roundedness of Being" and to embody the spiritual principles we have spoke about throughout this book. In keeping with these purposes I call the Tai Chi and Yi Chuan dual-cultivation, self-defense methods a "Joining Hands, Self-development Practice."

Joining Hands practice is one method of cultivating the Golden Ball; but many spheres of development are encompassed by the symbolic expansive meaning of the Golden Ball spoken of through this book. Standing Mediation helps us to hold the Golden Ball, develop its spiritual base and dissolve into the source from which the creative energy of life arises. The Bodymind Healing Qigong practices help us to cultivate the ability to energize, heal and move with the Golden Ball. Two person exercises help us to play with, test, roll with, and develop the substance of the Golden Ball and share our practice with another. The transmuting of our leaden emotional and mental issues that cloud us from glowing gold in life are another essential part of the sphere of the Golden Ball. All facets of the Golden Ball are part of its wholeness, and are equally essential to our "well Being," helping us to draw from the wellsprings of our potential. Developing each facet of the Golden Ball adds to the other facets.

In the next Chapter, we will explore the psychological cultivation of ourselves regarding our life patterns and life stances as another significant part of the Chuan Fa, and the development of the Golden Ball. From the perspective of the associated arts of the Chuan Fa, *Yi Chuan and Tai Chi Joining Hands Self-development Practice* is a metaphor for our everyday encounters with others. How do we empty the spheres of ourselves of our dysfunctional life patterns; and how do we deal with our fears of being bullied? How can we develop the strength and flexibility of a tree in order to endure the emotional storms and stresses of life? How can we cultivate the ability to yield appropriately when verbally assaulted, and empathize with the wound in the other; or how do we discharge the verbal attacker's critique with the least force necessary. How do we find cohesiveness when we are criticized, or when our psychological patterns fragment us? What do you need to empty yourself of at such difficult moments?

Dealing with our inner emotional demons, according to the thesis of this book, is a deeper purpose of the Internal Marital Arts. The inner work, from this point of view is to find our Stance, and to cultivate our deepest Selves as we practice Joining Hands with everyday emotional life. When we face an outer force or off-centered life pattern, can we psychologically Roll Back, sink down into the psychological roots of our issues, stick to our inner process, and through inner reflection alchemically transform our issues into a new way of Being? Perhaps you will add your story to those in the next chapter.

Section III:

Rebirthing the Tradition in Modern Times

I swear the earth shall surely be complete
to him or her who shall be complete.
The earth remains jagged and broken to him or her
who remains jagged and broken.

—Walt Whitman

STANDING UP FOR YOURSELF:
The Psychological Ground Beneath Standing Meditation

Healing is not just a property of the physical body...
we are all mind-bodies, so that healing,
like health and illness, must also be psychosomatic.

—Andrew Weil, M.D.

...classical man saw psychological and physical sickness
as the effect of a divine action
which could be cured only by a God or another divine action.
When sickness is vested with such dignity,
it has the inestimable advantage
that it can be vested with a healing power.
The divina afflictio then contains its own diagnosis,
therapy and prognosis,
provided of course that the right attitude toward it is adapted.

—C.A. Meier,
Ancient Incubation and Modern Psychotherapy

Changing your Life Stance: The Transformation of our Self-Identifications

Though I had the utmost gratitude for finding Standing Meditation and Qigong, as a psychotherapist I knew that this experience was no more than "a divine high" unless it was grounded in the psychological dimension. How "the golden ball" rolls through real life is the work of *the opus*.

In the first Chapter we spoke about how in the *Ksatreya* warrior class, to which Buddha's parents belonged, the Standing Meditation tradition was a holistic practice— a martial art, a healing and spiritual practice. It was also a method for working on the psychological *klesas*—the envy, jealousy, greed and other issues that are a part of psycho-spiritual practice. We spoke about how the holistic dimension of the practice was lost through invasion, dispersion and time. We are now ready to open the final chapter, coming full-circle to re-vision in modern times what a holistic vision of this practice might be.

In the last chapter we focused on the spiritual and alchemical transformations in the body that come from Qigong and Standing practices. These cannot be separated from the psychological inner work that occurs during the practices. In this chapter we will shift our focus of attention to the psychological level. In truth, all of these levels occur simultaneously, though sometimes one or the other comes to the forefront. The more we are aware of the multidimensional layers of affect, the more whole is our practice.

Sigmund Freud stated that "the ego is first and foremost a bodily ego."[1] In developmental and object relations theory today, as well, there is increasing awareness of how the primary experience of the body is a conveyer of the individual sense of Self. Male children who mature late with late-developing pubic hair or small penises, or girls who are small-breasted, may begin life with an identity of being small, inadequate or late bloomers. They may feel that they don't "measure up" to their peers.

As a practicing psychotherapist, I have seen the body image of childhood remain fixated as part of a person's identity many years later in life. A small man in the film industry, who works so compulsively that he is in danger of losing his family, admits that behind his stance as a high-level achiever are memories of being unable to stand up to his big brothers. He says, "Now it's me who's standing up tall in the world. I'm making more money than all of them." A gay man who risks his life at sex clubs smiles coyly as he talks about liking to be seen as attractive; he goes on to tell about how he felt he was ugly as a child. He says, "Now I'm making up for lost time." A small-breasted woman, and frequenter of Sex and Love Anonymous groups, gradually became aware of the price she paid for her early sense of pride in being the most intelligent girl in her high school. She discovered that it compensated for her inadequacy feelings stemming from other girls in gym making jokes about her small breasts. She said, "I thought I could find love through sex."

Margaret Mahler says that "the core of ego development, the first orientation toward external reality, is the differentiation of the body image, which is the psychic representation of the bodily self."[2] A major part of the psychotherapeutic process is to integrate the old representations of the Self that are encoded in the body, and to transmute them through awareness and new self-representations.

In combining Standing Meditation practice with consciousness of our psychological Selves, the practitioner has an opportunity to bring into awareness the old representations that the Self has been built upon, and to form new identifications. If a person identifies with being small and weak, in the process of Standing and Push Hands practice the person may discover that being small means they have a lower center of gravity and a greater ability to uproot larger practitioners. If a person identifies with being strong and superior, Standing may give a more balanced, gentle and humble sense of Being. If a person has identified with being an intellectual, a new stance is gradually discovered as the Qi sinks to the Tan Tien and a new center is experienced there. Impulsive personalities begin to experience a new sense of rootedness. Standing Meditation is a practice of experiencing our imbalances until, in time, a new posture and a new identity take root.

In *Psychological Standing Meditation* we meditate upon the lifeforce as we directly experience it in ourselves as a way to develop our connection to a wider sense of Self. For example, when doing *Zhan Zhuang* (standing like a tree) practice, we may experience the organic potential in ourselves to reach and grow to spiritual heights, and at the same time we may direct our intentionality to cultivate rooted connection to the ground of ourselves. This is referred to as *raising the spirit and sinking the Qi.*

When we Stand with an awareness of our whole psychological Self, we practice finding a Self that is able to hold the centerline in the midst of archetypal patterns that manifest in our emotional bodies and break our connection with the ground under our feet. Can we find our ground when our siblings put us down and we feel ourselves falling apart inside? Can we remain centered when we are exhausted at work and we are asked to do one more thing that could "break the (proverbial) camel's back?" Can we find our way to our heart of hearts when our partner doesn't meet our expectations?

The practice of Standing Meditation involves finding a felt sense of Self that is at the physical center of our ball of energy. In Zhan Zhuang practice, our self-identification can be with the centerline of our inner tree trunk. Our stance, bodily feelings and associated thoughts may lead us naturally to penetrate to the core of a given psychological issue. We may sense the psychological gravity of the situation, or become aware of fragmenting thoughts; then we can use our awareness to go back to the meditation on our solid foundation, and on the centerline of the body as it finds a balanced equilibrium, even if we are pushed.

In my two decades of practice as a psychotherapist and as a practitioner of the internal marital arts including Standing Meditation, Tai Chi and Qigong, I have grown to appreciate the value of the interweaving of these Eastern and Western traditions. The contexts for my observations have included students of mine in the classes that I have taught, students of my teachers and my psychotherapy clients. In each of these areas there have been times that I have watched the two traditions both used together with an individual, as well as used separately.

I have seen those who have practiced Standing Meditation and Qigong for years without psychotherapy change psychologically. I have seen overly aggressive practitioners of the interal martial arts, who were not involved in therapy, soften over time; and I have seen withdrawn people increase their assertiveness. I have been particularly moved to see women who have been abused in their childhood (with fears of being assaulted evoked by even a soft touch) transform their fears and become adept at Joining Hands practice.

But, Standing Meditation, Tai Chi and Qigong are not panaceas,[3] nor are they the only paths to self-transformation. I have seen people in therapy with the same characteristics listed above change their stance in the world without practicing Standing Meditation or Qigong. Also I have seen people who practice these arts and don't change their basic patterns, or change them to a lesser degree than others. Most commonly for most of us, there are times that changes are apparent and other times when we fall back into old patterns as stressors increase.

So, as a scientist, I can not say that it was the traditions themselves that changed the people, and not time or other factors. As a practitioner and empirical witness, I believe that there is a very special catalytic combination that comes from integrating both traditions. Being aware of the alchemical transformations that are happening to our psyches while we practice Qigong brings an integated wholeness. Likewise for those involved in psychotherapy, Qigong and Standing practices may enhance the degree to which intellectual and emotional insights are embodied.

I have chosen three cases for illustrative purposes that represent various degrees of integration of psychotherapy and the internal martial arts traditions.[4] After discussing my experiences integrating the two traditions, I will discuss a bullied young man who did both psychotherapy and Tai Chi and Standing Meditation classes with me. Then we will discuss a night-shift worker who was my psychotherapy patient, but studied Tai Chi with another teacher. Finally, we will discuss a university student who took my Tai Chi and Standing Meditation classes, and who was in psychotherapy with another therapist.

My Experience: Bullies, Qi and the No-sword School

Being reared as an intellectual, not big or very muscular, I could not stand up to many of the aggressive boys in my high school. My father told me it was not worth fighting with ignorant bullies. For many years I suffered from running away from bullies, not only during daylight hours, but at nighttime in my dreams. For years, I had a recurring dream that I was running away from bullies; sometimes I would take out a gun, but its bullets weren't powerful enough to harm my attackers. After about a year of Standing practice, I had another one of my recurring dreams. The same attacker came after me, but this time instead of running away, I faced him. I put my hands up in the Opening the Golden Sphere of the Heart posture and an energy came out of my chest and arms that was like a vacuum cleaner turned in reverse. The energy was so powerful that the person was literally blown back a few feet into a wall. This dream felt like a major turning point in my therapy, in my life and in my Standing Meditation practice.

In my lineage of training for over two decades with Sifu Fong Ha, Standing Meditation practice has been integrated with the practice of Tai Chi Chuan. They are seen to be part of an integrated whole balancing the cultivation of groundedness as well as a fluidity in yielding. In Tai Chi training, we are taught not to use any more force than is absolutely necessary. The training in the internal arts is to be like the famous swordsman, Bonzi, of "the no-sword school."

> One day Bonzi was on a ferry and a bully was having fun unsheathing his sword and showing off his prowess by cutting nicks in people's ears. Sometimes he wouldn't be that accurate and he would cut off a piece or a whole ear. Everyone on board was cowering. When the bully did this to an old woman on board, it was too much for Bonzi to bear. He said to the bully "You shouldn't be doing this to these kind people. I don't want to get into a fight with you, but I pray you will stop." The bully replied to Bonzi, "Unsheathe your sword you

little man and I'll teach you a lesson for daring to speak up to me." Bonzi replied, "Oh I couldn't do that sir, I am Bonzi the Swordsman, practitioner of the no-sword school, and I've never lost a fight. I wouldn't want either of us to be harmed, or see our blood shed all over the deck of this beautiful boat."

The enraged bully said, "You have no choice, for if you don't unsheathe your sword, I'll kill you." Bonzi replied, "Then I have no choice but to show you my art. But I have one condition, and if that is met you can have your way of fighting me—I do not want anyone on this ferry to get harmed from one of your missing sword thrusts, or to have any of these kind people have to witness a bloody scene, so I ask you to be honorable enough to go with me on that attached rowboat to the island off the stern of this boat. "You will meet your just fate there." The Bully, steaming by now, agreed. Two passengers helped take down the small rowboat and put it into the water. Bonzi bowed to the killer, motioning to the boat said, "After you, sir." As the bully stepped into the boat, Bonzi removed the oars and with a graceful push from his foot he pushed the boat into the current of the river leaving the bully to float downstream. The ruthless cutter of ears was humiliated as everyone on board laughed. The bully yelled out his final curse calling Bonzi a coward and in a screaming, yet cracking voice, said, "I thought you were such a good swordsman." Bonzi, replied, "No sir, I am not a braggart like you. I told you I was a practitioner of the no-sword school, and I had never lost a fight. Now you know why."

In the practice of the internal martial arts, we likewise do our best to avoid fights. Instead we practice with other students by playing Push Hands, learning not to contend with others. This is called Wu Wei (effortless effort). It has been an emotionally reparative experience for me, and many others like me, to find that by yielding and neutralizing another's force and then absorbing it, that those with undeveloped musculature or small size can uproot, and actually make fly a few feet in the air, those who are much bigger and stronger (called Fajing). It's nothing special. It's a matter of learning how to find our ground, sinking our Qi to the earth and being sensitive to our fellow classmates. The power of this energy (Fajing) is like an exploding ball of Qi that many practitioners experience after a time of practice. It is really a form of mutual play that many students can understand the beginning stages of in about six months to a year of practice with a teacher who has expertise in this method. The psychological effect of this practice gives self-confidence, and a new bodily identification with integral force, the ability to feel the different parts of the body in alignment.

In my two decades of practice, I have been able to avoid any major physical confrontations except on two occasions. I remember once in Hawaii when I had practiced for about four years, I was in a bar naively doing Tai Chi dance with two women friends. This apparently angered one of the locals who looked like he was on drugs. He was about 5 feet 10 inches, very heavy set and muscular; his eyes were emblazoned with a scattered kind of rage as he cursed at me on the outskirts of the dance floor. He said, "Come on, do you want to fight?" I assured him in my gentlest voice that I had nothing against him and didn't want to fight. He raised his fists and kept yelling, "Come on, come on." I took a step away and tried to make eye contact with his friends to help me avoid a fight. His three Samoan friends, who each must have weighed over 225 pounds, looked at me without expression and said, "Take care of it yourself." I could feel that my Standing Practice was barely with me as my fear response shot up through my 5 foot 7 inch, 135 pound body; then I barely had a chance to exhale "sinking my Qi," trying to get grounded. As the man swung at me, one of the first movements of Tai Chi, called Roll Back, instinctively came to me. It is the most basic Tai Chi movement used to take another's force and not contend with it. We adhere to the attacker's fist, shift our weight backwards and circle the force out of the way (as in the Pa Kua Fish Tai Chi movement in Section II). The angry man flew into one of his friends. He came back at me one more time, and I did a variation on the same movement again. This time, he was uprooted as I did the Tai Chi movement called "Roll Back and Push" (as seen in Section II); he flew into a table, breaking a glass on the floor. I didn't want to stay around for the next event with him and his friends; so I left with my two companions to avoid further needless confrontation.

Though I felt the adrenaline rush of power that came from my years of Standing and Tai Chi practice, I was fully aware of my fear and limitations as a lightweight scholar who had minimal Tai Chi and Yi Chuan training under his belt. One never knows how good their art is, and there are always people more adept than we are. I certainly don't identify myself as a martial artist; and I believe, like Bonzi, it is better to practice the no-sword school and to use the gift of the internal martial arts for healing, rather than fighting.

It's said that training in the internal martial arts takes a lot longer than training in the external martial arts, and that those who want to be fighters shouldn't bother with it. It takes very long to master anything, and those that want to learn self-defense might do better to study an external martial art. I certainly experienced this when confronted in the bar, and didn't feel particularly self-confident, even after four years of practice, though I was grateful that the movements I had learned had saved me from at least a black eye, and maybe severe injury.

Another Bonzi story tells of Bonzi as a young man,

Bonzi heard about an eccentric swordsman who lived alone way out in the woods. Bonzi went to study with this old gruff man, while many of Bonzi's friends studied sword forms with other teachers. The Old Master in the woods told Bonzi to come and live with him and just cut his vegetables every day. Bonzi kept asking when his sword lessons would begin, and the Master said, "Just learn to cut vegetables." Bonzi's friends were bragging about learning their whole second sword set, not even having to cook or prepare meals for their teachers; and Bonzi hadn't even learned one movement yet. Occasionally the Master would correct his stance as he was cutting vegetables, or lightly hit him on the buttocks with his sword and show him how to turn, but this seemed like nothing much to the young, impatient Bonzi. But from this foundation of the caring stance of cutting vegetables, learning how to turn, and after developing a loving relationship with his Master, Bonzi was able to master many forms of Sword and later became one of the greatest sword-masters of China.

My second story about being physically attacked came after practicing Standing and Tai Chi for about 23 years. One day I was at a local reservoir waiting for a parking place. At this popular site, many sit in their cars waiting in front of the diagonal spaces for a parking spot to open, because the pleasure of the nice walk in the woods is worth the wait. Sometimes the wait is considerably long, and is a test for anyone's patience. After a long wait, a car pulled out right in front of the place for which I'd been patiently (OK, I admit, not so patiently) waiting. Before I could get into the space, another car weaved around me and pulled in. The young man who had exercised this devious maneuver, turned around and mockingly smiled at me. I honked my horn, and he turned around again with a wide grin.

With tenacious intent to not give up "my space," I laid my hand down on the horn (not very non-attached, I must admit). After a few moments, it bothered the driver enough so that he angrily got out of the car. I got out of my car and "just stood" there. When I saw him get out of the car, I wondered whether my old issue with tenacity was a mistake. The young man, probably in his late 20's, was about 6 feet tall and solidly built. I was 52 years old, 5 feet 8 inches and 145 pounds, He was huffing and walking fast towards me with rage in his face as he yelled, "You shouldn't be honking like that, man," and he began to grab towards my collar as if to shake me.

It was interesting to me that his assault was not frightening to me. I didn't feel any fear as I was "just standing" there. My standing practice was rooted in my body; instinctually my tailbone slightly curved under sinking my Qi to the belly (Tan Tien) as my lower back (Ming Men) spread out. I automatically lifted my hands into a variation of the Yi Chuan "Opening the Sphere of the Heart "posture that has been shown earlier in the book."

As the enraged man grabbed for my collar I instinctively changed this Standing posture to split his oncoming force along with a variation of the "Crane Opens the Heart" and "Crane Opens the Door to the Heavens" postures of the Animal Qigong set. My hands opened like a Crane's wings, contacting and splitting his outstretched hands. As my hands turned around, they faced his exposed neck and chest.

Assuming these "no- force postures" leaves the aggressor feeling exposed as if the energy has been sucked out of him. The aggressor knows that he is totally, vulnerably exposed to any strike from the defender. Of course I didn't take advantage of his vulnerable position, being constitutionally, and by training, a kind soul. I just stood there holding this potential; but was ready to do whatever was needed. The young man, feeling this potential, immediately changed his stance toward me and apologized, "I wasn't trying to do anything to hurt you, I.... um, um, was just trying to get you to stop honking the horn."

Though I was grateful for the skill and sense of ground provided by my years of training, it is a very important part of the training in internal martial arts not to be overconfident. Events of road rage and confrontation can lead to unforeseen consequences. This event did serve as another major moment in my psychological transformation. Using "no-force" techniques from Standing may seem impressive on a physical level; but the real, everyday work is how we respond and sink our Qi when attacked emotionally by those at work or in our personal lives, and whether we lose ourselves, our balls of divine energy, in the process.

How do we find the stance of Opening our Hearts and "split" the oncoming force of emotional assault in every day life? Through our body stance and our psychological awareness we look into our own heart, and through its reflection in the mirror of our own hands; we breathe and begin the process of working through our issues. We "come to terms" with the feelings that we and others have—of fear, jealousy and anger. We form our words and feelings and embody new life stances.

The feeling of being collapsed like a victim begins to change as words of self-empowerment arise from our depths. Blaming others and extending over our center-lines changes as we begin to take responsibility for the ways we respond to our anger. As we spoke about in Chapter One, the role of the divine creator is to shape reality by our words and our postures.

I remember a story from a Buddhist journal from Spirit Rock Meditation Center in San Geronimo, California, about a young girl who was teased by a classmate who kept calling her, in a mocking, singsong phrase, "four eyes, four eyes... you're so ugly."

> *The young girl went home crying, got some advice from her mother, who was a Mindfulness Meditation practitioner, and learned a new stance to take. The next day when the boy attempted to humiliate her again, she said, "You're right, I have four eyes, two regular ones, another one here in between my two eyes, and another one in my heart. You might want to try to develop your other two eyes. "*

Finding the stance of empowerment through our meditative awareness has the capacity to change us, and others around us, at our core. Hopefully, the little boy's cruelty was changed to kindness by this little girl standing up for her Self. But, we cannot control another's evolution; all we can do is find our own ground.

Life's emotional cross-currents give us an opportunity everyday to find new stances. This is the real practice. This is "Internal Marital Arts."

The following cases are presented to illustrate the interface of Psychotherapy and Standing Meditation Qigong. I am grateful to each of the following people for the depth of their inner work; and I recognize that much more transpired in the sessions with each of the following people, to which a brief vignette barely does justice.

Case Example: The Bullied Boy

Perhaps because of my history, I have attracted patients who have also been bullied. I like to say that my greatest referral source is "the Cosmic Coincidence Control Center." It is the way of the Tao to respond with mysterious accuracy, bringing to us the people with whom we resonate, for we are all "Energy Beings" magnetizing to us those with whom we have lessons to teach and to learn.

As a young boy, Sam (not his real name) was the smallest of all of his classmates, and was a gentle and sensitive child. When other kids engaged in cruel jokes and hitting contests, Sam shied away. Because he was so small, kids enjoyed bullying him when he wouldn't fight back. Sam's stance was, in part, constitutional, his mother remembered that he was a gentle child even in his first few years of life.

Contributing to fixate this stance into a characterological pattern was an older brother who would beat Sam up on a regular basis, and told him "I'm better than you at everything." Sam's father's attitude was to say, "Let it roll off of you." Sam developed an attitude that a man is one who doesn't stand up to his peers.

By the time he was in his late teens, Sam felt so paralyzed that he developed a social phobia, and feared contact with his peers. He dropped out of college once, and complained of multiple somatic issues including developing arthritis in his fingers.

Sam did a combination of internal martial art classes and psychotherapy with me over a period of about a year. A major turning point in Sam's life was when he found a stance to stand up to his brother through his internal marital arts practices including Standing Meditation; but though this was important in giving him sensitivity and power, the verbal dimension of power was equally crucial. One of the more significant moments in our therapy was when Sam found his verbal stance to his brother's message about being better than him at everything. This message had always made Sam cower with anxiety in his stomach. I remember the day in therapy when Sam found his stance and said, "You're not better than me at everything, you're not better at being a kind brother." According to Sam, when he said this to his brother there was a long pause and it stopped his brother in his tracks; after apologizing for the way he had treated Sam in his childhood, a new relationship developed between them.

With a combination of his study of the internal marital arts, which emphasize the power of softness, and his therapy, over time Sam transmuted his identification with being an ungrounded, wimpy male. He learned that another male archetype who was like him was Ghandi, a man of peace. He realized that his sensitivity was a gift, and then used this sensitivity to excel at Tai Chi Push Hands and to become a brown belt in Aikido. He was able to work through his social phobia and remain in college; and over time I witnessed Sam harness his sensitivity to begin to pursue a career in the healing arts. He learned to affect his arthritis in his hands with the power of his mind, and through the use of Acupressure points and the visualization methods that are a wider part of the practice done in Bodymind Healing Qigong practice. He was able to get off the anti-anxiety medication he was taking and discover how his breath and his new stance helped him alleviate his anxiety.

This was no "total cure," but "a healing." Issues still arise, but Sam cultivated a stance toward them, and a way of working with them. He now has a clear vision of the path ahead of him, whereas before, his ground was paved over. Sam now recognizes that just like his internal arts work takes practice, so does finding his psychological stance. He is aware of how the abusiveness of his brother scatters his energy; and as he watches thoughts arise, he practices "cognitive restructuring."[5] Instead of his old thought, "I'm no good and can't stand up for myself," his new restructured thought and stance became, "I don't deserve to be treated badly despite any of my shortcomings; and I will stand up for myself." Then he breathes and practices returning to his grounded stance of power and kindness. It also helps that he is now able to use his Tai Chi Push Hands practice to play with his brother and demonstrate the power of his softness. Sam became "a Chuan Fa Warrior."[6]

Case Example: The Exploding Karate Kid

Arnie was a 30-year-old night-shift worker at an industrial firm with whom I worked in therapy. I did not have Arnie as a Tai Chi student, but in the course of therapy I referred him to another teacher in order to keep our therapeutic container unencumbered and uncontaminated by two different types of relationships.

Arnie came to me on referral from his company's employee assistance program for "exploding on two separate occasions"—one time he put his fist through a window, another time he threw a vial of industrial fluid across the room.

As part of our therapy, I had Arnie focus on his breath, then follow his breath down into his body to be more aware of kinesthetic sensations and bodily holdings. A key moment in the therapy occurred when Arnie was "focusing"[7] on his body and tried to identify the tightness that was there. He noticed how puffed out he was in his chest. A memory surfaced of being in gym class as a child and noticing that his chest was caved in and his posture was slouched, whereas all the other boys' chests were more filled out and their postures more erect. The belief that ruled Arnie's life for the next 10 years was forming, "A man is one who doesn't slouch, a real man's chest is pushed out proudly."

This was Arnie's way of expressing a common male theme that "a man is one who doesn't show his vulnerabilities and doesn't cave into the pressures of life." Many people gave Arnie validation for being able to tolerate more than other guys could. He worked longer hours than any of the other workers. When anyone needed someone to take over one of the late night shifts, Arnie was the one that would readily volunteer. He was very well-liked for his "helping out" anyone who had a problem.

Since Arnie would never "stoop so low" to admit his vulnerabilities or ask for help on his late-night shift, when things bothered him he would oftentimes build up resentment and explode. Also, Arnie started to realize that he had little true intimacy in his life where his true feelings could be expressed and his real feelings known.

Arnie had been a longtime practitioner of Karate; and at first he balked when I suggested that he might consider trying Tai Chi, an oriental internal marital art that emphasizes balancing strength and softness. I didn't push this idea on him, but when he saw a man practicing it in a park one day he was struck by its grace and asked me for a referral. I gave him the name of a local teacher I respected. After six months of practice, Arnie began to discover a new type of strength. On one occasion he told me of the insight he had just gotten from his practice of Push Hands with another student; he found that "the softer you are, the stronger you are."

The insights he gained went along well with the psychotherapeutic work we were doing. Arnie realized how he never had room in his family of origin to speak of his vulnerabilities. His father was a Marine captain who had a very stoical view of what it meant to be a man and "trained" Arnie in this attitude.

Arnie began to develop a new stance in his life, "A man is one who balances strength and softness. A man is one who can be with his whole Self—vulnerabilities and all."

Identifying and working with his old and new life stance was a significant part of a larger psychotherapeutic process. Arnie learned to become more aware of the feelings in his body, and he learned how to explore their deeper meaning. The psychotherapeutic process as a whole led to better containment of his feelings and the ability to express them more often. At a later point in our therapy, Arnie was proud of himself on one occasion for expressing to a co-worker that he was exhausted and irritable on the late-night shift. He asked the co-worker to help him out by letting him catch a twenty-minute catnap and wake him! To the best of my knowledge he never "exploded" at work again.

Case Example: Finding "the Right Man"

Rachel, a bright, vivacious student in her early 30's, learned Standing Meditation as part of a psychotherapy training process I gave at a local university. The following is a synopsis of a term paper she wrote and discussions I had with her.

Rachel had a history of many short-term relationships. During the time of her training, after a boring evening with her current partner, the thought arose, "He's not stimulating enough for me." Cross-currents of feelings then took her away from her own center of gravity: "Life is depressing;" "There must be something wrong with me to be in a relationship that's not more alive;" "Maybe I shouldn't stay in this relationship any longer."

Rachel reported after two months of practice that Standing Meditation was helpful to ground her on her own "Island of Being" in the midst of waves of conflicting thoughts and emotions—waves that in the past made her criticize her partner with derogatory remarks. On this island she had room to cultivate her awareness with some of the methods of Bodymind Healing Psychotherapy.

When Rachel felt that her partner wasn't stimulating enough, she "focused" on the bodily feeling that emerged as she reflected on the above issue and asked the question, "What's this feeling all about?" By plugging into the roots of her own ground, she had room to feel her own loneliness that arose from not being met in the way she wanted to be. She felt a closed door in her heart. She felt deadness there and desperately desired to be saved from the feeling. She became aware of the thoughts, and precisely how they disrupted the flow of her Qi. She reported having difficulty going back to her breathing.

Specifically, when Rachel noticed the thought arise, "He's not enough fun," she become aware that her Qi went up into her head and an angry flushed feeling came into her face along with a contorted turn of the side of her mouth.

In Standing Meditation with psychological intent, we connect the feelings that arise while Standing with our family of origin issues. "Self-psychology" and "object relations theorists"[8] believe that many of our core patterns develop from introjecting representations of early objects such as our parents. Our parents' beliefs, or lives, live in us as self-representations that need to be transmuted in order for us to be our real Selves.

Rachel associated the roots of her feelings with her unhappily married mother who thought her husband was boring, and so gave the message to her daughter, "Be careful not to get involved with a boring man." Rachel became aware of the replaying tape of her early family experience; then she went back to breath, back to center, back to her own ground. This insight, and the resulting shift that happened in her body, led her to begin a process of therapy with a therapist that I recommended. She began the process of differentiating her own life from that of her parents; she began to take responsibility for making things fun in her relationship, instead of "expecting the man to do it."

In the third quarter of her training program, Rachel reported that while practicing the "Opening the Golden Sphere of the Heart" exercise she found a sense of her own ground, and a sense of her Self as a Golden Ball of energy that was sending out love to her mother. She realized that her mother's message was just a well-meaning attempt to save her daughter from a similar fate. Rachel's resentment of her mother started to melt away as her therapy continued, and she started to take responsibility for initiating humor-full interactions with her boyfriend. The last time I heard from Rachel she reported that once she began to let go of her mother's fear, she was able to see that her boyfriend actually had a dry sense of humor with which she could play.

A Concluding Perspective on Psychological Standing Meditation

> *As you ought not to attempt to cure the eyes without the head,*
> *or the head without the body,*
> *then neither ought you to attempt to cure the body without the soul*
> *... for the part will never be well unless the whole is well.*
>
> —Plato

When facing life, sometimes we are weak-kneed, sometimes we are inflated and puffed up in our chests; sometimes we are collapsed. Sometimes we try so hard to please our partners that anxiety fills the ball of heart energy we hold; and we lean too far forward.

Sometimes, with our partners we are constricted; and we hold ourselves too far back. Other times we simply let go and feel a sense of relaxed peacefulness pervading every cell of the body. It can be like a process of learning to ride the animals and demons on the Merry-Go-Round of life, and from "our Horse Stance" we reach out and perhaps get hold of the Golden Ring.

Standing, while being mindful of our psychological processes is a practice for keeping in touch with the center of the wheel of life and recognizing what our inner work is. Standing practice helps us find the ground beneath our emotional bodies. We practice using our stance to find and play with the Golden Ball of Energy that we hold in the midst of life's cross-currents. We just Stand, and in the process we may find health and live younger longer as we cultivate our psycho-spiritual Selves.

And you may want to join my prayer that your stance helps to kiss the eyes of other sentient Beings, helping them to heal and actualize their Qi-full life stance.

THE TAO OF EVERYDAY LIFE

The ordinary is the extraordinary.

—Wang Xiangzhai

Once upon a time, or as the great storytellers like Michael Meade say, once before the time of digital time, once in a time when people had the time to be in tune with cosmic time…there lived a disillusioned young man (or woman) who was discontent with a life that had lost its meaning.

Feel yourself time travel into the realm of mythic tales and reconnect with the cosmic time that's still alive in this very moment.

The young man decided to go on a quest to the Taoist sacred mountain of Hua Shan to see if his life's meaning could be restored. Although he vowed to fast from all food and wait until a vision came, after three days, nothing had happened. Weak from starvation, he fainted in the middle of his prayer circle and gave up.

As he let go of trying, it was then that the founder of Tai Chi Chuan, Chang San Feng, appeared and offered to teach him how to move like the animals to restore his vital energy, and how to find his Primordial Self by filling his body with the powers of the heavens and the earth.

And so this initiate learned how to move like a Snake Creeping Low. In addition to learning the physical movement, the snake taught him to descend into his darkness and find the way through his pain. Another week was devoted to watching and imitating the movements of a White Crane Spreading its Wings. Mimicking the crane, the initiate put one foot in the water, and spread his not-so-imaginary wings. Into his awareness came a vision of how to step into his pain, and yet find a Transcendent Self that could observe his emotional process with non-attachment.

After 40 nights on the mountaintop learning from the animals, studying the ways of nature and being visited by the spirit of various Taoist Masters, he knew it was now time to leave. As he traveled down the mountain, he was very excited about all he had to teach.

The first person he passed was an old lady who was washing off a glass window with a circular motion. The initiate felt a wave of disenchantment come over him as he realized that she was doing the Tai Chi movement, Making a Circle between the Heavens and the Earth (also called Taoist Immortal Paints a Heavenly Rainbow), just like he had learned it from Yang Luchan, the founder of the Yang lineage of Tai Chi.

"Maybe everyone knows what I know already, and will not want to learn anything from me," he thought.

After walking a little further, he saw a man drop something on the ground and bend down to pick it up.

"How does this man know the secret movement called Grasping the Needle at the Bottom of the Sea, which I learned from Yang Cheng Fu? It's supposed to be a secret way to open the lower Tan Tien and ground the body's energy. What I know is nothing special; everyone knows it," he said to himself dejectedly.

Walking a little further he saw a couple in an argument, the woman's arms were outstretched in the shape of a ball in front of her heart as she exclaimed to her husband, "Why can't you just listen to me?" The young initiate now reached his limit, for she was doing the special Opening the Heart Meditation posture that he learned from the founder of the Yi Chuan system, Wang Xiangzhai.

Just as he was ready to give up and fall back into the sea of depression he knew so well, he realized that yes, everyone he saw was doing sacred movements, but most were unconscious of their sacred character. Then he realized that his path was to teach people to appreciate the meaning and beauty of what they were already doing in their everyday lives…that our human movements, and our very Being, are divine gifts—if we could just see them as such.

Adapted and Retold from Shamanic Oral Teachings
—Michael Mayer

When I tell the teaching story above in workshops I ask people to notice how their body is positioned, and for readers now, I advise the same. Maybe your feet are crossed at the ankles, preventing the energy of the feet from dissipating. Maybe you are touching your head at the temples, unconsciously instilling some idea further into your mind through touch. What is the sacred purpose of your current posture?

As in the days of old, hearing a story like the one above has the capacity to induce us into an awareness of the Tao—the Way of Harmony with the elements of the universe. We remember that there is a sacred quality of Being that lives in each of us, ready to emerge into awareness at any moment, as it lies beneath the surface of ordinary life.

The aspirant of "the Way" asks, "Where do I go to learn about this Way, how hard will I have to study, how long will it take, and how much will it cost me?" The response from Masters of "the Way" is that there is a paradox because, on one hand everything we do, if viewed from a higher perspective, is already sacred; therefore you don't have to study at all, it is right here in this moment and costs nothing…it is free, if you are free. And yet on the other hand, we all feel out-of-sorts quite a bit of the time, and it seems as if all of the training by the greatest masters in the world would not help us find our way.

Everyday life presents us with an opportunity to practice reclaiming the awareness of who we are—we "re-member" (putting ourselves back together into the whole Beings we are) how every moment, and every movement, is an opportunity to be mindful of the gift of life.

Standing in Lines: The Grocery Store, Bank, and Department of Motor Vehicles

The river of our everyday lives often feels like it runs into a dam when we have to stand in lines. We do not just stand in a line, we become one. Though it may not be as bad as old Russia where people waited in line for a loaf of bread for the better part of a day, our bodies take on a linear form. Our pelvises become locked and lower back problems become a signature of a society whose everyday lack of energized rituals make the root of the spine weak. The rivers of Qi get blocked as we enter the mindset of "waiting until." We become a "linear world" thinking about time, impatiently or resentfully waiting for the next step forward, rather than being content in the space we occupy.

We were well prepared for our lives as consumers. Our "educational" system taught us to tighten our bodies and sit in uncomfortable positions with no regard for how we felt. We were talked at, and then we waited for graduation, for our ticket to the supposed "good life," for the diploma. Most of us have become so accustomed to living in the future that we do not realize how the light of our Being decreases in strength through the years as the natural, energized child within us loses his Golden Ball.

No wonder a vast number of spiritual practices from the East have come West to teach us the importance of living in the present. Many meditative traditions sponsor weeklong retreats to teach people how to be in the present in their everyday lives. It may seem incongruous to have to leave the world in order to learn how to stay present in it, but unlike more indigenous societies where singing, chanting and frolicking were part of everyday work life, our specialized society has split life into segments. Just as religion is not allowed in the schools, nor sacred practices allowed in the workplace, so has meditation often been relegated to a workshop away from everyday life. Our everyday world may be politically correct; but it is psycho-spiritually sanitized.

Standing Meditation is an ideal remedy, particularly for waiting in those dreaded lines at the grocery store or the bank. Wherever we go can potentially be a perfect place to practice. We just go into our Standing Meditation posture, bend our knees, stay aware of our centerline, and watch our breath. We can practice any of the methods associated with Standing Meditation described earlier in the book. For example, we can practice Microcosmic Orbit Breathing, noticing the breath come up the spine on the inhalation and descending down the front of the body on our exhalation. We may practice Macrocosmic Orbit Breathing allowing the breath to come in from our feet, up over our heads, and then back out through the feet. Or we may practice circulating Qi with "the Circle that Arises from Stillness," moving our hips in a circular motion around the centerline as our weight shifts over each foot. We do these practices while "not trying" to do anything; they arise from "just being." We "do no-thing" while the world is doing so many things. We move from Wuji to Tai Chi.

Since the nuances of our practice are so slight, no one is likely to notice what we are doing as we practice self-healing with the power of our awareness. One good practice is to shift our weight slowly from side to side while maintaining our centerline. Then, when the weight is 100 % over one foot we can slightly lift the other foot off the ground practicing maintaining our balance, and strengthening our legs one at a time. For the first few weeks of practice, we can keep the lifted foot slightly touching the ground while we develop our legs' strength. We count how many breaths we can comfortably stand on each leg. By slowly increasing the amount of time we balance on each leg, we may add our names to The Journal of the American Association study that found Tai Chi as the best method to increase balance and decrease falls among the elderly.

Another practice is to simply enjoy time and make use of the powerful energy that arises from our stillness. Imagine sending healing light out to our environment on our exhalation, and allowing the light to revitalize us on our inhalation. Instead of being a chore, "standing in line" becomes transformed into "standing in the sphere of cosmic energy."

Children oftentimes seem to be the only ones who notice, and are curious enough to engage in what we are doing, like the cute four-year-old blond boy the other day with whom I was able to "energy play."

After standing a while on a long line at the Department of Motor Vehicles, little Jonathan peeked out from behind a pole to see what I was doing. I slowly moved my hands up from the earth as if I was throwing a ball to him in slow motion. He pretended to catch it and throw it back. After a while of back-and-forth playing with him, we began to throw the imaginary ball to others in the room. Pretty soon scowls turned to smiles on the faces of many of the people who were watching. Some participated, and one older lady, who must have been in her early 70's, even threw the ball from her heart.

What a beautiful world it could be if we could play more while we work, and make room to be alive while we are alive. Perhaps Joseph Campbell said it best:

> *People say that what we're all seeking is a meaning for life. I don't think that's what we're really seeking. I think that what we're seeking is an experience of being alive, so that our life experiences on the purely physical plane will have resonances within our own innermost Being and reality, so that we actually feel the rapture of being alive.*

Traffic Jams on the Freeway: An Opportunity to Clear Clogged Arteries of Qi

There is almost nothing more irritating for most of us than getting stuck in traffic on the highways of the modern world. Just when we have an expectation that we will be flowing smoothly, flying along at least at the posted speed, the traffic stops, or slows down to a turtle's pace. We feel stuck. Tension builds up inside, and sometimes we may feel like screaming. We are controlled by the forces of modern life regardless of how important we may think we are. "This isn't a 'free-way,' it's "a constricted way" of living.

The Taoist practitioner knows that not only are there outer road blocks and traffic jams, but there are inner blocks and jams as well. We remember that psychological health is a question of attitude. As James Russel Lowell said, "Mishaps are like knives that either serve us or cut us as we grasp them by the blade or the handle."

One handle for the apparent mishap of "being stuck in traffic" is to use our time to play a musical tape, finding the kind that fits with the rhythm with which we want to resonate. Maybe we'll choose a beautiful, relaxing tape or an up-tempo one. If we are prepared for the situation, we may have an educational tape that we haven't had time for in our busy schedule. Ah, how nice to have a chance to stop and listen!

Another way to "get a handle" on the situation is to feel what we need to do at this moment. Being with our Selves may mean screaming to let some of our pent up anger out. Catharsis on the freeway can be one of the pleasures of modern life. If due caution is exercised so that one doesn't lose concentration and get into a car accident, we can use the modern car as an emotional release chamber when we're driving with the windows down and no one can hear us. We can practice making more sublte sounds for healing the internal organs that we spoke about earlier.

> *As you are driving, allow your breath to turn into sound. Try experimenting with various sounds to see which sound connects with which organ, or part of your body, that is in need of healing. Do you need a nice pleasant Hum or Aum sound, or a louder growl after a long day at work?*

We may use the situation as an opportunity to practice letting go—of our own importance, of our schedule. During a moment of being most impacted by modern life, we can practice detaching ourselves from it by "Being in the world, but not of it." We begin to breathe and choose a form of practice appropriate to the moment, while keeping our attention on the road.

We may appreciate having a chance to watch our thoughts. We can notice just how critical we are of ourselves, and of the situation. We practice not judging our judgments; we just notice them and go back to our breath.

> *Practice Microcosmic Orbit Breathing, inhaling up the back of your spine and down the front of your body, pausing after your exhalation as described earlier. Feel your Qi grounding you and at the same time imagine extending your centerline up through the top of your head to the heavens above. So that you don't get too relaxed, practice "sung," relaxed awareness, like a cat at ease, yet ready for whatever comes. Become aware of the ball around your car and extend your awareness in all directions. Notice the other cars, their colors, and the people in them that are sharing our journey in modern space. What comes to your attention as you become more present to your surroundings like a martial artist, readying yourself in all directions?*

Freeways that are like a parking lot give us an opportunity to work with stagnant Qi. The expression "clogged arteries of traffic" is more than just a saying; it can be the reality of sitting in "stuck Qi land." Stopping and starting again as the traffic moves, we are teased with the possibility of freedom of movement, then it is taken away at the next moment, turning us into mechanical devices. We are turned on and off by an inhuman hand. Control is in the hands of others; we are cogs in someone else's machinery. Or are we?

To "get a Taoist handle" on the jolting stop-and-start we can do a meditation on speed. Instead of going along at the pace of everyone else's stop- and-start, we can play with finding just the right speed, pacing ourselves so that we minimize stopping and starting in a jerky manner. Sometimes this requires leaving a few car lengths between ourselves and the car in front of us. We slow down from the herd mentality, and "shift into another gear," a gear of inner peace.

Some people mistakenly think that Taoist practice is about a pseudo-spiritual notion of "letting go of control," but as the practice of Tai Chi teaches, sometimes we keep the ball of Qi in our hands, and other times we let go of controlling it. It depends upon what is appropriate to the situation, and what form we want our practice to take. In Walking Meditation, for example, we practice the turtle step. Instead of moving at the fast-paced speed of others, the turtle raises its foot with Qi, like a piston raising and lowering slowly, rather than compulsively all at once. We feel our own rhythm. Maybe this is why turtles live so long. As discussed earlier in this book, slow movement that focuses on where it is coming from and going to is called *reeling silk* in Tai Chi.

When we find this speed, particularly listening to just the right music and just the right breath, we may find the way to clear the arteries of Qi inside ourselves. There are some people who might get angry that we are leaving extra space between ourselves and the car in front of us. In their rush, fighting for their idea of control, they may honk or move to another lane. But when we look into our rear view mirror, we realize that we may have done an act of service for many others, for there are hundreds of cars behind us who may also decide to choose *the slow moving Qi lane* over the frustrating stop-and-start lanes.

The Alchemy of Everyday Life—At Home and at Work

We have all had the experience of having some cleaning to do around the house when it feels like too great an effort to begin. Yet a few minutes later we put some music on, dance a little, and the cleaning seems like just the thing to do. We clean the kitchen counter effortlessly, the push and pull of the vacuum cleaner becomes part of our exercise program—we are in the flow of things. At these moments we understand what is meant by Lao Tzu's statement in the *Tao te Ching* which says,

> *In the pursuit of the Way one does less every day,*
> *one does less and less until one does nothing at all,*
> *and when one does nothing at all*
> *there is nothing that is left undone.*

Doing "no-thing" does not imply a lazy attitude; it means that when we are in the flow of the river of life, work takes place without effort. In Taoist practice this is called *Wu Wei*, or effortless effort. In Western Alchemy this state of Being is called *The Great Round*. We find a way to catalyze the elements of creation, creating gold from the lead of everyday life. The four elements in the Western alchemy tradition are fire, earth, air and water.

In our everyday life, when we are in touch with the Tao, the Way of Harmony with the elements of nature, we naturally move from one element to another. We may start the day by moving, activating the fire element with a walk, stretching, or going for a nice jog. When we are out of touch with our natural energy and pump up our adrenal glands by drinking a cup of coffee, we may pay the price of a crash down later in the day.

Throughout the day we can reactivate the fire element just from the movements of performing some daily tasks of life like cleaning the kitchen or taking care of bills. When we feel like we have done enough, we may move into the air element by learning new information through reading, or getting on the internet, absorbing information from the airwaves of life. Perhaps afterwards we may instinctively enter into the water element by taking a sip of water, or by taking a shower to refresh ourselves. The water element is also activated by meditation, which gets us in touch with the still pond of our deepest Selves and where we tap into the vital energy of the reservoir of life. Likewise at work, try to find opportunities within the parameters of you work situation to harmonize with your natural Self. Taking breaks where we return to stillness can prevent carpal tunnel syndrome and other work-related disabilities. The Taoists call this Wuji, and as we have discussed, without this stillness, movement takes more effort and is less healing. From our stillness, we are made ready to move back into the fire of life or work.

> *Find ways to move wherever you are; the beauty of Qigong is that you can make very small circles or larger circles. If it is not appropriate in your work environment, you can do much of the Bodymind Healing Qigong system with movements so small no one will notice you are doing them. Remember "The Circle that Arises from Stillness," can be practiced standing or sitting at your office desk on the edge of your chair. Listen to the signals that your body is giving when you are at the computer, or engaged in other repetitive work, whether it is at home or at the office. Which Bodymind Healing Qigong movement would your Taoist medicine man prescribe as an antidote?*

As we learned form the Taoist initiate at the beginning of this chapter, all people are already living the Way of the Tao. There is nothing to teach and nothing to learn. When we are in touch with the natural movements of our lives, we can sense from our own bodymind the next thing to do to bring peace and golden, glowing energy into our lives. But even though we all know this, we still need to be reminded of "the Way."

Food, Eating and Fasting[1]

Food as Medicine: Our Body's Wisdom

Oh Sinnah Fast Wolf, a Native American Medicine Woman with whom I studied many years ago, told me that the word for food and the word for medicine were one and the same in the Apache (Dineh) dialect. Anyone who hears this may instantly recall a truth that they have always known. Yet we all listen to the "experts'" latest news telling us what is good and not good for us.

If we could truly feel our own bodies, we would know what, when, and how much to eat. The Taoist belief is that every time we need food, it is for nourishing a part of us that is out of balance. Our tongues, stomachs, and minds are in perfect harmony with the Tao in the most subtle and intricate ways. With a reservoir of millions of years of stored knowledge, it is ready to be put to the test as we stand in front of the refrigerator, after a long day of work, and we make a choice about what food to eat.

Our biochemistry speaks a non-verbal language with our bodies, helping us to decide what foods we need to nourish us at particular moments It says, "Hmm, I'm feeling very scattered after a long day of work and not having eaten since lunch,...I think I'll have a piece of that left over chicken…no that's too heavy, I think I'll have a piece of fruit. That orange looks great. No, that's too sugary, I think I'll have a banana. Yup, that's perfect, grounded but light enough not to weigh me down too much so I can go for a walk before supper." Our body's ability to know which food is medicine for us at what moment is an awesome wisdom.

The other part of this yin-yang equation is that some of us are allergic to certain foods that we crave, some of us are addicted to certain types of food, and some of us have a tendency to overeat. Learn to read your body's signals to differentiate between your body's wisdom, your body's allergies, and your bodymind's compulsive cravings.

When we overeat or eat a food not suited to our systems, we pay a price. Rich sugary deserts, and meat and heavy proteins need to be consumed in moderation, or at least with mindful awareness of their effect on our energy. Each human being is different and our personal history and our ancestral lineage speaks through our stomachs' preferences in a way that is amazing to behold.

Overeating, Diet and Eating Disorders

Just about everyone is guilty of overeating from time to time. We all have learned that if we overeat, we get a feeling similar to a plane crashing...thus the term "crash down." When we are not weighed down by food and our Qi is flowing as it should, the natural experience of being human is like "flying high."

An important question to ask ourselves is, "What are we eating for?" Many times, we eat to fill an emptiness. The alienation of modern life, which leaves us unplugged from community, also leaves us with a desperate need to fill our bellies. Food grounds the disconnected wire of our psycho-physiological state that is dissociated in psychic space.

Bodymind awareness is the missing ingredient in modern dietary propaganda. Being aware of our bodies is the first step out of the shark-infested waters of mass ideas that swallow us up telling us what is good for us as individuals. To lose weight, the Atkins diet of high protein, low-carb is useful for many people. I found aspects of this diet to be particularly good for me, however the idea of eating as much meat as you want created pain in my kidneys, so I adapted my diet to include more fish instead of meat. Listening to our bodies is key.

It is interesting to note that thousands of years before the Atkins diet suggested lessening the use of grains and cereals this was a common Taoist practice. In the Taoist Cannon (Daozang), abstaining from cereals, swallowing the breath and exercising (Daoyin) were methods practiced to "eliminate bad energies and induce good energies to stay in the body," and were methods associated with long life.

Regarding overeating, the Taoist approach is first to fill ourselves by sinking the Qi to the Tan Tien and filling ourselves with breath and Qi from our connection with the universe around us. This is done through Microcosmic Orbit Breathing (see Chapter 2). Focusing on the exhalation helps to fill the stomach (Tan Tien) with Qi.

Other traditions also are a part of the natural Way of eating. It helps to be psychologically aware of "what we are eating for." Are we feeling emotionally stressed, empty or lonely when we shovel in that fast food? It is essential to have awareness of our psychological issues, and to be able to have a compassionate relationship to those issues. Mindful practice is the key. When we lose this key and eat to fill the void, our stomach becomes bloated with an overweighted physical ball rather than with a ball of golden energy.

One antidote to overeating, and a healthy way to eat in general, is to eat slowly, chewing the food many times until it turns to liquid. This makes digestion easier and gives us a chance to really taste and appreciate what we are eating.

The same goes for drinking, as consuming too much liquid can be a problem as well. The Taoist approach is to listen to the body's needs and drink only the amount necessary to satisfy ourselves. Oftentimes this is just a sip.

Allergies

Another way our body demonstrates its wisdom and speaks to us about our personal history is through food allergies. Some, whose families or early lives involved over-consumption of milk proteins, have milk allergies. These people get congested after consuming even minimal milk products. But you don't need to listen to anyone who tells you to eat or not eat milk products. Notice your own body's reaction and look at your tongue a little while after eating. In Chinese medicine, tongue diagnosis is an art. You can start your course of study by noticing if you get a thick white coating on your tongue within a few hours or a day after eating milk products or other foods.

How do you get rid of the congestion? Many go to a doctor or pharmacy not even realizing that their congestion was due to eating milk products many days in a row. They take a decongestant and add to the multimillion-dollar drug industry. If you listen to your body, you may be able to relieve the congestion by eliminating the food to which you are allergic. As we will discuss below, fasting for a period of time may help you to discover to which foods you are allergic.

Fasting

Fasting for a short period of time is a great way to experience the free-flowing, natural energy in our bodies. It is important to remember that fasting can apply to more than just abstaining from food. Fasting gives us a chance to appreciate Wuji, the void from which Qi is created. Doing "no- thing" in any arena helps us break down reification and appreciate life. Fasting from talking for a day makes us appreciate and savor the sanctity of speech. Fasting from sex for a period of time may help us to approach making love in a more sacred manner. Fasting from the conveniences of the modern world through vision questing or backpacking makes us appreciate the conveniences of the modern world, and stop taking things for granted. Try adding television and news to your fasting menu. Fasting helps us return to primordial awareness.

Be particularly circumspect when receiving advice on food fasting. One of my patients many years ago was in a religious commune and was told to fast for a month. It led to a psychotic breakdown. Experiment with listening to your body, and choose the type of fast that is right for you whether it's one day a week, one day a month or year, or not at all. Even not eating a single meal, like breakfast, can be cleansing. A sensible way to experience a minor fast is to have only a piece of grapefruit in the morning and then wait until you are hungry before eating anything else.

Don't let rigid ideas lead your way; let your body be your guide. In general, I like to use fruit during the day for cleansing and either vegetable juices or warm vegetable soups at night. Warm foods are easier to digest because our bodies don't need to use as much energy to process them. For those with yin constitutions, sometimes protein like fish or meat or a little warmed grain is needed to keep your energy grounded so you can continue the fast.

Our understanding of why we fast is increased by Taoist philosophy in general and Tai Chi in particular. By emptying, and then filling again, secrets of life are discovered. In the transitional movement from Double Ward Off (Yang) to Roll Back (Yin) and back to Press (Yang), the practitioner empties (Roll Back) and fills (Double Ward Off, and Press). Awareness of letting go and filling the sphere of our life energy is heightened by separating Yang and Yin movements into Standing Meditation postures. The strength of our legs increases by keeping the weight in each separate position and holding our posture there for a few exhalations; new energy and appreciative awareness comes when we link the movements back together. When we fast, we empty ourselves; and when we fill again we become more aware of our allergies, and of which foods give energy or take it away. Our bodies react in their own unique ways.

When I fasted and re-introduced wheat back into my diet, my belly bloated. When I re-introduced my favorite soymilk to my breakfast, my tongue got a thick white coating that lasted for days after I finished eating; and I became more lethargic. What are the foods that give your body problems? How can filling and emptying your stomach increase your awareness of which foods add to the sphere of your life energy and which foods deflate it.

The Water Element in Eating

We are so programmed to think the outside world will cure us of our maladies that we may forget that we have a natural drinking fountain within—our saliva. A secret Taoist exercise to calm the body's fire is to swallow saliva. More subtle than even drinking water, we can get a sense of fulfillment by moving our tongues around the mouth enough times to create an excess of saliva, and dividing it into three portions. Then exhale and swallow the saliva. While in your awareness, follow it down to the Tan Tien. This helps calm our internal fires and can help in quenching thirst.

Temperature is also a key variable in drinking. Warm water relaxes the body and gives us a feeling of expanding. Morning is a great time to cleanse with a glass of warm water and a bit of lemon or honey.

How we combine eating and drinking is important. When we feel dryness in our mouth while eating we often use drinking to solve this problem, but then the saliva doesn't get to fulfill its purpose — to moisten and aid digestion.

Experiment with drinking before the meal to clear the way for the food, and to reduce your water intake afterwards. If you drink in the middle of a meal, check whether it makes you feel more bloated. If you feel the need to drink after a meal, try having some warm liquid like tea rather than a cold drink, which constricts the belly after it has expanded to eat. Feel out how much you can trust your saliva to do the work of watering your meal and activating the alchemical process of dissolving you food. Experiment with your own body to see when it needs to drink and how much.

Food Combinations

Combination of foods is also something that your body knows a lot about, if you just listen to it. If you have a lot of fruit after a meat meal you may get indigestion, because meat takes a long time to digest, and the fruit will get stuck in the tunnel of digestion. It's like putting a race-car stuck in fifth gear behind a slow moving truck in the Lincoln Tunnel. No wonder your body feels a crash!

Feel out how much meat protein or carbohydrates your body can handle, once a day, not at all? People with Yin constitutions may need more animal protein for their strength; those with more Yang constitutions might try to experiment with reducing meat protein. After eating your big meal do you need to take a siesta as they do in warmer climates, or maybe a light walk? Only your body knows the truth of your energy level. Listen to what nutritionists have to say, but then take the advice back to your body to make the final decision.

Bringing Qi to your Food: A Sacred Eating Ritual

Incorporating Yi Chuan meditation while sitting down to a meal is a great way to make eating into an enlightening experience.

- Begin by using "Natural Long Breath and Microcosmic Orbit Breathing" discussed earlier. Let go of the stress of the day on your exhalation.
- Position your hands as if resting them on an imaginary balloon over your food.
- Incorporate the food into your balloon of Qi.
- To further transform your food into medicine, maintain your Yi Chuan stance and add the Mindfulness Meditation practice that follows: As you are holding the food in your imaginary balloon, open your heart to appreciate the food.
- Notice the colors of each living thing. Appreciate the kingdoms from which each morsel derived. Your heart ball of energy then sends appreciation to the ground that grew those green vegetables, the water, minerals, and other elements that created your meal.
- Then if you have fish or meat, appreciate the sacrifice that these living things made for you to be nourished; and remember the *dharmic* purpose for which you are being refueled—whether you'll be using the energy toward some creative project on which you are working, or a family member or friend to whom you want to send some extra love.
- Next bring into your awareness the people who have contributed to bringing the food to you—the farmers, the truck drivers, the grocery clerks. Then finally, and foremost, bring into your energy balloon an awareness of that force, that is non-force, in the universe that created all of these things including you. Imagine that there is a bigger ball around you that is being held by the elements of life itself.

- Notice the shift in your awareness and energy, and notice how the food tastes as you take the first bite.

I adapted this ritual as an Internal Martial Arts practice for my students in my Eastern Perspectives on Healing class at San Francisco State. I tell them to bring in a piece of fruit for our next class on Mindfulness Meditation. Then I have them do the above ritual with their hands in the Yi Chuan ball position and their eyes closed. Before they bite into that fruit and after they have appreciated the fruit and all the places from which it came, I tell them I'm going to do something that they might not like. I tell them this right when they are in a blissful altered state. I ask them to be mindful of what is going on in their bodies and minds when we do the next practice.

- Give your piece of fruit to the person in the class next to you. Feel what comes up in your body and mind.
- Open your eyes just for a moment to exchange fruit with a class member. As you close your eyes again feel what is happening in your body and mind.
- Once again appreciate this fruit and the places from which it came, as you are holding it in your hands and imagining sending energy to it.
- Open your eyes and appreciate the fruit as you take your first bite. Chew it many times taking in the flavors.

After getting past their initial anger at having to give away "their fruit," virtually all of the students appreciate the lesson learned in letting go, non-attachment, and dealing with their feelings brought on by this exercise. From an Internal Martial Arts perspective, Eastern practices aren't just about going into a blissful state. Internal Martial Arts are about dealing with our inner opponent—our attachments and our difficulties with jealousy and desire that take us away from ourselves. The issues that come up for students are a reflection of deep life beliefs such as, "What I have is better than others, and I'm getting a raw deal when I interact with others." Or, "What others have is better than what I have, and I don't deserve to have these better things." Issues of being overly rigid or being overly giving are brought into awareness. The exercise makes us aware of these beliefs, and of how these beliefs sometimes hinder our ability to feel and savor the gifts of life. This is "Yi Chuan Eating Practice," finding what is in our ball of Qi and watching it transform through awareness.

Guarding Shen (our spiritual energy): At Parties, in Psychotherapy and in Everyday Encounters

One major purpose of Taoist practice is to transform Qi into Shen, the spiritual energy of the bodymind. One of the ways that Shen is manifested is through the eyes. In many of our professional lives, our Shen is drained by the way we use our eyes.

Practitioners of psychotherapy experience this when they look at a client for a long period of time. As the therapist looks at the client and empathizes with him or her, the spiritual life force, Shen, goes out through the eyes. One of the reasons it feels so good to be seen with compassionate eyes is that the life force of the other is nourishing us with that divine energy that is the fruit of being human. Authors in the field of Self-Psychology believe that this empathic mirroring may be the most important ingredient in nourishing and building the Self of a child.

However, the consequence of excessive empathic mirroring, for the sender, is that, as with any natural resource, if it is over-used the resource becomes depleted. Then we lose touch with ourselves, and lose ourselves in the other. This happens in more subtle ways every time we get stuck at a party, listening to a person who talks on and on, without sensitivity to our circle of communication. If we keep looking at them, our Shen becomes drained.

A Taoist's antidote for the draining of Shen in everyday life is a process called *Sinking the Plumb Line,* as when a house builder drops a line with a weight on a hilly terrain to find the center line of gravity. The teachings of Qigong tell us that the center to which the plumb line drops in the human body is the center of our bodies in the Tan Tien. When we are practicing Sinking the Plumb Line, we don't actually look at the Tan Tien; we find it as a feeling by dropping our eyes, while they are open.

In *The Secret of the Golden Flower* we are told that the location of the plumb line is along the line of the nose. But if we don't try too hard to find it, we will discover that the secret place is actually very easy to locate. It is the place to which our eyes naturally drop when we are reflecting upon our lives or our encounters with others.

By dropping our eyes to this place after looking for a long time at a psychotherapy client, or at a person at a party who is not our cup of tea, we experience coming back to our center. This is the feeling of being in the Tan Tien, the reservoir where our life energy and power is contained. Just as we look into a body of water, this reservoir can provide a resource for reflecting within. It provides a psychic space that reflects back how life is. If we open the dam of our inhibitions, we can release just the right amount of this stored energy to water the fields of awareness. Having our eyes connect with the Tan Tien, we combine the activation of two important energy centers—our observing Self (located in the area referred to as the third eye), and our gut feelings about a particular encounter.

For example, one very sensitive psychotherapy intern with whom I do supervision, reported being drained by a female client who was complaining all the time. The intern's heart always went out to the client with great empathy, and the client felt very supported. After I suggested he allow his eyes to drop occasionally during therapy, Sinking the Plumb Line, he gained great insight into her case. He became aware that the reason why quite a few friends of this client were abandoning her was because of her victim stance in life.

He found a new level of honesty in himself, and realized the client's whiny voice drained him as it did her friends. He now had the insight into how she learned this pattern of behavior as a child, to get attention within her large family. Specifically, when her brother was overpowering her, she whined to her parents got them to side with her. Through finding his separate observing Self, this intern was able to help the client work on her "victim stance" in life. She began to take responsibility for her stance's effects on others, and to find other ways of being with her power as an adult.

Sex, Qi and Making Love with Life—The Play of Tao

I see my teachers, alive and departed, smiling at me as I approach this section. "Michael, are you going into one of you long explanations about something so natural?" The wisdom of my teachers speaks through me, saying, "There is no-thing to do, just be natural."

In line with the shamanic teaching story beginning this section, while it is important to just "be natural" when having sex, it is equally important to be aware that every movement and every touch of our sexuality holds a sacred purpose.

In Michael Gach's book, *Acupressure for Lovers,* he shows how virtually every point on the body, not just our sexual orifices, is an energy gate through which lovers may enter into bliss. Intention is the key to opening the gates of life. As you make love with your partner, try "circling, touching and feeling" various points on one another to open these energy gates. Imagine that your intention is healing, is pleasuring, and is opening the two of you to merge with the ocean of divine bliss. This exercise parallels the Qigong exercise of the Circle that Arises from Stillness.

Your Qigong practice has taught you the importance of moving from stillness to movement and back to stillness. This same theory can be applied to sexuality. Stopping and starting sexual play can shift sexual lust to divine embrace. The Taoists speak of transforming sexual energy (one aspect of Jing) into Qi, and then into spiritual energy (Shen). In the middle of making love, return to stillness and try practicing Microcosmic Orbit Breathing in sync with your partner. It is said that the Shen comes out of the eyes, so integrate the spiritual energy into your lovemaking by looking gently into your partner's eyes. As one of you inhales, the other exhales. Imagine the energy moving in a circle between the two of you. This has been called "dual cultivation" in Taoist Sexuality.

Qigong and Taoist concepts add a sacred depth to our understanding of lovemaking in "the play" of Tao. In Act I, the Taoist Yin-Yang symbol takes center stage. The small black dot of Yin in the larger white Yang half circle, and the small dot of white Yang in the bigger black Yin half circle becomes a useful metaphor to enhance the Tao of our lovemaking. Put anything onto the stage and its meaning will be sacralized. Yin and Yang tendencies in two people meet in lovemaking and then their Yin and Yang elements engage in the dance of opposites, waxing and waning. Hidden in the strong elements of ourselves is a dot of deep gentleness; hidden in the soft parts of ourselves is a dot of deep strength.

Figure 43: Yin-Yang: Adapted Symbol of Taoist Philosophy

The "spiritual" and "soulful" aspects of ourselves are a spinning Yin-Yang symbol intertwining in the play of lovemaking. At one moment one is in the foreground, and then they reverse.

Being aware of "darker," less-evolved elements of your sexual patterns is equally important to being aware of the "lighter," more spiritual aspects of yourself. Are you just taking care of your needs? Are you making love when you don't want to, just to please your partner? These are things that can drain Jing (libido). Use Eugene Gendlin's "focusing" method to become aware of energy blockages, find what they are about, and share that information with your partner. "Dark" feelings can be equally important as the light in adding depth to the intimacy of lovemaking. Discussing our limitations and vulnerabilities adds "soul" to the "spirit" of lovemaking.

Opposites have the potential to be resolved in lovemaking. For example, one paradox of sexuality is that on one hand we need to be self-gratifying to enjoy sexuality, on the other hand making love is for the giving and intimate "I-thou" connection with our partners. All opposites dance and join within the symbol of the Tao—at one moment we are aware of our own pleasure with a dot of awareness of the other, at the next moment we give pleasure to our partner with a small dot of awareness on ourselves. Like the Taoist yin-yang symbol, there is a dot of the Yin (self-centeredness) in the Yang (desire to satisfy the other), and a dot of the Yang (desire to satisfy the other) in those moments that we are Yin (satisfying ourselves). Then, distinctions between self and other dissolve; the separation between giving and receiving disappears as we move from Tai Chi to Wuji.

In Act II of the Tao of Lovemaking, The joining hands practice of Tai Chi Push Hands moves to center stage. The movements that we make in our bodies and our minds in lovemaking are like the dance of Tai Chi Push Hands. Let's take the sequence Roll Back, Press and Push for example. The dance of lovemaking takes a step as we symbolically "Roll Back," breathe in and satisfy ourselves. Then we exhale giving to our partners; as in Tai Chi "Press" we make contact with the circle of the ball of our heart; and then as in Tai Chi "Push" we give ourselves from our Tan Tien as our energy moves upward and outward, giving from our hearts. The energies of lovemaking can be sacralized, balanced and enhanced by the ingrained wisdom of this ancient art.

Another part of the Taoist family of arts is Tui Na, a type of bodywork similar to doing Tai Chi Push Hands-like movements to massage another. We can transpose this practice to the partner with whom we are making love. We Press the skin of our partner sending healing energy to them, or we make snake-like movements pulling our partner's energy blocks out with our Roll Back movements. Lovemaking can be a bodymind healing experience.

In Act III of the Play of the Tao, the idea of stance is transposed to lying down by being aware of what "stance" you are taking as you are making love. In Chinese literature, we hear the act of love described with rich metaphors of the natural world such as galloping steeds, flying seagulls, late spring donkeys, and silkworms spinning a cocoon. In the Greek mythic tradition we hear of Zeus sometimes taking the form of a swan with Leda, or taking the form of a bull with Europa. Lovemaking transforms us into all elements of creation, if we can just be aware of the transformations. As it is said in the Kaivalya Upanishad, "Seeing the Self in all Beings and all Beings in the Self, the Absolute is obtained."

In Act IV of the Tao of Lovemaking, we shift our intention from the personal to the universal. The Baal Shem Tov's (the founder of Hassidism) viewpoint on the meeting of making love is expressed in the following quote,

> *From every human being there rises a light that reaches straight to heaven,*
> *And when two souls that are destined to be together find each other,*
> *Their streams of light flow together and a single, brighter light goes forth from*
> *their united being.*

This quote from the Baal Shem Tov lets us know that Qigong is not only a Chinese tradition; the energy that is felt when two souls meet is a universal experience. A world away, and a time apart, the Baal Shem Tov expresses well in this quote, the dissolving practices that are fundamental to Qigong. By letting go of our narrow selves we dissolve into the light of the universe. What is the light that is coming to the world from your lovemaking?

Imagine when you are doing your Qigong that you are making love with the divinely created life forms around you. The space around you transforms as the trees, the land, and the sky above become included in your dance. We shift from *anima personalis* (love of another person) to *anima mundi* (love of the ensouled world).

When you are making love with your partner, particularly after orgasm, imagine you are dissolving into the multifaceted elements of creation. Likewise, when practicing Tai Chi, shift your movements into acts of lovemaking with the surrounding universe.

In the Emerald Tablets of Hermes, the Bible of the ancient Egyptian mystery schools, it was put this way:

> *It ascends from the earth to the heaven, and descends again to the earth, and*
> *receives the power of the above and the below.*
> *Thus you will have the glory of the whole world.*

Sleep and Insomnia

We spend approximately one-third of our lives in sleep, yet we receive little education on how to sleep. The position that we sleep in is as important as the position in which we meditate. Finding the right posture for your individual body is the difference between waking up with a sore back or feeling well rested. If one side of your body is overly yang or swollen, it may be best to keep that side upward when lying on your side. While going to sleep, meditate on balancing the energy by visualizing the Qi moving downward with the flow of gravity, and upward to connect to spirit.

When you sleep, do you keep the heat on? Try sleeping in a room that is a little colder, without artificial heat, and add a few more blankets. Notice the difference in your state of mind upon awakening.

If we suffer from insomnia, Western psychological research tells us that it is usually from "trying to go to sleep." The Taoist remedy to this problem is to practice our Microcosmic and Macrocosmic Orbit Breathing. If we are worried that we need to sleep, and not just to meditate, we say to ourselves that during meditation we activate theta and delta rhythms of the brain, which are very healing to the body. We tell ourselves that even if we don't go to sleep we will be relaxed in the morning if we can just relax all night.

We start counting our exhalations and look at our time before sleep as an opportunity to practice any of the visualization or meditations we have learned in this book or elsewhere, enjoying the opportunity to travel to places our busy lives have not allowed. If there is something worrying us, as we watch our breath we see if we can find a compassionate relationship to ourselves. Many of my clients have reported having success with placing one hand on the heart and the other on the Tan Tien. See how many breaths it takes you to feel a sense of calm, balanced energy—even love—entering into your body.

Standing and Walking in the Woods at Night: Activating the Primordial Self

The basis of all Taoist practice is the return to our primordial Self. Before civilization gave us the comforts of, and protection against the elements, humans slept outdoors. For many millenniums, a natural part of the cycle of the day was to stare into the stars at night and get reconnected to our place in the vast and wondrous universe of which we are a part. This is encoded in our ancestral memory, and when we sleep outside, we can be so restored.

No wonder so many people backpack. But few people make sleeping outdoors or taking a walk in the woods at night part of their everyday lives. In the cities, in particular, this is understandable in that there is so much danger from our "fellow human beings." Nowadays we can't be sure whether some knife-wielding maniac, rapist, or otherwise aggressive person may attack us. One of the undiscussed, major hardships of modern (so-called "civilized") life is that we've been cut-off from "Being" with the night. No wonder one of the first sayings associated with the radical feminist movement was "Women take back the night." For it was the role of women in ancient times to hold nighttime celebrations at the mountain top of Acrocorinth, the Telesterone of Eleusis, and the palace of Knossis in order to bring participants into touch with the power and mysteries of night.

Qi is activated by danger, and we discover our natural potential to be brought to a state of full aliveness by facing dangerous situations. I like to walk into the park at night, doing a very slow stalking walk, from the Yi Chuan Walking exercises, and listening to the noises of the night.

I begin with a period of Standing Meditation, and then choose one or more Yi Chuan Walking Meditations, while holding the ball of Qi. My daytime practice of Walking Meditation is enhanced in the woods at night by my awareness of the wild creatures I see there. Each half moon step of the Yi Chuan Walking Meditation counts more at night, and its primordial purposes are revealed in a more basic way. I've been awed by experiences of walking up to deer this way. When they see me, I go into one of the Deer Qigong postures; the deer and I become hypnotized by our meeting, staring, and wondering. It's an invigorating and sacred experience to return to primordial awareness this way after a long day at the office being a civilized human being. Again, I am not suggesting anyone else try this practice; obviously there are real dangers in the woods at night.

> *During the day when you practice, imagine that you are practicing Walking Meditation at night to enhance your practice. Become aware that your physical safety is dependent upon your quiet, centered steps. At any moment something may come from an unsuspected direction. Are you ready to turn or respond?*

When we walk in the woods at night it is different than during the day. Everything is animate and filled with mystery. What is that thing we suddenly see—a monster, an animal, or merely a broken branch? In seeing it, we walk differently—our knees bend, our center of gravity lowers. What is that cracking branch sound we hear a little ways away—a deer with whom we might play, or some animal or person from which might ensue a dangerous confrontation? There is a seductive charm about what's frightening. We become vigilant in ways that are beyond us during most daytime encounters. We are stretched beyond our normal limits by the normality of night? Our perceptions become more acute. We remember what it is like to be a warrior, even though we may have felt weak during the day. Nighttime forces us to pass through our fears in order to take the steps we need to survive.

Sleeping Outside to Activate the Primordial Self

When we are planning to sleep outside to cultivate our connection to our primordial Self, due caution must be exercised. One possibility is to choose the most rustic location close to our houses, where the greatest degree of silence and the ability to see the stars exists. Even a location right in your own backyard can serve to cut the cords to our normal lives, and open us to the experience of being part of the wild.

In the process of "modern day Vision Questing" many participants set up a buddy system where they can check on each person who is camping out alone. Sometimes a pile of rocks on the outside of one's territory is used; then our partner can come and check on us. Similarly when we are camping out, we may let a friend know where we are, and ask them to check on us if we don't call by a particular time the next day.

Though we think we live in a free society, being able to explore the beauty of nature during nighttime (approximately 50% of a day) is an exercise in "Civilization and its Discontents." In many places in the United States, modern laws forbid such retreats and adventures, as many state parks close at sundown.

There is obviously good reason for such laws. Civilization is built upon the protection of the masses. Inevitably, when people challenge the civilized safety zones, someone gets hurt, and laws get passed to protect "civilized man" from dangers and big institutions from lawsuits. Thus, we have rules like speeding limits, prohibition against swimming in certain bodies of water, and no trespassing in nature at night.

It is difficult to get a person at a local park to give you a permit, but it is worth investigating. I once had success speaking to the executive of a local park near my house who gave me such a permit for sleeping in the woods for forty nights.

When I cannot get a permit, I drive to a location near the spot I have chosen and leave a note on my car pretending that it has broken down. I let a friend know where I am, and arrange to check in at an arranged time. I walk to my pre-chosen spot and practice my Standing and Walking Meditation Qigong, as mentioned above.

When out in nature, as we lie down for the night, our mind projects our deepest fears out into space. One young man, who was a psychotherapy client, spoke about a three-day vision quest he was planning to take and about his fears of sleeping outside. He had fears of being attacked by people or animals. When we explored his fears, they felt similar to the ones he had as a small boy when he was beaten by his father. He realized how he had adopted a stance in life of fear and withdrawal, based on these early times. Though we did much work "systematically desensitizing" this fear through Bodymind Healing Psychotherapy, the ultimate test was his experience on his Vision Quest. He reported a "rough first night;" but then found "a strength in meeting the possibility that he might die in pursuit of his power." He stood up to a bear in the Sierra mountains; and after returning found the power he had always longed for…to stand up to his father and tell him how it felt to be beaten by him.

Sleeping in the woods at night should not be pursued frivolously. There are very real dangers. Even writing about such things in our litigious society opens the writer or publisher to potential lawsuits. Unfortunately, our self expression then become sanitized, The solution is that we all need to take responsibility for our actions and our choices as adults and think of the wider cultural effects of our actions when we sue someone for choices we've made.

When I began to sleep in the woods at night, filled with fear, I brought along three lines of defense. First my flute, second my staff, and third my knife, all close at hand. In all of my encounters with animals at night, I have never needed to go past my first line of defense, my flute. Once, during daylight hours, a growling wildcat approached me. Maybe I was in its territory. I played my flute, as I worked through my fear, and the wildcat was calmed. We need to use our own intuition at such moments, and call forth our deepest instincts.

In terms of the fear of animals, the way we look at animals and the postures we take can make all the difference. Finding a place of harmony and oneness with animals is an important key. After all, we are animals, and after the elements of civilization are stripped away from us, and we are left naked in the woods, we might look out carefully, or growl like this animal, if someone suddenly approached us in our territory. Remembering our animal nature helps us to remember our oneness with animals, and reduces unnecessary fear.

Native American shamans report that if we see a bear and turn on our axes, the bear will stop because this is something it can't do—don't take my word for it—this is an experiment with consequences. Oftentimes, animals are hypnotized by slow, Tai Chi-like movements made with the hands, or by the earlier Walking Meditation exercises. One of the most awesome experiences I ever had was dancing with deer in the woods using these slow non-threatening movements.

As you bed down, look up into the sky and become, once again, part of the natural world, stripped of civilized conveniences. Become more part of the greater scheme of things than you ever were when you slept protected inside of four walls. Enter into the ordinary, yet extraordinary realm of simply becoming a human...Being. Night becomes your initiator, illuminating what was dark and hidden within you. No wonder Night has been called the mother of all mystery!

Tree Climbing

It is a necessary and unfortunate by-product of the development of consciousness that we move from a state of a childlike wonder and unity with life into a state of *reification*. Reification means that an object becomes a thing in our minds rather than a living being. The experience that so-called primitive peoples had when they joined with nature has been called *participation mystique* or *animism,* because when we relate to nature in this way, a mystery unfolds where we become enlivened, animated, and filled with Qi. Our very state as a human being expands, and we begin to walk on the path to becoming our Primordial Selves.

When we were young we may have hugged a tree, rubbed our back on one, or climbed a tree. But as we learned language and found the names for them, we may have forgotten how to enter into participation mystique with them. Categorizing trees as objects has many civilized purposes. We can know which type of tree fuels long lasting fires, like oak trees and other hardwoods, but we lose something in the process.

We lose our natural experience of oneness, our participation mystique with the natural world. A basic tenet of cross-cultural knowledge is that healing comes from returning to the origin. If modern science is correct and our bodies evolved from the apes, then a key to healing our bodies may lie in being in the trees. For many millennia, our physical forms developed and adapted to climbing, swinging, and resting in trees. Normally when we exercise, we do so on flat surfaces. But the pelvic girdle loves to be stretched in multifaceted ways.

Tree climbing helps stretch our bodies in these multifaceted ways; but along with its benefits come potential dangers, such as falling from the tree. Returning to our Primordial Selves has its benefits and risks. Anyone who has felt energy rushing through their bodies after aerobic exercise, stretching in yoga postures, or dancing with a loved one knows that the energy that is latent in the human body is one of life's greatest gifts.

Perhaps the greatest amount of our potential energy is released when we face a situation where our life is in danger. This activates the fight or flight response. One of the greatest skills taught in Internal Martial Arts is the ability to relax under dangerous circumstances and cultivate *the neurophysiology of harmony.* Likewise with tree climbing, the higher we climb the more the fear of falling and death is activated. We need to stay with our breath at such times and, as in the elevator breathing technique described earlier, sink our Qi to our feet.

Tree climbing naturally puts the attention into our feet, because if we don't focus on our feet, we fall. As we climb and the energy moves to our feet, a more grounded sense of Self emerges within us.

To Climb a Tree

Once you choose a tree to climb, make sure that it is a good fit for your ability. As you climb one branch at a time, stay in tune with your breath. Feel the energy rising on the inhalation, then allow your breath to sink the energy back down to your Tan Tien, below your navel and then further down to your feet.

Every tree is its own unique exercise system providing various ways to stretch and strengthen our hands, feet, muscles and spine. Tree climbing helps us reconnect with our inner child, and reconnect with nature. Being with, and in, the tree can help heal blocked energy in the body. On your inhalation ask for healing and feel the energy transmitted by the tree. On your exhalation, feel yourself giving energy back to the tree.

Climb slowly, one branch at a time. Stay on each branch for as many breaths as you need to maintain your balance. For those with pelvic imbalances, experiment with stretching the legs by moving more weight into the weaker side. Allow the monkey in you to enjoy the various stretches of your legs and arms as you climb. Stop and breathe to feel the healing Qi of the tree. On the inhalation, draw in the energy of the tree that allows you to ascend in life. As you exhale, give back to the tree, appreciating the tree's support.

This gives us the opportunity to practice the elevator breathing technique from Chapter 1 and sink our Qi to our feet (Kidney 1). The tree keeps us honest and in touch with the ground of where we really are and how high we can really ascend. Perhaps next time we try to ascend too quickly in life we will be reminded to go one step at a time.

Nature is a teacher. As it is stated in the Upanishads, "By seeing all beings in ourselves and our Selves in all beings the Absolute is obtained." The tree is a beautiful starting place to learn this; but every element of nature is a potential place to understand and appreciate the way we and nature are one — created by that mysterious force that some call God and others call Tao. We constrict and expand like the rivers and seas, get high like the sky, and have low points like the valleys. Sometimes our branches get blown asunder as a difficult life situation confronts us, but if we remember who we are, we may find the roots that give us strength to handle the situation.

The Big Picture: Everyday Options for Living Younger Longer

Practicing Qigong is one part of a wider picture of "Living Younger Longer." Here are some tips that you might find helpful. Feel free to eliminate the ones that don't work for you, and find ways to adapt them to your own scheduling needs. Add ones of your own that are your personal "secrets to living younger longer." (Share your secret way to live younger longer with others by e-mailing them to drmichael@bodymindhealing.com and have yours added to the website list.)

- Set your alarm 20 minutes earlier than usual, and when waking in the morning practice Yoga in bed. The energy gates of the joints tend to close during sleep; yoga is one good way to get the energy moving, opening your energy gates. Breathe, and feel constricted joints opening.

- Listen to your dreams; they deepen your soul's aliveness. In the *Talmud* it says, "A dream left uninterpreted is like a letter left unopened." Open to the messages in your dreams. Get a book on dreams to help facilitate your process such as Dr. Eugene Gendlin's *Let your Body Interpret your Dreams*, Chiron Publications, 1986.

- Start every day singing in the shower. Song gets the vocal chords vibrating and gives the heart wings to create lightness of Being. Don't limit your self to the shower; there is a song for every occasion. When a song doesn't come to mind, make up your own chanting phrase, hum or whistle. Allow a song or tune to emerge from your inner musical archives to fit your mood. It doesn't need to be a happy song; "blues" enable transformation of consciousness as well as uplifting songs. Human singing is a primordial way to bring passion to the soul and create aliveness. Language is a late comer to the party of life, having its uses and abuses. To experience the difference between a song's language of energy and the limitations of everyday speech try this practice: *Speak about what a wonderful world it is, then sing a song like Ray Charles's, "What a Wonderful World."* Now you know why Qigong's definition of ways to cultivate the energy of life includes sound. Practice Qigong by increasing the percentage of your day spent in the vibratory sphere of song.

- After a morning shower, eat a piece of fruit to your liking (I like half a grapefruit) to help to refresh and clean out your system to ready it for food later.

- After doing a few of your favorite stretches (perhaps some from the Bodymind Healing Qigong system), go for a walk up a hill or sprint to get your cardiovascular system stimulated.

- While you are going for your morning walk, or at other times of the day, listen to the sounds of animals and birds and imitate them. Experience what opens in you. Learn "the language of birds" through finding how to shape the elements of life in your mouth to create their tune. Even imitating a dog's barking or growling can have healing and empowering effects. (Do your dog-imitation practice with conscious discretion at an appropriate distance from the dog, as you are walking away, so you don't antagonize it.) If animals or birds are not in your everyday environment, imagine becoming your favorite one and make its sound.

- Do some weight bearing exercise to change fat into muscle. Balance stretching and building exercises in your daily physical exercise routine.
- Practice Bodymind Healing Qigong as appropriate to your schedule. A general guideline is to practice at least once a day; let your Qi tell you for how long to practice. For a more dedicated approach, practice two or three times a day before meals. Each time of the day has its own beautiful purpose to be discovered. Late in the peaceful hours of night can bring serenity which, for some people, can be just what is needed to enter into the world of sleep; for others, the activation of energy can be overly stimulating and disruptive to sleep. After work is a great time to relax and revitalize your Self with Qigong and Tai Chi. Eventually you'll find the practice as a center post, a heavenly axis, a sacred space to be tapped into, a way to relax and re-energize and a way of Being in your everyday activities.
- Have love and hugs in everyday life.
- Give yourself the gift of some bodywork/massage as often as possible.
- As the old saying goes, "Work like you don't need the money, love like you've never been hurt and dance like no one is watching."
- Arteries aren't the only thing that calcify. Try to eliminate reification (approaching life as "things" to do). Maintain freshness of perception so that you see things as if you are a child seeing them for the first time. Appreciate life! Do at least one body exercise a day as if you are a child for example: crawl, lie down on your back and squiggle on the carpet, move and make sounds as if you are your favorite animal.
- Bring a water bottle with you when you go out to work in a non-toxic (non-leaching) type of plastic or glass container. Water is the juice of the rivers of life.
- Bring along some healthy snacks with you when you go out: fruit, dried fruit, nuts, and seeds reduce tendencies to addictive eating of junk foods. One of my personal favorites are carob clusters from the health food store that have no refined sugar, and have nuts, seeds and peanut butter.
- Reduce intake of refined carbohydrates, white refined flour, fast foods, trans fatty acids and refined sugar. Follow the eating methods mentioned above in the section on "A sacred Eating Ritual." Make informed choices about vitamins and food.
- When issues come up between you and others, practice "constructive communication of negative feelings" rather than holding on to things or dysfunctionally communicating. (See my *Trials of the Heart* book for an easy four-step method for Constructive Clearing.)
- Save the last portion of the day for a spiritual activity such as meditation, reading a spiritual book or playing a peaceful musical instrument.
- Before going to sleep, as you are lying in bed, put one hand on your heart and another on your belly sending healing energy and compassion to any leftover emotional stuff from the day. Imagine that any key life issue that you are carrying from the day in your bodymind is being played from a motion picture camera creating a dream. Ask your inner dream-weaver for a healing dream to to help resolve the issue.

Internal Star Gazing: Big Dipper Meditation

If there is anyplace in this world that has the potential to awaken us from our reified state, it must be the starry night sky. For who can gaze at the stars without being filled with the mystery of life? What shaped the Big Dipper in its pattern? The awesome power of the universe that created the stars is no less than the forces that created us, and the patterns that created the constellations of our life patterns are equally a miracle.

When we look at the stars at night, we may wonder whether the same miraculous forces that created patterns in the cosmos, created the patterns of our human lives. By looking in awe at that mystery reflected outside, we may be induced into an altered state of consciousness where we can become healed by our relationship to the universe. Thus, Taoists go to the stars to commune with the powers that reside there, and use Qigong practices to make the body a receptacle to receive the energy of the stars. To begin, practice the following exercises at night and in a seated posture.

1. Big Dipper Chakra Meditation: Inhale and exhale through just your nose. Imagine the Big Dipper overhead, its bowl overturning. It's filled with purple amethyst light, which enters through Bai Hue at the top of your head and fills your body. Breathe in and out as it fills the base chakra, and imagine the light circling around that area 5 times. Then breathe in as you imagine light from the base chakra rising up to the genitals and circling there 5 times. As you breathe out, it drops back down to the base and springs back up, this time to the navel on the inhalation. Then the purple Qi descends down to the base on the exhalation. On the inhalation it springs back up to heart, circling 5 times. On the exhalation it drops to the base; it shoots up to the throat on the next inhalation, circling 5 times. And so on...up to the third eye and the crown chakra. Finally it drops down the centerline of the body on the exhalation, and on the inhalation it springs up to the crown chakra out of the top of the head joining with universal Qi. On the exhalation, it descends down outside the body like a shower. To end, allow the image to dissolve and come to rest. Take in your experience and feel your energy level.

2. Big Dipper Journey: This exercise comes from the Taoist Cannon (Daozang), it goes as follows: In a Sitting Meditation posture, imagine the Big Dipper in your body. Picture the handle going from head to solar plexus, the bowl of the dipper is located in your lower abdomen. Visualize that the bowl is filled with purple mist, Qi. You are standing inside the bowl of the dipper, within your body, surrounded by purple Qi, dressed in white robes. Standing in the middle of the dipper, there are rings of fire under your feet. The fiery wheels turn slow, and then more quickly. Swirling, they rise up through your body, through the handle of the dipper, and you rise up. Wheels of fire carry you aloft, up into space, as you are protected by purple Qi. You go up toward your natal star. Rest in stillness in front of the star, with the rings of fire under your feet. Maybe some information from the star will come to you concerning your life path. Then you descend back through space, back to your body, through your head, descending down the handle into the bowl, and you return to sitting. Finally, dissolve the image into emptiness, and return to your breath.

The more we experience ourselves in and as nature, the more we become our wider Selves. We can find the place where the methods above are not an exercise, but a way to exercise our higher faculties—our hearts, our minds and our imagination. When we break through the reification of these exercises, we may find the light that shines from our very Being. Try these exercises for one moment, or in your meditation for 20–45 minutes, or on and off during just one day. Become like a star, or the Big Dipper, spilling light from your overflowing Self to the earth on your exhalation, and draw in energy and light on your inhalation. Become the star you are.

Gathering Starlight

Many students of Tai Chi learn a two-person exercise called Pushing, or Joining, Hands Practice as has been shown at the end of the Tai Chi set in the conclusion of Section II. Also, look in this book at the page where Grasping the Bird's Tail or Single Ward Off is shown.

The secret origin of this movement is said to come from a Taoist practice called Gathering Starlight.[2] Note the similarity between this movement and the Tai Chi movement Grasping the Bird's Tail, which reiterates the theme that Tai Chi has roots in shamanism, and that understanding these roots can deepen the healing potential of our practice. In Gathering Starlight, as compared with Grasping the Bird's Tail, note the difference of the rear hand in the lower back, by the Gate of Vitality (Ming Men). To practice this movement, circle around with your palm facing inward while simultaneously rotating your hips and imagining that you are gathering Qi from the surrounding area. Then do this same circle, starting slightly above the level of your head. Gradually circle down your body, lower and lower so that you create a spiraling motion down to your heart and belly area, then back up to the stars again. Imagine that you are Gathering Starlight and giving it to those you love, and to the world.

All human beings, according to modern physics, are composed of ancient stars. The space between the physical elements of our bodies is as open as the space between planets and stars. There are unfathomable energies moving in our inner and outer space, playing beneath the range of our conscious perception at all times with names such as neutrons, photons, electrons, quantum fields, neutrinos and quarks. In the deepest sanctums of our own inner space, wonderous energies can be held and gathered by our loving hands, and can stimulate us to move with cosmic awareness. We are heavenly space. Whether we are conscious of it or not, when we are still and when we move, in our cells and in our heavenly bodies, we all are Qigong practitioners. As we move in harmony with "Qi," we are expressing our appreciation of the divine force that creates life. The ability to cultivate this awareness is the universe's gift to us as humans, Being.

"Keep Shining like the Stars you Are."

APPENDIX 1

Exercises for Self-Healing

Sample of Selected Qigong Movements from Bodymind Healing Qigong
Organized according to Health Issues

*Essential Note: Gather Chi first before doing targeted techniques. From Wuji to Tai Chi. From Stillness to Movement.

Hypertension
- Check on Abdominal versus Reverse Breathing   44
- Standing Meditation   92–96
- Self-Soothing One hand on Heart, other on Belly (IDP)*   11
- Raising Qi to the Heavens and Bringing down to Earth—emphasize downward
  movement   81–88
- External Qigong—Extended Fan Palm Technique (Johnson) for cleaning
  Conception and Governing vessels   ——
- Dr. Sha Close Hand Above Head, Far Hand by Belly sound   98–99
- Acupressure self-touch points—CV 17, H-7/8, GB 31   ——
- Deer Double Ears, Deer Hooves Draw Inward, Deer Rutting and Butting   139

To Prevent Falls amongst the Elderly
- Crane Stands on one Leg, Golden Rooster Stands on one Leg   130, 171
- Walking Meditation—from Yi Chuan Qigong   146–50
- Elevator Breathing   45

Breathing Methods
- Abdominal Breathing   44
- Micro and Macrocosmic Orbit Breathing   46
- Elevator Breathing   45

Opening the Door to Trance State—Taoist Alchemy
- Beating the Heavenly Drum; Opening the Eyes to the Beauty of the World   142
- Tai Chi Ruler   89–90

Heart
- Cloud Hands—releasing old wounds (Tai Chi)   170–171
- Wild Goose Taps its Chest   103
- Buddha Opens the Heart to the Heavens   105
- Tai Chi—Taoist Immortal Paints a Heavenly Rainbow   158
- Yi Chuan Holding the Golden Ball in front of Heart   95
- Crane Animal Frolic   131–133
- Healing Sound—*Ha*   132

Lungs—Sound Ah or Shh
- Bending the Bow, Healing Sounds   108
- Tapping on Lung Points—Wild Goose Taps its Chest   103
- Tai Chi—Single Whip   164
- Animal Qigong: White Crane Spreads Wings (Taiji), Crane (BMQ)   130, 166
- Tiger Animal Frolic   135–137
- Healing sound—*Ah* or *Shh*   137

Kidneys

- Kidney—Rubbing and Sounds   109
- Tai Chi—Rolling the Ball/Transition to Rollback   90, 160
- Tai Chi Ruler   89–90
- Selected Movements from Wild Goose   124–125
- Wild Goose Searches for Food   125
- Deer Animal Frolic   137–140
  - Healing Sound—*Whooh* or *Chiree*   140

Stomach

- Cloud Hands   170
- Rolling ball—Transition from Tai Chi into Rollback   160
- Chi Nei Tsang (IDP)*   ——
- Monkey Animal Frolic   134–135
- Healing Sound—*Huh*   135

Liver

- Detoxifying Liver   110
- Tai Chi—Shoulder Stroke   165
- Bear Animal Frolic   126–129
- Healing Sound—*Sss* or *Shhu*   129

Some Self-Touch Points for Self-healing—*(See Gach, M., Acupressure's Potent Points)*

A. Computer Tension—for shoulders, GB 21
B. Revitalizing after running or physical depletion, St 36
C. Sinus Problems, St 3
D. Neck/Shoulder Release, GB 21, GB 20
E. Emotional Release points—Anxiety CV 17, Fear K1
F. Constipation, LI 4
G. Energizing/Balancing the Heart, CV 17
H. Immune System, LI 11
   General healing principle of self-touch—Tap to activate Yang energy. Circle,
   stop, and feel for Yin energy.

*(IDP) Stands for Integrative Depth Psychotherapy. See Mayer, M., "Psychotherapy and Qigong: Partners in Healing Anxiety," 1997.

APPENDIX II

Qigong: Selected Review of Research on Health and Longevity

*That which is looked upon by one generation
as the apex of human knowledge
is often considered an absurdity by the next,
And that which is regarded as a superstition in one century
may form the basis of science for the following one.*

—Paracelsus, Sixteenth Century

Introduction—Energy Medicine in the West

Though Qigong (dao yin) was recognized, and empirically shown, for thousands of years to be a method for improving health and increasing longevity, the groundwork in modern times for Qigong being a verifiable method for health improvement was first established in other fields of research.

Beginning with the work of Walter Cannon, who spoke of the stress response in the 1920's,[1] one of the grandfathers of Western stress physiology, Hans Seyle in the 1930's, showed that stress caused increased illness through its effect on the immune system.[2] There are many intricacies in the research, far too great to go into here in an appendix. For example, the stress response itself does not cause illness, it is the prolonged repeated stress without rest that damages the immune system and is correlated with disease.[3]

Dr. Herbert Bensen, who is president of Harvard Medical School's Mind/Body Medical Institute, and is most associated with coining the term "relaxation response," showed the role of the relaxation response in ameliorating hypertension and cardiac problems.[4] Dr. Benson now says "relaxation, meditation and prayer have begun to find a place in medicine, not only because of support in scientific studies, but because of the possibility that these techniques might reduce medical costs."[5]

From the early days of research on stress and the relaxation response, the whole field of bodymind medicine and psycho-neuroimmunology blossomed with solid evidence for the relaxation response and the mind to effect healing in a wide variety of conditions. Robert Ader, who coined the term psycho-neuroimmunology, showed that by using conditioning to affect animals' immune systems, their life spans could be extended.[6] The areas of bodymind medicine and hypnosis have now demonstrated the ability of the mind to modulate the autonomic nervous system and blood flow, and ameliorate the alarm response, Raynaud's disease, hypertension and cardiac problems. Bodymind healing methods can enhance the immune response.[7]

A key element in opening the door to using relaxation methodologies in the traditional United States health care system was a National Institute of Health panel (NIHTAP, 1996)[8] which concluded that "integrating behavioral and relaxation therapies with conventional medical treatment is imperative for successfully managing these conditions." The panel did not endorse a single technique, but said a variety of them worked as long as they included two features—"a repetitive focus of a word, sound, prayer, phrase or muscular activity, and neither fighting nor focusing on intruding thoughts." When done this way the panel concluded that they "can lower one's breathing rate, heart rate and blood pressure." Qigong fits these guidelines well.

Dr. Robert Becker was one of the grandfathers of the field of "energy medicine" in the west. He was one of the first modern scientists to measure the "current of injury" associated with healing wounds and bone fractures. In his early research on the healing and regeneration of salamanders, which some mark as the beginning of the new scientific revolution in energy medicine, he showed that the control system that started, regulated and stopped healing was electrical.[9] In research of his and others, the acupuncture meridians known since ancient times have now been measured as conducting current.[10] It is now commonplace to hear of athletes using TENS (transcutaneous electrical nerve stimulation) units to deal with the effects of pain. In Sweden, Dr. Bjorn Nordenstrom has experimented with electricity's effect on tumors, and reports a cure or prevention rate in 50% of 20 patients.[11] Differentiating the similarities and differences between the energy that is in electricity and the energy that is constellated in Qigong is part of the work of the field of energy medicine.[12] Some question whether the healing that takes place is a matter of energy, or a shift in consciousness itself.[13]

Western knowledge of the energy in the human organism has moved a long way from believing that nerves are the only part of the body that contain electricity. We now know that the body emits a broad spectrum of electromagnetic and acoustic radiation that has been measured by magnetic resonance imaging (MRI), electroencephalogram (EEG), electrocardiogram (EKG), electromylogram (EMG), thermography and ultrasound. These instruments are used to monitor and diagnose diseases. Furthermore, modern science has demonstrated that electromagnetic fields of the body are generated during various biological processes including rapid cell division during natural growth processes such as growth of bone cells following fracture, intense nervous activity associated with mental processes, and various pathological conditions such as abnormal cell growth with diseases like cancer. The distinction between conservative medical practitioners and the new proponents of energy medicine is summed up well by one of the forefront researchers in the field, Dr. Glen Rein:

> *It is now well known that the human body emits a broad spectrum of electromagnetic and acoustic radiation. Traditional medicine looks at these as by-products of biochemical reactions in the body. They are not considered by most biomedical researchers to be involved with the basic functioning (or healing) of the body. The basic tenet of Energy Medicine is that these fields are not only involved with functioning of physical/chemical body but regulate these processes.[14]*

The International Society for the Study of Subtle Energies and Energy Medicine (ISSSEEM) located in Colorado has complied hundreds of solid research studies on the uses of energy in healing.[15] Also in the United States, Dr Leonard Laskow, in a controlled study, reports measuring the ability of magnetic field emission from his hands being able to inhibit tumor cells 18% while practicing Microcosmic Orbit Breathing. He is doing groundbreaking research in exploring the effects of different states of consciousness and intentionality on tumor cells. In one of his comparative studies of biological responses to different intentions he discovered that focusing intention on the phrase, "return to the natural order and harmony," produced a 39% inhibition in tumor cells. The intention of "unconditional love" neither stimulated or inhibited cell growth, and Microcosmic Orbit Breathing produced a 41% inhibition.[16]

Some people consider the new movement to be a revolution, signaling a paradigm shift from a Newtonian to an "Einsteinian Medicine:"

> *Newtonian thinkers see the human body as a series of intricate chemical systems powering a structure of nerve, muscle, flesh and bones. The physical body is viewed as a supreme mechanism, an intricate physical clockwork down to the very cellular structure. Einsteinian Medicine sees human beings as networks of complex energy fields that interface with physical/cellular systems. There is a hierarchy of subtle energetic systems that coordinate electrophysiological, hormonal and cellular structure of the physical body. It is from these subtle levels that health and illness originate. These unique energy systems are powerfully affected by emotions, spiritual balance, nutrition and environment. They influence cellular patterns of growth.[17]*

Eastern Health and Longevity Methods

Eastern modalities have been entering into the mainstream of the Western health care system. For example, many Eastern methods of stress reduction have been used successfully with hypertension. In well-designed, randomly assigned studies, Transcendental Meditation (TM) has been shown to positively affect the blood pressure (BP) of hypertensives.[18] In other TM studies, even where the BP was measured at times after the meditation period, significant changes in BP were demonstrated.[19] Positive results have been claimed in combining Vipassana meditation and stress reduction techniques at the University of Massachusetts Medical Center.[20] When Yoga was integrated into an intensive, multifaceted lifestyle change program, including a low fat, low cholesterol vegetarian diet, daily meditation practices, moderate aerobic exercise and group support, hypertension and coronary disease were reduced (Ornish et al. 1990 a and b).[21]

Qigong

For primitive people the presence of energy and power
is the starting point of their analysis
and understanding of the natural world.
Primitive people felt power, but did not measure it.
Today we measure power, but are not able to feel it.[22]
—Vine Deloria

Like Yoga and other Eastern relaxation methods that have reported beneficial results in treating various stress-related diseases, Qigong is a tradition that combines relaxation, breathing and a mindful relationship to body awareness.

However, Qigong is unique in being a healing methodology that synchronizes breath and movement with the relaxation response; it combines relaxation and energizing methods. As discussed earlier, this unique combination is called Sung in Chinese.

We are now on the verge of a new millennium where science and esoteric healing knowledge are meeting and holding hands as partners. The acupuncture meridians known since ancient times have now been measured by modern researchers and shown to conduct currents.[23] Solid scientific research supports the case for the ability of Qigong practice to balance the energy of the Chinese meridians.[24]

As to just how Qigong works in healing the body, no one has the answer. Some of the Western studies mentioned above lay some groundwork,[25] and scientists are continuing to develop new studies and some interesting hypotheses. Dr. Jame Ma, professor of physics at the Chinese University of Hong Kong, postulates that Qigong movements are in the specific frequency range at which the proton, the nucleus of the hydrogen atom, will absorb energy from the Earth's natural magnetic field by means of nuclear magnetic resonance (NMR). He studied the effect of Qigong on organic chemicals that produced a well-characterized NMR and found that it did indeed change significantly.[26] Adding to this research, John Zimerman (using a superconducting quantum interference device)and A. Seto of Japan (using a special magnetometer) have demonstrated that healers emit pulsing biomagnetic fields at frequencies which fall within the alpha level of brain wave activity which corresponds with the earth's vibratory frequency of 7.8 Hz.[27] The healing effects of Qigong may be due in part to bringing brain wave frequency into coherence with the earth's natural vibration and thereby aligning with the energy of the earth. Top scientists have posited that low-intensity electromagnetic fields and biophotons (light emitted from human cells) are a key element in healing, and that these fields carry information, not just energy.[28]

Finally, an intriguing hypothesis emerges from the work of Dr. Emoto who has researched how art, music, words, thoughts and feelings seem to effect the molecular structure of water. For example, when a word like "despair" versus "hope" is focused upon in the presence of water, the crystalline shape of water molecules in the former case seems more broken, and in the later case seems more coherent and beautiful. (See masaru-emoto.net, or Dr. Emoto's book, The Message from Water III.) Since our bodies consist of high percentage of water, perhaps Qigong effects the very water molecules in our body.

Many psychophysiological measures may be effected by practicing Qigong. Some of these include: psychophysiological corollaries to the relaxation response such as changes in brain wave emission,[29] changes in the DC current in the brain,[30] photon emission changes, and release of various neurochemicals, such as endorphins. Research from Japan indicates Qigong's ability to affect the immune system and endorphin levels. In one such study, a sitting control group experienced a 35% decrease in endorphins after one hour of sitting, whereas the Qigong group showed an increase in endorphins after practicing Qigong.[31] In summary, a hypothesis for this stage of our knowledge is that Qigong practice induces effects in many areas of the human anatomy simultaneously: acupuncture energy meridians, brain wave functioning, water molecules, photon emission and neurochemical and biochemical measures. The healing effects of Qigong may be due to some combination of all of these factors.

Much of the clinical research on Qigong suffers from the problem that it comes from secondary source materials from China; the reports of the research are often presented at conferences where significant elements of the research is omitted. The Qigong Institute of San Francisco has copies of the proceedings since 1986 where over one thousand abstracts exist.[32] I have written elsewhere on a critique of Qigong research methodology.[33]

The following are some examples of selected research on Self-Healing Qigong Exercises[34] related to health and longevity:

Hypertension, Strokes and Death due to Strokes

Many research studies from China have shown that the practice of Qigong can have both long and short-term beneficial effects on hypertension.[35] For example, one twenty-year study was reported in the Journal of Traditional Chinese Medicine by Dr. Kuang at the Shanghai Institute of Hypertension. Two hundred and four hypertensive patients were randomly divided into a Qigong and control group. Both groups were given the same anti-hypertensive medications. The Qigong group of 104 patients practiced 30 minutes twice per day. During the 20-year time line there was a highly significant statistical difference between the two groups ($P. < .01–.001$). It was reported that 47% of the Qigong group was able to reduce the anti-hypertensive drug dosage due to stabilized blood pressure, whereas 30% in the control group increased the anti-hypertensive dosage.[36]

Figure 1 below shows graphically the effect of Qigong on blood pressure. The systolic blood pressure in the upper portion of the graph and diastolic blood pressure in the lower portion of the graph is plotted in millimeters of mercury as a function of time over a 20-year period. During the first two months the blood pressure of all patients dropped in response to the hypotensive drug. Subsequently, and over the period of 20 years, the blood pressure of the Qigong group stabilized while that of the control group increased at a highly significant level ($P. < .001$).[37]

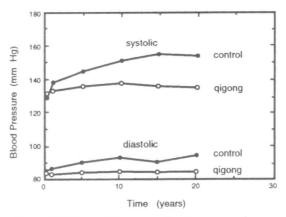

Figure 44: Effect of Qigong on blood pressure of
hypertensive patients over 20 years. Qigong group (n=104)
practiced 30 min/day twice/day.

The ability to track patients over 20 years is remarkable by Western standards; even
more impressive is the hypertension studies at the Shanghai Institute of Hypertension
that were done as a follow-up by Dr. Wang over a 30-year period of time. In this study,
242 hypertension patients were randomly divided into a Qigong and control group, and
all patients were given drug therapy. After 30 years of practicing for 30 minutes twice a
day, significant differences were discovered in many physiological measures.[38]

Figure 2 below shows how the accumulated mortality rate after 30 years was 25.41%
in the Qigong group and 40.8% in the control group (P. < .001). The incidence of strokes
was also significantly different in the Qigong practice groups as compared to the control
group, 20.5% and 40.7% respectively (P. < .01). The death rate due to strokes was 15.6%
and 32.5% respectively.

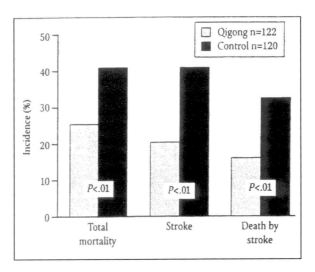

Figure 45: A 30-year follow-up of the effect of qigong on
mortality and stroke in 242 hypertensive patients. Both
groups received drug therapy.

Other Cardiodovascular Measures

A wide variety of other cardiovascular measures are reportedly improved by practicing Qigong. Fewer cases of congestive heart failure and acute myocardial infarction were reported (P. <.001), but the existence of control groups was not mentioned.[39] A shorter comparative study[40] was done on a randomly divided sub-grouping of 98 cases of hypertension accompanied by coronary heart disease. There was a comparable control group based upon age, gender and course of disease. Significant improvement was reported in the group practicing Qigong compared to the control group in retinopathy (P. < .05), and fewer cardiovascular lesions were found (P. < .05).

Wang reported that after one year, many significant changes took place in a subset of 80 elderly hypertensive patients with Heart Energy Deficiency (a Chinese Medical Diagnosis), which often presents as a weakened function of the left ventricle and a disturbance of microcirculation. Researchers evaluated the results of Qigong exercises on patients through measurements done by ultrasonic cardiography and indices of microcirculation. Subjects were divided into three groups: hypertensive patients with heart energy deficiency, without heart energy deficiency, and with normal BP. Left ventricular function (LVF) improved in the group practicing Qigong compared to the normal BP group (P. < .05-.01), and other cardiac measures increased, including ten indices of abnormal clinical blood conditions—for example, blood flow and petechiae (fragile capillaries creating red dots on the skin) (P. < .05).[41]

Reduction of Symptoms of Chronic Diseases Associated with Hypertension

Reports suggest Qigong practice affects other chronic diseases and physical complaints associated with hypertensive states. Aching, distention, dizziness and insomnia were reduced in a hypertensive group practicing Qigong compared to a control group.[42] In a group of chronic renal failure patients, swelling disappeared and fatigue was reduced (Suzuki, 1993)—both were attributed to Qigong exercises. In the Kuang study,[43] a sub-grouping of 16 male patients with hypertension associated with diabetes reportedly had, after six months of practice, significant reduction (P. < .01) in symptoms of polydipsia (excessive thirst), polyphagia (overeating), polyuria (excessive urination), fatigue, weakness, blurred vision and hyperesthesia (skin sensitivity); and when 40 patients from the Qigong group were examined by ultrasound, they were found to have better left ventricular function.[44]

Artheriosclerosis

A report from Zhejang College of Traditional Chinese Medicine reports clinical observation of the treatment of 158 cases of cerebral artheriosclerosis treated by Qigong.[45]

After 38 to 180 days treatment (with an average of 82 days) by conducting and respiration qigong. 91. 83% of the patients' symptoms were reported to have been relieved, and 82.82% of the syndromes alleviated. The unstable EEG cases declined to 36.36%

(48/132) comparing with 52.37% (69/132) before the training practice (P<O.Ol). The conducting and respiration qigong also had an effect on the wave amplitude of rheoencephalogram by recovering (P. < O.Ol) or lowering (P. < 0.01-0.O5) the cerebral blood flow to the normal level. The number of the sufferers whose total serum cholesterol and serum triglyceride determination were higher than normal had decreased to 72 (54.96%) from 113 (86.07%) and 75 (57.73%) from 118 (90.07%)(P. < O.01). The researcher states that obvious differences before and after the training practice were seen.

Cancer

127 Patients with medically diagnosed malignant cancer were divided into a Qigong and control group. All patients received drugs, and the Qigong group practiced Qigong for more than two hours a day over a period from 3–6 months. Both groups improved, but the Qigong group showed improvements four to nine times greater than the control group in strength, appetite, diarrhea free and weight gain. The phagocytic rate, which is one measure of immune function, increased in the Qigong group but decreased in the control group. This is an important study showing that Eastern and Western approaches do not need to be seen as conflicting choices; rather Qigong complements Western cancer treatment in reducing side effects of medication, and enhancing energy and strength.[46]

In a review of the literature on Qigong therapy for cancer treatment, Dr. Chen reviews clinical studies of human patients and discusses positive changes in immune system indicators after self-practicing Qigong; in-vitro studies and animal studies with external emission Qigong are reviewed to control for placebo. He discusses problems with research designs and limitations of the research.[47]

Long Term Disabilities

Dr. Trieschmann, a clinical psychologist who works in medical rehabilitation, discusses her own odyssey from being a clinician-scientist to a healer and why she began to incorporate Qigong with patients with severe disabilities. She discusses the transformative healing (not total curing) that took place with two of her patients for whom physicians offered no hope. A 52-year-old woman with multiple sclerosis and bilateral optic atrophy. After meditation and Qigong training Dr. Trieschmann reports the patient's eyesight improved so that she can drive in light traffic and is able to read, and is happier and healthier. Another case involved a 40-year-old spinal cord injured man who was in a wheelchair and had impaired bladder and bowel control. After Qigong treatment and meditation instruction, he was able to reduce his sympathetic nervous system arousal and control his pain, his bladder-kidney problem improved and surgery was eliminated as an option. Within six months to a year and a half, the patient was able to return to work, bike again, paint and engage in home repair projects. Research methodology issues are not discussed in this article.[48]

Diabetes

Ten inpatients with diabetes mellitus were studied on three different days. Either Qigong walking (30–40 minutes duration) or conventional walking was performed by the patients 30 minutes after lunch on one of the three study days. Plasma glucose levels and pulse rates were measured 30 minutes after lunch and again 20 minutes after exercising. These data were compared to those obtained on a day with no exercise after lunch. Results were plasma glucose decreasing after both exercise groups more than in the no exercise group. The pulse rates increased after conventional walking more than in the Qigong group. Researchers concluded that Qigong walking reduced plasma glucose after lunch without inducing a large increase in the pulse rate in these patients with diabetes.[49]

Senility

100 Subjects were divided into two groups, mean age 62.7 years who were pre-senile or with cerebral function impaired by senility. The Qigong group practiced a combination of static and moving Qigong. The control group exercised by walking, walking fast or running slowly. After 6 months, 8 of the 14 main clinical signs and symptoms in the Qigong group had improved more than 80% whereas none of the symptoms in the control group had improved more than 345%. Criteria for judging outcome were based on measuring cerebral function, sexual function, serum lipid levels, and function of endocrine glands.[50]

Fibromyalgia

28 Patients, 8 weekly sessions of 2 1/2 hours each with three components: #1. An educational component focusing on mind-body connection, #2. Focusing on relaxation response with mindfulness meditation and #3 Qigong. Outcome measures included Fibrolmyalgia Impact Questionnaire, the Health Assessment Questionnaire, the Beck Depression Inventory, the Coping Strategies Questionnaire, the Helplessness sub-scale of the Arthritis Attitudes index, etc. Results: Standard outcome measures showed significant reduction in pain, fatigue, and sleeplessness; and improved function mood state, and general health following the 8 week intervention.[51]

Asthma

30 asthma patients with varying degrees of illness severity were taught Yangsheng Qigong under medial supervision. They were asked to exercise independently if possible on a daily basis and to keep a diary of their symptoms for half a year. There was one teaching phase, a phase of self-practice and a refresher teaching course. Results shows an improvement in reduced hospitalization rate, less sickness leave, reduced antibiotic use and fewer emergency consultations resulting in reduced treatments costs. Subjects showed a decrease of at least 10% in peak flow variability between the first and 52nd week of the study. These changes occurred significantly more frequently in the group of exercisers than in a group of non-exercisers.[52]

Depression

The following study was a Doctoral dissertation investigating the use of Qigong with Depression. Here is the way the abstract reads:[53]

A pilot study with 39 subjects suffering from DSM-IV (Psychiatric Diagnostic and Statistical Manual 4th edition) diagnosis of major Depression, Dysthymia or Bipolar Disorder were treated with the Eastern Traditional Chinese Medicine technique of Qigong. Treatment included qi emission treatment by qualified practitioners, and subjects were required to practice qigong exercise for a two-month period. Significant improvement was observed, especially in the first month on the measurements of Beck's Depression Index-Revised (BDI-R) ($p<0.0000$) and Symptom Checklist-90R (SCL-90 R) Depression Index ($p<0.00003$), Interpersonal Sensitivity ($p<0.00003$), Scl-90 Somaticism indexes as well as three criteria from DSM-IV guidelines are also reported on indicating an overall trend of improvement over time. All subjects improved over the treatment period and it is determined that the qigong exercise is a highly effective complimentary and alternative treatment modality for depression and should be considered as an adjunct to psychotherapy treatment. No significant difference was seen in those subjects treated with Qi emission.

We started with 63 subjects and had 3 practitioners. 45 subjects showed up for treatment. We split them into 3 groups. The individuals in the study were screened for situational depression and psychosis. I only chose those individuals who met criteria for a long-term depression, one which would be considered biological in basis. Also, in consideration of the deviant syndrome which has been seen, I screened for any psychosis in depression. Some of the subjects had been suffering from major depression for 30 years. One individual had a brain tumor, and several had been victims of sexual abuse. These were very depressed individuals.

In the first session, half were given a Qi emission treatment for 10 min. There were significant decreases in BP for the treated group. The second and third time we met (30 days apart) all subjects were given a 10 min qi emission treatment. There was no difference between those who received the qi emission treatment the first time and those who did not. The qigong exercise seemed to be the main factor. There were significant decreases in other areas measured by the SCL-90 as well, such as anxiety, hostility, and psychoticism, however I reported only 3 measures—Depression, Somaticism and Interpersonal Sensitivity, which is a major factor connected with depression. The results are impressive. Some of the scores fell as much as 50% (40 points) when I was hoping to get at least 10 points on the measures.

We used Spring Forest Qigong—Chunyi Lin's technique. The subjects were told to practice 40 min a day and utilized video tape/audio tape to accomplish this. There was a marked difference in personal presentation between the first and last meeting—from somber, sad and discouraging faces to joyful and excited behavior. So there was also a significant effect with bipolar subjects (3) in the study and this is an important aspect.

Anti-Aging Research -Additional

In addition to the previous research, those who are interested in further exploration about Qigong, health and longevity may wish to examine some of the following sources:

1. Sancier K. "Anti-aging Benefits of Qigong," Jour. of International Society of Life Information Science Vol. 14, No. 1 March, 1996. Research on Qigong's positive effects on blood pressure, mortality and stroke, improvements in heart function and micro-circulation of blood, improvements in sex hormone levels, reversing symptoms of senility and enhanced activity of various anti-aging enzymes including Superoxide Dismutase (SOD).

2. Cohen, K., *The Way of Qigong*, Ballentine Books, 1997. An excellent review of Qigong research. Studies and discussion about how Qigong can improve a wide range of bio-markers of aging including bone density, immune function and increase in the enzyme Superoxide Dismutase (SOD). SOD protects cells against damage from Superoxide a highly toxic free-radical which causes aging of the body's tissues, including wrinkling and changes in skin pigmentation and age spots in the same way that air causes food to spoil. Superoxide can cause breakdown of cartilage and synovial fluid, the cushioning and lubrication between bones leading to arthritis and joint damage.

3. Feng, L Baylor University College of Medicine (see lfeng@bcm.tmc.edu). She reports on research showing increase in qigong practitioners compared to controls of the cell life of neutrophils measured in vitro. Neutrophils are the most abundant leukocytes in blood being the first line of defense against infection. She also reports that in vitro measures of telomeres of Qigong practitioners are longer compared to controls, and how shortening of telomeres is a sign of aging. Telomeres are structures formed by short DNA sequences that are essential for chromosome stability and protect chromosome ends from attack.

Anxiety:

As we have discussed, Qigong is a method of cultivating the energy of life through a variety of means, one of which is touch. We discussed earlier in Chapter 1 how self-touch of various points of the body is an important part of *Bodymind Healing Psychotherapy* and *Psycho-spiritual Postural Anthropology* in treating anxiety disorders (See Mayer M., "Psychotherapy and Qigong: Partners in Healing Anxiety"). We have shown how touch and tapping is incorporated in various parts of the Bodymind Healing Qigong system for example in Wild Goose Taps its Chest, Tapping the Belly Clock and in Beating the Heavenly Drum. However, only phenomenological/empirical rather than scientific/statistical research points to its healing effects.

The emerging field of "energy psychology" has recently been incorporating tapping touch and other energy healing methods into psychotherapy (See Gallo, F., *Energy Psychology in Psychotherapy: A Comprehensive Source Book,* W.W. Norton, 2002); and it is beginning to investigate the efficacy of energy-based, psycho-physiological approaches in a more scientific manner. One controlled study was conducted in Brazil by principal researcher Joaquin Andrade, M.D. (See

Feinstein D., *Energy Psychology Interactive*, W.W. Norton, 2002). Over a 5 1/2 year period approximately 5,000 patients, diagnosed at intake with an anxiety disorder, were randomly assigned to an experimental group (imagery and self-statements paired with manual stimulation of selected acupuncture points) or a control group (Cognitive Behavior Therapy/medication). Ratings were given by independent clinicians who interviewed each patient at the close of therapy, at 1 month, at 3 months, at 6 months and at 12 months. The raters made a determination of complete or partial remission of symptoms or no clinical response. The raters did not know if the patient was in the experimental or control group. At the close of therapy 63% of the control group were judged as having improved and 90 % of the experimental group were judged as having improved. 51% of the control group were judged as being symptom free and 76% of the experimental group were judged as being symptom free. At one year follow-up patients receiving acupoint treatments were less prone to relapse or partial relapse than those receiving CBT/medication as indicated by the independent raters' assessment and corroborated by brain imaging and neurotransmitter profiles from a sampling of the patients. Brain mapping revealed that subjects whose acupuncture points were stimulated tended to be distinguished by a general pattern of brain wave normalization which interestingly not only persisted at 12 month follow-up but became more pronounced. In neurotransmitter profiles with generalized anxiety disorder, acupoint stimulation was followed by norepinephrine levels going down to normal reference values and low serotonin going up. Parallel electrical and biochemical patterns were less pronounced in the CBT medication group. In a related pilot study by the same team the length of treatment was substantially shorter with energy therapy and related methods than with the CBT/ medication (mean = 3 sessions vs. mean =15 sessions. (See www.innersource.net)

Since this study was initially envisioned as an exploratory in-house assessment, not all the variables that need to be controlled in robust research were tracked, not all criteria were defined with rigorous precision, the record-keeping was relatively informal, and source data was not always maintained. Nonetheless, the studies all used randomized samples, control groups and blind assessment. The findings were so striking that the team decided to report them. More detailed reports of some of the studies are being prepared for submission to scientific journals. If subsequent research corroborates these early findings, it will be a notable development since CBT/medication is currently the established psychological standard of care for anxiety disorders. Since tapping is just one of the methods of Qigong, it will be interesting to see what happens when the wider range of Qigong methods are examined with sophisticated research protocols.

Conclusion

The studies above are a brief sampling of the vast storehouse of research on Qigong and health and longevity. For more information please see (www.qigonginsitute.org or, www.worldtaichiqigongassn.org) If you are interested in a discussion of the complexities of research methodology issues as they relate to Qigong and the research reported above, please investigate further, and see my peer-reviewed articles.[54] One issue is the Western need to say that one particular treatment helps more than others do. In the Eastern view of things, and in the Western new integrative health model,[55] different disciplines come together to contribute to the overall health of the individual. In this context, I conclude my research articles by saying that "whether Qigong alone can improve various health related issues is not necessarily the most important question. Further research will be required to better assess and understand the effect of adding Qigong into an integrated, multifaceted program that selectively incorporates diet, moderate aerobic exercise, relaxation training and social and psychological dimensions."

APPENDIX III

A Brief Summary of Tai Chi's Health and Longevity Benefits

I have little patience with scientists who take a board of wood,
look for its thinnest part,
and drill a great number of holes where drilling is easy.

—Albert Einstein

Balance and Falls Amongst the Elderly

Tai Chi has long been known to have many beneficial health and longevity benefits. Falls amongst the elderly are one of the greatest causes of fear, degeneration of health, and death amongst the elderly. Unintentional injury is the sixth leading cause of death in persons over 65, with the majority of these deaths attributed to falls. Health complications from losing one's balance, falling, and breaking bones is a severe risk factor of aging. Each year over 30% of persons over 65 years of age fall, about half of them experience multiple events. Approximately 15% of falls result in serious injuries with substantial morbidity and mortality resulting from these falls. Even two months after a fall, 40% of elderly victims who were seen in an emergency department report continued pain or activity restriction; and 40% of these continue to complain for a median of 7 months after the fall. In 1984 this was estimated to have cost 3.7 billion dollars; these figures are increasing due to the increase in the average age of the US population. This knowledge has spurred research in standing and postural balance by physicists, physiotherapists, neuromuscular researchers, and experts in bio-dynamics at universities such as the University of Colorado, Boston University, and Harvard.

A recent article in The Journal of the American Medical Association (1995) showed that Tai Chi was the most effective exercise system to prevent falls amongst the elderly.[1]

General Benefits: Modern research has shown that the benefits of Tai Chi extend to many areas involving health and longevity. Regular practice of Tai Chi helps reduce stress, increase body awareness, tone muscles, increase flexibility, and boosts the immune system.[2]

Immune System: A study conducted in China indicates that Tai Chi may increase the number of T lymphocytes in the body. Also know as T-Cells, these lymphocytes help the immune system destroy bacteria and are part of the immune system's arsenal used to potentially destroy tumor cells.[3]

Cardio-Respiratory Effects: has been long known to have beneficial cardiovascular effects. It helps to decrease hypertension, increase micro-circulation of the blood, and enhance cardio-respiratory effects.[4]

Arthritis: Adler et. al., studied the effects of Tai Chi on 16 older adults with chronic arthritis pain. An experimental group of 8 participants attended 10 weekly 1-hour Tai Chi classes and were encouraged to practice these exercises daily. A control group of 8 participants did not attend the classes. Pain intensity scores decreased in the experimental group but remained constant in the control group.[5]

Tai Chi has been reported to be helpful with arthritis in many Journals.[6] In a study reported in Geriatrics, patients with osteoarthritis demonstrated improved balance and coordination, increased range of motion, muscle strength and flexibility, improved conditions in joint tenderness, and swelling without increased damage to joints.[7]

Rheumatoid Arthritis: No significant exacerbation of joint symptoms using this weight bearing system of exercises was observed. Tai Chi exercises appear to be safe for RA patients ...weight-bearing exercises have the potential advantages of stimulating bone growth and strengthening connective tissue.[8]

Support Groups Recommending Tai Chi: Multiple Sclerosis, Fibromyalgia, Parkinson's Disease, Lupus, Migraines, Chronic Pain and Aids. Dr. Laurence E. Badgley, M.D. Psychology: "Tai Chi is a natural and safe vehicle for both clients and staff to learn and experience the benefits of being able to channel, concentrate and co-ordinate their bodies and minds: to learn to relax and to "neutralize" rather than resist the stress in their personal lives. This is an ability which we greatly need to nurture in our modern fast-paced society. Dr. John Beaulieu, N.D., M.T.R.S. Bellevue Psychiatric Hospital, N.Y.C.[9]

Psychological Benefits: Relative to measurement beforehand, practice of Tai Chi, relative to baseline level subjects reported less tension, depression, anger, fatigue, confusion and state-anxiety; they felt more vigorous, and in general they had less total mood disturbance.[10]

The research on both Tai Chi and Qigong is currently being put to the test of the most exacting scientific standards. Although discussing such research is beyond the scope of this book, more information can be found in my previously cited articles.[11]

APPENDIX IV

List of Chinese Names and Terms*

Names

(Pin Yin)	(Wade-Giles or other spelling)
Cai Songfang	Ts'ai Sung Fang
Fong Ha	Cheung Fong Ha
Han Xingyuan	Han Hsing Yuan
Wang Xiangzhai	Wang Hsiang Chai
Yang Chengfu	Yang Ch'eng Fu

Terms

(Pin Yin)	(Wade-Giles)
bai hui	bai hui
dan tian	tan t'ien
huiyin	hui yin
laogong	lao kung
mingmen	ming men
qi	ch'i
qigong	ch'i kung
quan	ch'uan
renmai	jen mai
taiji	t'ai chi
taiji quan	t'ai chi ch'uan
wuji	wu chi
yi	i
yi quan	i ch'uan or yi ch'uan
zhan zhuang	chan chuang

* Throughout this book we shall use Chinese spellings from the two Chinese-to-English translation systems (Pin Yin and Wade-Giles) in accordance with the way they are used colloquially, feel appropriate to Western sensibilities, convey appropriate symbolic meaning or fit with ease of usage. Pin Yin will be used sometimes, and at other times Wade-Giles spelling. For example, the Pin Yin term *Qigong* is used in this book instead of the Wade-Giles term *Ch'i Kung* or *Ch'i Gung*. But, the Wade-Giles term *Tai Chi Chuan* is used instead of the Pin Yin term *Taiji Quan*. The choice was made because most Westerners, in colloquial usage, are more familiar with the terms *Qigong* from the Pin Yin and *Tai Chi Chuan* from Wade-Giles; and furthermore in the main text of the book we discuss how the letter "Q" conveys a symbolic meaning better fitting with the deep meaning of *Qigong* and *Qi* than does the "C" in *Ch'i* or *Ch'i Kung*. It is important that the reader's attention is brought to the fact that many people assume that the "chi" in Tai Chi refers to life energy; but rather the Chinese character *Chi* in *Tai Chi* (Wade Giles) or *Ji* in *Taiji* (Pin Yin)

refers to the meeting place of opposites where the shady and sunny side of a mountain meet. Please note that Ch'i (with the apostrophe is Wade-Giles for life energy (Qi). Chi (without an apostrophe) means a ridgepole where Yin and Yang meet, or the celestial pole leading to the North Star, as is discussed more fully in the section on the Shamanic origins of Tai Chi. The term *Chuan* from the Wade Giles is used since, the term *Quan* is not common in Western usage, nor does it fit with Western senibilities. In some instances in this book, in a single phrase Pin Yin and Wade Giles are combined as can be seen in the choice of spelling of term *Yi Chuan*; the Yi comes from Pin Yin and *Chuan* comes from Wade Giles. The spelling *I Chuan* (Wade-Giles) or *Yi Quan* (Pin Yin) does not fit Western sensibilities as well. There could easily be confusion about the pronunciation of the "I" in I Chuan; The pronunciation of the term I or Yi is *yee*. Therefore the hybrid term *Yi Chuan* is chosen.

APPENDIX V

Glossary of Some Common Qigong Terms**

Bai Hui (Point of one hundred meetings). The twentieth acupuncture point on the Governing Vessel, at the crown of the head, in line with the apexes of the ears. In Standing Meditation this point is in alignment with the hui yin, the point between the anus and the genitals.

Chuan (also spelled quan). Fist in colloquial exoteric usage, as Tai Chi Chuan (quan). Esoterically, it means taking the five elements and bringing their power into one's grasp.

Tan Tien (Field of Elixir). Also called Dan Tian, or hara in Japanese. Two or three finger widths below the navel. The center of gravity of the body, and a key place of focus for activating Qi, according to the Taoists.

Dao (also called the Tao). The way of harmony with oneself, others, nature and the universe.

Hui Yin (Meeting of yin). Acupuncture point where the Conception Vessel ends, between the genital organs and anus.

Jing is usually defined as essential energy. Qigong practitioners talk about the purpose of Qigong training as transforming jing into qi and then into spirit. There are many kinds of jing: sperm, the jing that comes from the earth and jing from our ancestors. In the internal martial arts one can speak of fa jing (the explosive power of the ball), Ming jing (obvious). An jing (hidden) and Hua jing (mysterious), Ling kung jing (empty force) and hung jing (empty force without touching another).

Lao Gong (Palace of Work). Acupuncture point Pericardium 8, in the center of the palm. Found by bending the fourth finger into the palm.

Ming Men (Sea of Vitality). The fourth acupuncture point on the Governing Vessel. Approximately opposite the navel. Associated with kidney energy. An important place of focus for lower back problems. Stretching this area of the lower back during Standing Meditation is a key to activating the vital energy and opening the sphere of the Self.

Qi. The vital energy of life, which runs through our body and our meridians.

Qigong. The art and science of cultivating the internal energy through breath, movement, posture, touch, sound and awareness. In early usage it was called dao-yin (leading and guiding), xing qi (moving the Qi), tu gu na xin (expelling the old, absorbing the new), nei gong (inner work) and yang sheng (nourishing life), according to Taoist scholar Ken Cohen.

Tai Chi. A term meaning the unity of yin and yang, where the yin, shady side of a mountain meets the yang, sunny side. It refers to a state of consciousness where the opposites of the universe unite in harmony. The term "chi" in Tai Chi also means celestial axis.

Tai Chi Chuan (also spelled T'ai Chi Ch'uan or Taiji Quan). Often translated as the "Supreme Ultimate Fist." On the esoteric level this is a system for finding harmony with the universe through the ability to balance all opposites (such as strength and gentleness, and hardness and softness) and activate the forces of the elements to heal the body, mind and spirit. Some argue whether Tai Chi Chuan is a martial art, a healing technique or a spiritual path; depending upon one's intention, each and all of these are fundamental parts of the art's wholeness. The major schools of Tai Chi Chuan are the Chen, Yang and Wu families.

Wuji. The void, undifferentiated state prior to the origin of opposites (Tai Chi), the mother of Qi. Wuji parallels the idea of "Ain Soph" in the Jewish Caballah, from which all creation derives.

Yi Chuan (also spelled Yi Ch'uan or Yi Quan). The Standing Meditation system founded by Wang Xiangzhai (1885–1963). Literally translated as "Mind Boxing." (Esoteric meaning: the intention behind the use of the five elements.) A system that is said to be the essence of the three systems of internal arts—Tai Chi Chuan, Xingyi Chuan and Bagua Chuan. It can be used for self-defense, as a martial art, for healing, self development, alchemical psychophysiological transformation or spiritual unfoldment. Its uses are only as limited as our intention.

Zhan Zhuang. Literally translated as "standing stake." Commonly referred to as "standing like a tree." Another name for the fundamental posture of the Yi Chuan system.

Endnotes

Preface

[1] Sherman L., Zuckerman M., and Weil, A., *The Canyon Ranch Guide to Living Younger Longer: A Complete Program for Optimal Health for Body, Mind and Spirit*, Simon and Schuster, 2001.

[2] For an excellent review of Taoist literature on longevity methods in classical scholarship see ED: Kohn, L. *Taoist Meditation and Longevity Techniques*, University of Michigan, 1989. Also see , Maspero, H., *Taoism and Chinese Religion*, University of Massachusetts Press, 1981.Ni, M., *The Yellow Emperors's Classic of Medicine*, Shambhala,1995. Blofeld, J., *Taoism: The Road to Immortality*, Shambhala, 1978. Saso, M., *Buddhist and Taoist Studies I*, The University Press of Hawaii, 1977. Cohen, K., *The Way of Qigong*, Ballantine Books, 1977.

[3] Cohen, K. *The Way of Qigong*, Ballantine Books,1997, p.13. Reference: Despeux C., *The Marrrow of the Red Phoenix: Health and Long Life in 16th Century China*, Guy Tredaniel: Paris, 1988, p.10. Taoist scholar Livia Kohn credits the origin of modern Qigong to Jiang Weiqiao (or Master Yinshi) who in a desperate effort to heal himself of tuberculosis, began to follow the regimen outlined in an inner alchemical text, practicing meditation, breathing and slow movements. He reportedly achieved complete recovery and described his techniques in biomedical terms in a treatise entitled Quiet Sitting with Master Yinshi (Yinshizi Jingzuo Fa), dated 1914. See Kohn, L., *Daoism and Chinese Culture*, Three Pines Press: Cambridge Mass., 2001, p. 195.

[4] Throughout this book we shall use Chinese spellings from the two Chinese-to-English translation systems (Pin Yin and Wade-Giles) in accordance with the way they are used colloquially, feel appropriate to Western sensibilities, convey appropriate symbolic meaning or fit with ease of usage. Pin Yin will be used sometimes, and at other times Wade-Giles spelling. For example, the Pin Yin term *Qigong* is used in this book instead of the Wade-Giles term *Chi Kung* or *Chi Gung*. But, the Wade-Giles term *Tai Chi Chuan* is used instead of the Pin Yin term *Taiji Quan*. The choice was made because most Westerners, in colloquial usage, are more familiar with the terms *Qigong* from the Pin Yin and *Tai Chi Chuan* from Wade-Giles; and furthermore in the main text of the book we discuss how the letter *"Q"* conveys a symbolic meaning better fitting with the deep meaning of *Qigong* and *Qi* than does the "C" in *Chi* or *Chi Kung*. It is important that the reader's attention is brought to the fact that the term *chi* (Wade-Giles, *Qi* in Pin Yin) is not the Chinese character in the Wade-Giles spelling of *Tai Chi*. Many people assume that the "chi" in Tai Chi refers to life energy; but rather the Chinese character *Tai Chi* (*Taiji* in Pin Yin spelling) refers to the meeting place of opposites where the shady and sunny side of a mountain meet. The term *Chuan* from the Wade Giles is used since, the term *Quan* is not common in Western usage, nor does it fit with Western senibilities. In some instances in this book, in a single phrase Pin Yin and Wade Giles are combined as can be seen in the choice of spelling of term *Yi Chuan*; the Yi comes from Pin Yin and *Chuan* comes from Wade Giles. The spelling *I Chuan* (Wade-Giles) or *Yi Quan* (Pin Yin) does not fit Western sensibilities as well. There could easily be confusion about the pronun-ciation of the "I" in I Chuan; The pronunciation of the term I or Yi is *yee*. Therefore the hybrid term *Yi Chuan* is chosen.

SECTION I

[1] The *Yi Chuan* or mind/intentionality behind the various systems of Chuan originated with Wang Xiangzhai who lived from 1886-1963 and taught it to Han Xingyuan, who in turn taught it to a group of Fong Ha's students, including myself.

[2] There are three main systems of Chuan, Tai Chi Chuan, Hsing Yi Chuan, and Pa Kua Chuan.

[3] Eliade, M., *The Forge and the Crucible*, University of Chicago, 1956, pp. 79–86. One of the derivations of the word *shaman* is the Vedic *sram*, to heat oneself. According to an Eskimo shaman, "Every real shaman has to feel an illumination in his body, in the inside of his head or in his brain, something that gleams like fire..." Evan Wentz says the same thing about Tibetan Yogis who produce a psychic heat that renders them impervious to temperature, even to long-term exposure to snow while wrapped only in sheets dipped in icy water. See Achterberg, J., *Imagery and Healing*, op.cit., p. 34.

[4] See later discussion and footnote in this chapter on *Zhan Zhuang* (standing like a tree) developed by Wang Xiangzhai. Also see the Book by Master Lam Chuen, *The Way of Energy,* Gaia Books, 1991.

[5] The ability to bounce another into the air when they push on a practitioner is called *fajing.* For more information, see feature article on Sifu Fong Ha in Tai Chi Magazine, Vol. 5, #4, August 1991, and also a book by Paul Dong.

Chapter 1

[1] Suares, C., *The Sepher Yetsera,* Shamballa, 1976. According to the *Sepher Yetsera* (The Book of Formation), the Hebrew letters are connected to the formation of the world. According to the ancient science of Gematria, each letter corresponds to a number, which governs the formation of the archetypal energies of the universe from the *ayn sof* (the void prior to creation).

[2] This interpretation of the Old Testament comes from Winkler, G., *Magic of the Ordinary: Recovering the Shamanic in Judaism,* North Atlantic, 2003. He refers to interpretive texts such as Sefer Hazoharn Midrash Ha Ne'elam 16B. The story of the Native American fisherman comes from, Gore, B., *Ecstatic Body Postures,* Bear and Co., Santa Fe, p. 14.

[3] At the Aesclepian temples it was reported and engraved in stone that miracle cures took place from curing people who were blind from birth, the lame could walk again, and there were even stories about Aesclepius raising the dead—like Glaucos the son of Minos, and Hippolytos the son of Theseus. The mind, "noo-therapeia," was key in the healing process. Papadakis, T., *Epidauros,* Verlag Schnell and Steiner Munchen, Zurich and Athens, 1988.

[4] Chopra, D., *Quantum Healing: Exploring the Frontiers of Mind/Body Medicine,* 1990, p. 122, reporting a study that Psychologist Daniel Goleman describes.

[5] Braun, B., *Psychophysiologic Phenomena in Multiple Personality and Hypnosis.* American Journal of Clinical Hypnosis, Vol. 26, 1983, p. 124–35. Murphy, M., *The Future of the Body: Explorations into the further Evolution of Human Nature.* Jeremy Tarcher, pp. 242–245, 1992. For more information on the ability of the relaxation response, psychoneuroimmunology and Qigong to effect healing, see Appendix 2 of this book. The most current term in the DSM-IV for multiple personality disorder is "dissociative identity disorder."

[6] The case of Milton Erikson's patient with the orange juice allergy is reported in, Rossi, E., *The Psychobiology of Mind-Body Healing: New Concepts of Therapeutic Hypnosis,* W.W. Norton and Co., 1986, p. 65. James Braid first defined the "State-dependent Memory hypothesis," which is a building block for modern medical hypnosis. Dr. Rossi gives and extensive review of the literature on state-dependent learning and mind-body healing in the above cited book and in *Mind-Body Therapy: Methods of Ideodynamic Healing in Hypnosis,* W.W. Norton, 1988. Also see Weil, A., *Spontaneous Healing,* Alfred A. Knoff, 1993.

[7] Gore, B., *Ecstatic Body Postures,* op. cit., p. 32.

[8] Goodman, F., *Where the Spirits Ride the Wind: Trance Journeys and other Ecstatic Experiences,* Indiana University Press, 1990. The quote in the text comes from one of her students, Gore, B., *Ecstatic Body Postures,* Bear and Co., Santa Fe, 1995, pp. 15, 32.

[9] Gore, ibid, p. 14.

[10] Gore, B. op. cit., xi., Goodman, F., op. cit., p. 107.

[11] Goodman, F., p. 119. I had used this posture in the psychotherapy approach I developed, Integrative Depth Psychotherapy, before learning of its anthropological origins; and I wrote about it in, "Psychotherapy and Qigong: Partners in Alleviating Anxiety," Psychotherapy and Healing Center, 1997. The spontaneous arising of postural forms in different people, in different locations and cultures lends some credence to the viewpoint that at least some healing postures are primordial and transcend culture.

[12] Goodman, F., *Where the Spirits Ride the Wind:* Trance Journeys and other Ecstatic Experiences, Indiana University Press, 1990, pp. 118–119. Gore op. cit., pp. 60–1.

[13] "Psychotherapy and Qigong: Partners in Alleviating Anxiety," Psychotherapy and Healing Center, 1997.

[14] Goodman, F., *Where the Spirits Ride the Wind: Trance Journeys and other Ecstatic Experiences,* Indiana University Press, 1990, p. 22.

[15] Rossi, E., *The Psychobiology of Mind-Body Healing,* Norton & Co., 1986, Rossi, E., *Mind-Body Therapy: Methods of Ideodynamic Healing in Hypnosis,* Norton & Co., 1988; Ader, R., *Psycho-neuroimmunology,* New York, Academic Press, 1981; Achterberg, J., *Imagery in Healing,* New Science Library, 1985.

[16] Cohen, K., *The Way of Qigong*, Ballentine Books, 1997. See discussion about healers' physiological changes while being in trance, i.e. changes in EKG, EEG surges in electricity from 4 volts to 221 volts, etc. pp. 47–50.

[17] Gore, B., op. cit, reporting on research of Mueller, p. 12.

[18] Yang Sihuan, 2nd World Conference for Academic Exchange of Medical Qigong, 1993.

[19] Gore, B., *Ecstatic Body Postures*, Bear & Co., Santa Fe, NM, 1995, p. 91.

[20] Despeux, C., Gymnastics: the Ancient Tradition, in ED. Kohn, L., Taoist Meditation and Longevity Techniques, University of Michigan, 1989, pp. 237–40.

[21] Cohen, K., *The Way of Qigong*, Ballentine Books, 1997, p. 13.

[22] Cohen, K., Ibid., p. 18.

[23] Despeux, C., "Gymnastics: the Ancient Tradition," ED: Kohn L., Taoist Meditation and Longevity Techniques, University of Michigan, 1989, p. 235.

[24] Gwei-Djen, L., and Needham J., *Celestial Lancets: A History and Rationale of Acupuncture and Moxa*, Cambridge University Press, 1980, p. 80.

[25] Tomio, N., *The Bodhisattva Warriors*, Samuel Weiser: Maine, 1994, p. 158.

[26] Nagaboshi, T., op.cit., pp. 173–174.

[27] Coomaraswamy, A.K., "The Dance of Shiva," The Dance of Shiva, Noonday Press, New York, 1957, quoted in Huntington, S.l. The Art of Ancient India, Weatherhill, New York, 1985, p. 536.

[28] Tomio, N., p. 168.

[29] Tomio, N., op.cit., p. 166.

[30] Tomio, N., op cit., p. 168.

[31] Tomio, N., pp. 184–185

[32] Tomio, N., op cit., pp. 220.

[33] *Shili*, meaning practicing strength. See Diepersloot, J., The Tao of Yi Quan, Vol. 2, Center for Healing and the Arts: Walnut Creek, 1999.

[34] For a more complete discussion of the use of Standing Meditation as a tool for developing the more subtle abilities of the internal martial arts including *kong jin*, empty force, see Diepersloot, J., Warriors of Stillness, Vol. 2; *The Tao of Yi Quan*, particularly Chapter 10.

[35] Tomio, N., *The Bodhisattva Warriors*, Samuel Weiser, 1994.

[36] See Mayer, M., *Trials of the Heart*, Celestial Arts, 1994, for an exploration of the use of such metaphors in healing. Also see Houston, J., *The Hero and the Goddess, Ballentine Books,* 1992.

[37] Tomio, N., Op. Cit., p. 398.

[38] Mayer, M., "Qigong and Behavioral Healthcare: An Integrated Approach to Chronic Pain," Qi Magazine, Winter 1996/7.

[39] Tomio, N., op. cit., p 229.

[40] Diepersloot, J., Vol. II., Op. Cit. p. 21.

[41] Tomio, N., p 173.

[42] For a more complete discussion of Wang Xiangzhai's life, see Diepersloot, J., *Warriors of Stillness*, Vol. 2, pp. 53–103.

[43] Wang Xiangzhai, *The True Course of Yiquan*, Li Ying, Arn, ed., Hong Kong: Unicorn Press, 1983, as quoted by Diepersloot, J., Warriors of Stillness, Vol. II. p. 68.

[44] It is analogous to the *ain soph* of the Jewish *Kaballah* and the state of potential of creation to which cross-cultural creation myths speak when they speak of the darkness before the creation.

[45] The internal schools of the martial arts are usually considered to be Tai Chi, Xingyi and Baqua Chuan.

[46] Kingsley, P., *In the Dark Places of Wisdom*, Golden Sufi Center, Invernesss, CA, 1999.

Chapter 2

[1] The Story of The Frog Princess, also called The Frog King, can be found in Colum, P., *The Complete Grimm's Fairy Tales*, Pantheon Books, New York, 1972, p. 17. The Iron Hans story is told by Bly, R., *Iron John: A Book about Men*, Addison Wesley, 1990, as well as in the previously cited Grimm's edition, p. 612.

[2] Perhaps the best known of these is the Tarot, which was a deck of cards in which was encoded esoteric knowledge to protect it from discovery by the inquisition.

[3] Wilhelm, R., *The Secret of the Golden Flower,* Harcourt Brace and Jovanovich, 1962, p. 23. Also see Claery, T., *The Secret of the Golden Flower*, Harper San Francisco, 1991, and Yu, L. K., *The Secrets of Chinese Meditation*, Samuel Weiser, NY, 1972. It is not being claimed that the practices in *Secrets to Living Younger Longer* are the same as those put forth by authors' Wilhelm and Cleary for cultivating Golden Light or the Golden Ball.

[4] See Eliade, *Myth and Reality,* Harper & Row, 1963, pp. 14–38.

[5] Diepersloot, Jan, *Warriors of Stillness*, Center for Healing and the Arts, Walnut Creek, l995, p. xi.

[6] Tulku, Tarthang, *KumNye Relaxation*, Dharma Publishing, 1978, p. 12.

[7] Parabola Magazine, Spring 1993, *The Kung Approach to Healing,* by Richard Katz. Halifax Shamanic Voices, Dutton, NY, 1979, p. 55.

[8] Krippner, S., "Energy Medicine in Native American Healing Practices," Volume 5, No. 1, *Newsmagazine of ISSSEEM*, Golden, CO, p. 8.

[9] Cohen, K., Bridges, "Native American Healing Touch," Volume 5, No. 1, Spring 1994, *Newsmagazine of ISSSEEM,* Golden, CO. Also see his excellent book, *The Way of Qigong*, Ballentine Books, 1997.

[10] For a method of self-transformation through being with our felt experience of the moment, see Gendlin, E., *Focusing,* Bantam Books, 1978. Dr. Mayer served as Dr. Eugene Gendlin's Focusing Training Coordinator of the San Francisco Bay area for 10 years. To integrate psychological "focusing" with Qigong see Mayer, M., *Psychotherapy and Qigong: Partners in Healing Anxiety*, Psychotherapy & Healing Press 1997, available at 510–849-2878, drmichael@bodymind healing.com.

[11] For more information, check with the Association for Transpersonal Psychology in Menlo Park, California. I helped to co-found the Transpersonal Psychology Department at JFK University, and taught there for 12 years.

[12] Gerber, R., *Vibrational Medicine*, Bear & Co., 1996, pp. 39–60, is a good introduction to recent evidence in physics that has been transposed into the field of Energy Medicine that we are, in fact, frozen light. Also, see the journal, *Subtle Energies,* Golden, Co.

[13] Cleary, T., *The Secret of the Golden Flower,* Harper and Row, 1991, describes the sensation of Sitting Meditation and Microcosmic Orbit Breathing as like taking a bath in golden light. The Jewish practitioners of Hassidism, followers of The Baal Shem Tov, activate the energy that comes from standing and rocking the pelvis while chanting, to experience divine ecstasy.

[14] The Tan Tien energy gate is located in the front of the body, three fingers below the navel; the Ming Men is located in the back of the body, below the second lumbar vertebra, behind the Tan Tien.

[15] Qigong exercises after Standing are an important part of the family of traditions that help to disperse stagnant Qi. See Section II of Bodymind Healing Qigong—Exercises for Dispersing Stagnant Qi.

[16] See for example, Edinger, E., *Anatomy of the Psyche: Alchemical Symbolism in Psychotherapy*, Open Court, IL, 1985.

[17] For more on the healing elements of Standing Meditation done in conjunction with other methods, see Mayer, M., "Qigong and Behavioral Medicine: An Integrated Approach to Chronic Pain," *Qi: The Journal of Traditional Health and Fitness*, Winter, 1996/7. For example, psychotherapy, acupressure and chiropractic care were very helpful in healing my neck along with the Standing.

[18] See Kremer, J., "Indigenous and Euro-American Science: Two Perspectives on Native American Healing," *ISSSEEM Newsmagazine*, Golden, CO, Vol. 5, No. 1, Spring 1995, p. 11.

[19] Gendlin, E., *Focusing*, Bantam Books, 1978. For an example of the integration of Focusing with energy work, see Mayer, M., "Qigong and Behavioral Medicine: An Integrated Approach to Chronic Pain," *Qi Magazine*, Winter 1996/7.

Chapter 3

[1] The Wuji system of Standing Meditation was learned by the author from Cai Song Fang, Qigong Master of Canton Province and from Master Fong Ha. For a description of this method see *Wuji Qigong and the*

Essence of Taiji Quan, and *Warriors of Stillness*, Diepersloot, J., Mount Diablo Tai Chi Center, Walnut Creek, CA, l989; and *Wujishi Breathing Exercise*, by Men Den and Tin Shen, Medicine and Health Company, Hong Kong, l986.

[2] Eliade, M., *Myth and Reality*, Harper and Row, 1963, p. 83.

[3] For beginners, it's best to stay with the most basic practice (Wuji Standing) for at least a short period of time before progressing on to the other exercises in the Yi Chuan system. Even for more advanced practitioners it is advisable do the simpler forms of practice for a greater amount of your practice time, adding on more complex methods gradually. Listen to your body's signals. In actual practice sessions in my Tai Chi classes, we do Wuji and Yi Chuan Standing Meditation for about 20 minutes—first just standing, next, standing in various fixed postures, then internal organ and animal posture Qigong, Walking Meditation and Moving Meditation (long style Yang Tai Chi). Finally we practice two-person exercises, and when the spirit moves us, Tai Chi dance. The Wuji posture is continually returned to, and is kept in awareness through all stages of movement practices. For beginners, start off standing for short periods of time (5 minutes). Gradually increase the time, listening to your body.

[4] Brunton, P., *The Quest for the Overself,* Samuel Weiser, Publication, Reissued by Larsen Buditt, NY.

[5] Though I have studied with recognized Masters of the Wuji Standing Meditation tradition such as Master Cai Song Fang and Master Fong Ha for two decades, as I have said in the Preface, I am not making a representation that the exercises imparted here are exact duplications of their teachings. In the decade that I have been teaching it, I have developed my own unique way of finding "the void, the mother of Qi," as does each practitioner. My orientation comes from my experience as a practitioner, psychotherapist and hypnotherapist.

[6] See Cohen, K., *The Way of Qigong*, Ballentine Books, 1997; and Sancier, K., "Medical Applications of Qigong," *Alternative Therapies*, Vol. 2, No. 1, 1996.

[7] The awareness of the knees here comes from the Yi Chuan training, more than from the Wuji tradition; the latter emphasizes just standing naturally.

[8] Keeping the eyes and mouth half open is an example of something that I didn't learn from my Standing Meditation teachers. The half smile I learned from Sitting Meditation with the Buddhist teacher, Thich Nat Hahn. The eyes half open is a common esoteric technique for entering into an altered state.

[9] See Diepersloot, J., *op. cit.*

Chapter 4

[1] *Elevator breathing* is a the most simple variation on the commonly used Taoist breathing practice called *Macrocosmic Orbit Breathing*, which emphasizes circling the breath up the back from below the feet, over the top of the head and down the front of the body.

[2] For a more complete explanation of the integrative method I developed for working through energy blocks, see *Psychotherapy and Qigong: Partners in Healing Anxiety,* Psychotherapy & Healing Press, 1997, phone 510-849-2878.

[3] There are numerous sources for descriptions of Microcosmic Orbit Breathing: Huang, Wen-Shan, *Fundamentals of Tai Chi Chuan*, South Sky Book Company, Hong Kong, 1974; Chia, Mantak, *Iron Shirt Chi Kung*, Healing Tao Books, Huntington, NY, 1986.

[4] There are now scientific studies on the ability of Microcosmic Orbit Breathing to effect bacteria and cancer cells in vitro. See Laskow, L., *Healing with Love*, Harper & Row.

[5] See, for example, the classic book on this by Western Psychologist Lee Sanella called "Kundalini Psychosis."

[6] *Co-dependence* is a much used term which originated in alcoholism literature, and grew to apply to taking care of another in any relationship in an unhealthy, unconscious, symbiotic manner which made "helping" detrimental to the other, and to our relationship with that person. Co-dependent people are those who have a hard time setting boundaries with others and owning their reality. See Mellody, P., *Facing Love Addiction: Giving Yourself the Power to Change the Way you Love*, Harper: San Francisco, 1992.

In my first book, *Trials of the Heart* (Celestial arts 1994, p. 42), I discuss the ancient psycho-mythological roots of "co-dependency" in the myth of "Amor and Psyche" when Psyche needs to learn to say "no" to a lame man on a donkey and a dead man floating. Her learning to set boundaries prevents her from distraction on her journey to complete her task in the underworld.

[7] For more on this point see Lade, A., *Acupuncture Points, Images and Functions*, Eastland Press, 1989. For more on the method of touch which I call "circle, stop and feel," see Mayer, M., "Qigong and Behavioral Medicine, An Integrated Approach to Chronic Pain," *Qi Magazine*, 1996/7.

[8] I heard this term from Kumar Francis, a Qigong teacher in Marin county.

[9] A more literal translation is "standing like a post;" but it seems that the more organic idea of a tree is preferable as a translation even though not as literally correct. I first learned it from Han Xingyuan with whom I spent two summers in 1976 and 1977 on invitation from my Sifu, Fong Ha. The actual visualization of being like a tree was not so much a part of the practice as was holding the ball of energy in eight fixed postures and then doing Walking Meditation and Push Hands. I have taken the liberty from my own experience with hypnosis and transpersonal psychology to add the particular visualizations of the tree. Another one of Wang Xiangzhai's students, Professor Yu Yong Nian, passed the Yi Chuan on to Master Lam Chuen. See the book by Chuen, L., *The Way of Energy*, Gaia Books, London, England, 1991. He discusses many exercises to develop the ball of energy, and calls it *Zhan Zhuang* (standing like a tree method of Qigong).

[10] Single case studies on a variety of medical conditions from the practice of standing meditation are reported in a booklet, Shen, T., *Wujishi Breathing Exercise*, Medicine and Health Publishing Co, 52 Tanner Rd., 11F Hong Kong, 1986. Some examples of positive results are with patients with hypertension and rapid heart beat, partial paralysis, Parkinson's nerve syndrome and habitual constipation. Thirty-two cases are reported; but inadequate research methodology limits interpretation of the results.

[11] Yang Sihuan, 2nd World Conference for Academic Exchange on Medical Qigong, 1993. The EEGs of the Qigong group were analyzed every half-year in meditation, and the EEGs were also recorded before learning Qigong. The students in the control group did not take part in the Qigong training and their EEG's were investigated at rest twice within an interval of one year. In the test, eight channels of EEGs were simultaneously processed by a computer on line for 20 minutes. The program, "computer evaluation system for the Qigong state" was provided by the Laboratory of Bio-Control, Department of Electrical Engineering, Zhejiang University.

After one year of Qigong training, total coherence between the left and right frontal regions increased from 0.84~0.07 to 0. 87~0.06 (p<0.05). Before Qigong training, the total coherence between the left and right occipital areas was 0.68~0.14. After half a year's training, it increased to 0.79~0.10, and after one year's training, it was 0.76~0.10. Self-comparison showed the probability was less than 0.001. The total coherence between the left and right temporal areas before Qigong training was 0.48~0.17; half a year after Qigong training it was 0.55~0.13, compared with that before Qigong training (p<O. 05). One year after Qigong training it was 0.64~0.12, compared with those before Qigong training and half year after Qigong training (p<0.001). Qigong training had no significant influence on coherence between the left and right central regions and between adjacent anterior and posterior brain regions (F3–C3, F4–C4, C3–01, C4–O2). It had no significant difference between the Qigong group without learning and the first recording of the control group at the same time. The data from the two tests of the control group showed that the total coherence did not change significantly between the left and right corresponding brain regions and between the anterior and posterior adjacent brain regions.

He states, "The results showed that Qigong training had affected coherence of EEGs between the two frontal regions, between two occipital regions and between two temporal regions of the Qigong group in meditation. The most significant is that, with the increase of training period, the total coherence value between the left and right temporal areas went up. It seems that there is certain dosage-effect relationship."

This study was supported by the National Administration of Traditional Chinese medicine.

[12] For more information on this technique see Mayer, M., "Qigong and Behavioral Medicine: An Integrated Approach to Chronic Pain," *Qi Magazine*, Winter 1996/7.

[13] This method is a variation of an exercise discussed by Master Lam Kam Chuen in *The Way of Energy*, Gaia Books, 1991, p. 136.

Chapter 5

[1] Master Lam in his book *The Way of Energy,* Gaia Books, uses a similar visualization to build Qi.

[2] See for example, Sugano, H., et al, "A New Approach to the Studies of Subtle Energies," *Subtle Energies*, Vol. 5, No. 2, p. 143, 1994; or Wirth, D., "The Effect of Non-contact Therapeutic Touch on the Healing Rate of Full Thickness Dermal Wounds," *Subtle Energies*, Vol. 1, No. 1, 1990. Yount, G., "Is it more than a beautiful form of hypnosis?" *Health and Spirituality,* Summer, 2001. The reference to Lao Gung emission comes from Saucier, K., "Medical Applications of Qigong and Emitted Qi on Humans, Cell Cultures and Plants. Review of Selected Scientific Research, American Journal of Acupuncture, Vol. 19, #4, 1991, and reported by Benor D., *Ibid,* pp. 216.

[3] This posture comes from the Yi Chuan tradition. I learned it from my Sifu, Fong Ha, and from my training with Han Xingyuan. I added the name "The Golden Ball of the Heart" and the visualization to bring out the posture's healing qualities.

[4] MacCraty, R., "Science of the Heart: Exploring the Role of the Heart in Human Performance," Heart Math, 2001. Also see Russek, L., and Schwartz, G., *Energy Cardiology: A Dynamic Systems Approach for Integrating Conventional and Alternative Medicine,"* Advances: The Journal of Mind-Body Health, Vol. 13 (4), Fall, 1996, p. 13.

[5] See Hall, M., *The Secret Teachings of all Ages*, Philosophic Research Society, Los Angeles, 1962, p. 37.

[6] Rinpoche, S., *The Tibetan Book of Living and Dying,* Harper: San Francisco, 1993, pp. 214–217.

Chapter 6

[1] James Braid (1797–1860) originated "the state dependent theory" of mind-body healing. *The Physiology of Fascination of the Critics Criticized*, Manchester, England: Grant and Co., 1855. The state dependent methods of hypnosis have been used extensively by Milton Erikson and Ernest Rossi. A good summary of this research is in Rossi, E., *The Psychobiology of Mind Body Healing,* W.W. Norton: New York, 1986, pp. 37–38.

[2] Webster's Collegiate Dictionary, 1977 ed.

[3] A common experience of those who have practiced Qigong for a period of time is "bone breathing." As we breathe in and out, it is as if the whole body is breathing, not just the lungs. The bones, and even the skull feels as if they are expanding on the inhalation and contracting on the exhalation. The sense of relaxation is very profound.

[4] A vast number of modern research studies in the area of bodymind healing show the mind's ability to create an altered state that can influence "the physical world," thereby fundamentally changing our conception of the static nature of material reality. For example, in the area of the psychobiology of bodymind healing it has been shown that our images of our diseases effect our neurochemistry, and can be used for healing. See Ackterberg, J., *Imagery and Healing,* op cit., and Rossi, E., *The Psychobiology of Mind-Body Healing,* op. cit.

[5] Edinger, E., *Anatomy of the Psyche*: *Alchemical Symbolism in Psychotherapy,* Open Court: La Salle, IL, 1985, p. 80 quoting Jung, C.G., *Psychology and Alchemy*, CW12, par. 336.

[6] *Spiritus mercurius* is said, by the alchemists, to be imprisoned in matter. And one of the purposes of the opus is to free the matter to obtain the philosopher's stone, the glorious body, the *corpus glorificationis*. Eliade, Mircea, *The Forge and the Crucible,* University of Chicago Press, 1978, Second edition, p. 225.

Chapter 7

[1] Wilhelm R.,*The Secret of the Golden Flower*, HBJ: New York, NY, 1962.

[2] Quotes from various alchemical texts from Edinger, E., *Anatomy of the Psyche: Alchemical Symbolism in Psychotherapy,* Open Court, 1985, pp. 49–51. The idea of the reduction to "prima materia" is one of the reasons why in psychotherapy that psychodynamic therapists place an importance on returning to the symbolic origins of certain psychological issues where they derived in childhood. Likewise, when we practice Standing Meditation, memories may arise of the origins of our body-blocks thereby beginning the

process of alchemical transformation. In Eastern spiritual practices, the Prima Materia is returning to the void, or "emptying your cup" before the teacher can fill it with new wisdom.

[3] Gendlin, E., *Focusing*, Bantam Books, 1978. Focusing is a six step process to find the "felt meaning" of a life issue, with a "felt shift" resulting. 1. Clearing a space 2. Felt sense of the issue 3. Find a handle word or image 4. Resonate the handle word/image with the felt sense 5. Ask questions such as "What's the crux of this issue?" 6. Receiving.

[4] Sha, ZG, *Zhi Neng Medicine*, Zhi Neng Press, Vancouver, 2000.

[5] Sha, ZG, *Zhi Neng Medicine*, Zhi Neng Press, Vancouver, 2000.

[6] Gore, B., *Ecstatic Body Postures*, op. cit., p. 14.

[7] Cohen, K., *The Way of Qigong*, op. Cit. p. 18.

[8] Quoted from Chief Seattle in Beinfeld, H., and Korngold, E., *Between Heaven and Earth: A Guide to Chinese Medicine*, Balentine Books: New york, 1991, p. 7.

[9] Bienfeld, H., Korngold, E., *Between Heaven and Earth: A Guide to Chinese Medicine*, Ballentine Books: New York, NY, 1991.

[10] For information about the Penetrating and Belt Strange Flow Meridians see Teeguarden, I.M., *Acupressure Way of Healthy: Jin Shin Do*, Japan Publications, Inc.: Tokyo, 1978, pp. 61–62. For a more in depth analysis see, Readman, P., *A Manual of Acupuncture*, Journal of Chinese Medicine Publication, 1998.

[11] See "Using Tai Chi to prevent Falls in Senior Citizens,"(Qi Magazine, Vol. 6, No. 1, Spring 1996, p. 30).

[12] For more information about the Great Bridge Channels see Teeguarden, I.M., *Acupressure Way of Healthy: Jin Shin Do*, Japan Publications, Inc.: Tokyo, 1978, pp. 61-62. For a more in depth analysis see, Readman, P., *A Manual of Acupuncture*, Journal of Chinese Medicine Publication, 1998.

[13] Hahn, T.N., *A Guide to Walking Meditation*, Thames Printing Co., Norwich, CT, 1985.

[14] Yi means the mind or intention behind the system of Chuan. *Chuan* literally translates as fist; but its esoteric meaning is based on the fact that when we make a fist we take our five fingers and bring them together. The five fingers represent the five elements—fire, earth, metal, water, and wood. Thus when we practice Yi Chuan techniques we find the mind that can bring the five elements together and make us whole.

[15] See Hahn, T.N., *A Guide to Walking Meditation*, 1985. The Vipasana Buddhist mindful meditation tradition also emphasizes the importance of Walking Meditation. The Taoist tradition contributes a specific method of hand and leg movements, and the positioning of the body to maximize the healing effects of the Qi. The emphasis in the Buddhist tradition is on the mindful opening of the heart and mind. Both traditions can be combined quite nicely as in the heart chakra meditation above.

[16] Wile, D., *Tai Chi's Ancestors: The Making of an Internal Martial Art*, Sweet Chi Press, 1991; and Wile, D., *Lost Tai Chi Classics from the Late Ching Dynasty*, State University of New York Press, Albany, 1996.

[17] The discussion about the term "chi" meaning a ridgepole and a celestial axis to the Polestar comes from integrating research from the following sources: Wilhelm, R., *I Ching: The book of Changes*, Princeton University Press, 1997, p. 318; LaChapelle, D., *Return to Mountain: Tai Chi*, Hazard Publishing, 2002, pp. 15; Wile, D., *Tai Chi's Ancestors: The Making of an Internal Martial Art*, Sweet Chi Press, 1999, pp., 82; Ulansey, D., *The Origins of the Mithraic Mysteries*, Oxford University Press, 1989, p. 104; Needham, J., *Science and Civilization in China*, Cambridge University Press, Vol. 2, 1956, p. 464 ff.; Eliade, M., *Patterns in Comparative Religion*, World Publishing, 1958, pp. 367–388.

[18] Wilhelm, R., *The Secret of the Golden Flower*, HBJ: New York, NY, 1962.

[19] In actuality, the whole set of 108 movements of Tai Chi can be practiced as a form of dual cultivation with another. As previously mentioned, this set is called *San Shou*, one of the great treasures I received from my Sifu Fong Ha. I teach it as part of the process of Bodymind Healing Qigong, Level 3. I view this practice as a further step in the cultivation of the Golden Ball. The student learns how to use the 108 Tai Chi movements to take a force coming from many different directions to practice with a partner embodying the appropriate element (fire, earth, metal, water and wood) and various Taoist principles such as yielding. The experience of moving the energy in various ways through the integrated ball of the body with another helps to further cultivate the practitioners' Qi, work through body blockages, and develop flexibility, adaptability the ability to flow with another. It should be noted that there are a wide variety of ways to count the number of movements in our Yang style Long-form. Depending upon the repetitions of certain

moves that are eliminated that number can be 85, 88, etc. 108 is a sacred number—12 x 9. 12 is the number of the zodic signs and 9 is the Ennead, the number of completion.

[20] Yang, J.M., *Advanced Yang Style Tai Chi Chuan*, Vol. 1, Yang's Martial Arts Association: Jamaica Plain, MA, 1986.

[21] Ha, F. and Diepersloot, J., *A Discussion of the Realities of 'Empty Force,'* T'ai Chi: The Leading International Magazine of T'ai Chi Chuan, August 1991, Vol. 15, No. 4, pp. 8–11.

[22] Though in the context of martial arts the ability to discharge another person without touching them has no scientific proof, there is interesting scientific data to support the hypothesis that external emission of energy from the body does exist. Emission of infrasonic (acoustical) waves were measured coming from the hand of a Qigong practitioner between 6 and 167 hertz (Hz) in a well-controlled study. Interestingly, the frequencies emitted during these studies fell in the alpha range of brain activity (8–14 Hz), which is associated with spontaneous healing. (Fang, L. Y., *Scientific Investigations into Chinese Qigong*, Ed: Richard Lee, China Healthways Institute, San Clemente, 1999). Experiments are taking place at the California Pacific Medical Center by Garrett Yount exploring Qigong Masters Use of "External Emission" on brain cells in cultures (Yount, G., *Distant Intentionality, Qigong Masters and DNA*, Esalen-Noetic Sciences Conference on Subtle Energy and Uncharted Mind, Esalen Center for Theory and Research, www.Esalenctr.org, 2000. Yount., G., *Is it More than a Beautiful Form of Hypnosis?* Health and spirituality (Summer, 2001). Finally, in the Copper Wall Project in peer-reviewed papers significant surges in electricity were measured coming from healers while they were in the process of doing their healing work. Green, E., *Anomalous Electrostatic Phenomena in Exceptional Subjects*, Subtle Energies, 2:3, 1991, pp. 69–94.

[23] When Person A moves toward Person B, the adept Person B moves back while still sticking to Person A. The result is an involuntary startle reflex in Person A due to the feeling of the vacuum in space. This leads Person A to pull back, and Person B follows this retreating movement with his integral force. It is a game intentionality, that two Push Hands practitioners play to cultivate the interplay of awareness between their two energy spheres.

Chapter 8

[1] Freud, S., *The Ego and the Id,* London: Hopgarthe Press, 1923.

[2] Mahler, M., *On Child Psychosis and Schizophrenia*, Psychoanalytic Study of the Child, 7, 1952, pp. 286–305.

[3] It should be noted that in recent years, culture-bound psychiatric disorders associated with Chinese Qigong practice have been reported in China and have been accepted by the Chinese Classification of Mental Disorders (CCMD-2).

The syndrome "Qi-gong Psychotic Reaction" has also been encoded in the 4th edition of the American Psychiatric Association's Diagnostic and Statistical Manual of Mental Disorders. This term is defined as "an acute, time-limited episode characterized by dissociative, paranoid, and other psychotic or nonpsychotic symptoms that occur after participation in the Chinese folk health-enhancing practice of Qigong (exercise of vital energy). Especially vulnerable are those who become overly involved in the practice."

It is difficult to determine to what extent Qigong causes such disorders or are concomitant with them. There have been reports that improper training causes psychotic-like symptoms, for example when a person focuses intensely for prolonged periods on the third eye area. This is easily remedied by shifting the focus to the belly (tan tien). Likewise, in my experience I have seen a few patients on very rare occasions in my 25 years of practice as a psychotherapist, who have had adverse reactions concomitant with Qigong practice. For example, one patient referred to me by a local Qigong master, obsessively practiced Qigong 6 to 7 hours a day as an escape from his relationship problems, and developed obsessive/compulsive psychotic symptoms. This was remedied by psychotherapeutic intervention. As with any exercise, due caution, common sense, moderation, and learning from a qualified teacher are important.

[4] Due caution should be exercised in integrating other modalities with psychotherapy. This relates to the issue of "dual relationships." It's possible for material from one tradition to spill out from its container and "contaminate" the other; for example, if a patient feels awkward or not proficient in their Qigong movement and doesn't talk about it, a negative influence can spill over into the psychotherapy. This can create an

unwanted "negative transference." Thus, some argue for a "sterile container" in order to protect the patient; in particular, damage can occur to people with limited ego strength. On the other side of the issue it is said that if such feelings arise when mixing disciplines, those feelings can become a subject to deepen therapy, and they can increase the growth potential of therapy. This is called "the Grist for the Mill" approach to therapy. This issue is a more complex one than can be addressed here in a footnote. When I train doctoral psychology students in the integration of Qigong and Psychotherapy, this subject takes up a good part of a three-hour lecture. Suffice it to say here that due caution should be exercised because of the legal and clinical issues involved.

Some of these issues involve: a careful assessment of the patient's ego strength, written, informed consent and choice, letting a patient know the experimental nature of the discipline that is being introduced, an explanation of the theoretical framework behind the treatment, a clear agreement that the patient can say "no" at any point in doing this practice, an agreement that an honest debriefing will take place after the treatment is tried to assess its efficacy, weighing the advantages of introducing the patient to another practitioner who does the practice to avoid dangers, weighing potential legal consequences, and problems in mixing different theoretical orientations involving "transcendence" in Eastern practices versus "working through," which is more emphasized in Western psychotherapy.

Some advantages of mixing the two traditions involve: adding a relaxation method that can be a useful adjunct to psychotherapy (as is discussed more fully in my article on anxiety), the use of a many-thousand-year-old empirical healing technology that can be useful in behavioral healthcare and pain relief (discussed in my article on chronic pain), and bringing a body-centered method into therapy that helps the person to be more whole. (See "Psychotherapy and Qigong: Partners in Healing Anxiety," Fourth Edition, 1997; Qigong and Behavioral Medicine: An Integrated Approach to Chronic Pain, 1996.)

[5] Reference is being made to the term *Chaun Fa* from Chapter 1. See Tomio, N., *The Bodhisatva Warriors*, IBID.

[6] Gendlin, E., *Focusing*, Bantam Books, 1978.

[7] For a good descriptiion of "cognitive restructuring" see Shapiro, F., *Eye Movement Desensitization and Reprossing*, Guilford Press, 1995. Cognitive Restructuring is the fifth method I have incorporated into my "Bodymind Healing Psychotherapy."

[8] For background in this literature see, Greenberg, J., et. al, *Object Relations Theory in Psychoanalytic Theory*, Harvard University Press, 1983; Horner, A., *Object Relations and the Developing Ego in Therapy*, Jason Aronson, NY: 1884, Kohut, *The Analysis of the Self*, International Universities Press, NY: 1971.

Chapter 9

[1] The correlation between eating and good health and longevity is an extensive subject. It goes beyond the scope of this book. For more information on diet and longevity, see Dr. Frank Shallenberger's book, *Bursting with Energy*, In Med, Carson City, Nevada, 2002, www.bioenergytesting.com. For healing the body naturally through eating and avoiding medications, see Dr. Hyla Cass and Patrick Holford's book, *Natural Highs: Feel Good all the Time*, Penguin Books: New York, 2002, www.cassmd.com. She discusses the importance of amino acids, and phyto-chemicals (plant-based) from natural sources to enhance mood, energy, memory and brain chemistry. For a holistic perspective on food, nutrition and a spiritual approach to eating, see Kesten, D., *Feeding the Body: Nourishing the Soul*, Canari Press, Berkeley, 1997, and Kesten, D., *Healing Secrets of Food, a Practical Guide to Feeding Body, Mind & Soul*, New World Library, 2003. For a broad overview of anti-aging research see Klatz, R., *The Anti-Aging Revolution*, Basic Health Publications 2003, www.worldhealth.net.

[2] I learned this the movement Gathering Starlight from Arnold Tayam and Shoshanna Katzman at a National Qigong Association conference. The move was inspired from Dr. Maoshing Ni's set called Eight Treasures (See Seven Star Publishing). It is designed to pull in the energy of the constellations down through the three Tan Tiens.

Appendix II

[1] Cannon W., The *inter-relationship of emotions as suggested by recent physiological research*, American Journal of Psychology, 25, 1914, p. 256.

[2] Mason, J., *A historical view of the stress field*, Journal of Human Stress 1, p. 6; part II: 1, p. 22. Seyle, H., 1975. *Confusion and controversy in the stress field*, Journal of Human Stress, 1, p. 37.

[3] Sapolsky, R., *Why Zebras Don't get Ulcers*, W.H. Freeman and Co., 1998.

[4] Benson, H., *The Relaxation Response and Norephinepherine: A new study illuminates mechanisms.* Integrative psychiatry 1, 15–18, 1983. Benson, H., *The relaxation response: Its subjective and objective historical precedents and physiology*, Trends in Neuroscience, July, 1983, pp. 281–284.

[5] Qi, Journal of Traditional Eastern Health, Vol. 5, #4, 1995, p. 45. Reference to an article in the New York Times by Phillip Hilts.

[6] Ader, R.; Felton, D.; and Cohen; *Psychoneuroimmunology*, Academic Press: San Diego, 1991.

[7] Rossi, E., *The Psychobiology of Mind-Body Healing* W.W. Norton & Co., 1986. Rossi, E., and Cheek, D., *Mind -Body Therapy: Methods of Ideodynamic Healing in Hypnosis*, W.W.. Norton, 1988.

[8] Reported in *Qi, Journal of Traditional Eastern Health*, Vol. 5, #4, 1995, p. 45. Reference to an article in the *New York Times* by Phillip Hilts.

[9] See Becker, R. *Cross Currents:: The Promise of Electro Medicine*, Becker, R., Jeremy Tarcher, 1990, pp. 136 for a review of literature.

[10] Becker, R., *The Body Electric*, William Morrow: New York, l985, pp. 235–236. For reports of research of the measurement of the current flowing through the meridians and the acupuncture points, see also Becker, R., *Cross Currents: The Promise of Electro Medicine*, Jeremy Tarcher, 1990.

[11] Nordenstrom, B. E. W, *Biologically Closed Electric Circuits: Experimental and Theroretical Evidence for an Additional Circulatory System*, Nordic Medical Publication, Stockholm , Sweeden l983. See Heilberg, E., ISSSEEM Vol. 4, No. 4, Winter 1993 p. 5. One must be cautious about interpreting this research because electricity has been shown to increase as well as decrease tumors.

[12] For example see Becker, R., *Modern bioelectomagnetics and functions of the central nervous system*, Subtle Energies, Vol. 3., No 1, pp. 53–71. For easier reading see Gerber R., *Vibrational Medicine*, Bear and Co ., 1996.

[13] Dossey, L., *But is it energy? Reflections on consciousness, healing and the new paradigm*, Subtle Energies, Vol. 3, no. 3, pp. 69–81, 1992. *Healing Energy and consciousness: Into the future or a retreat to the past?*, Subtle Energies Vol. 5., No 1, 1994.

[14] Rein, G., *Quantum Biology* QBRL, Northport, NY 1992, p. 7.

[15] For copies of their materials and conference proceedings contact ISSSEEM, 356 Goldco Circle, Golden, CO. 80403.

[16] Laskow, L., *Healing with Love*, Harper and Row, 1992, p. 306.

[17] Paraphrased from Gerber, G. *Vibrational Medicine*, Bear and Co. 1996.

[18] Schneider, R. H.; Staggers F.; Alexander, C. N.; Sheppard, W.; Rainforth, M.; Kondwani, D.; Smith, S.; King, C. G.; *A randomized controlled trial of stress reduction for hypertension in older African Americans*, American Heart Association 1995; Hypertension 1995; 226: pp. 820–827.

[19] Benson, H.; Rosner, B.A.; and Marzetta, B.R.; *Decreased systolic BP in hypertensive subjects who practice meditation*, Journal of Clinical Investigation, 1973; 52: 80.

[20] Zinn, J.K., 1990, *Full Catastrophe Living: Using the wisdom of your body and mind to face stress, pain and illness*, Bantam Doubleday, New York.

[21] Ornish, D. M.; Brown, S. E.; Scherwitz, L. W.; et al., *Can lifestyle changes reverse coronary artheriosclerosis?* Lancet, 1990a; 336: pp. 129–133. Ornish, D.1990; *Dr. Dean Ornish's Program for Reversing Heart Disease*, New York: Random House, 1990.

[22] Quote from Eisenberg, D. *Energy Medicine in China*, Noetic Sciences Review, 1990 Spring, pp. 4.

[23] For a discussion of research supporting the acupuncture points and meridians electrical characteristics and measurements of their DC potential see: Becker, R.., *Cross Currents*, 1990, pp. 46–48; Becker, R., *The Body Electric*, William Morrow, l985, pp. 234–5; Reichmanis, N., Marino, A., Becker, R., "Electrical Correlates of Acupuncture Points," IEEE Trans. Biomed. Eng, Vol 22, 1975.

[24] Electrical conductance of the skin above acu-points is measured by a machine called the Vollmeter (Electroacupuncture according to Voll). Subjects were examined in a blind protocol where the operator did not know whether a subject had practiced Qigong before the examination, Sancier, K., *Medical Application of Qigong*, Alternative Therapies, 1996, Vol. 2, No. 1.

[25] For an excellent review of the wide variety of well-controlled Western studies on consciousness, energy and spiritual healing see Benor, D., *Lessons from spiritual healing research and practice*, Subtle Energies, Vol. 3, No. 1, 1992, pp. 73–87.

[26] Becker, R. *Cross Currents*, op. cit. pp. 112.The chemical treated with qigong was o-n-propyl-o-allylthiophosphoramide. The extent of alteration in the NMR spectrum could be increased by repeating the Qigong exposure. Similar studies are going on in the U.S. at this time to rigorously attempt to validate this study.

[27] Zimmerman, J., *Laying on of Hands Healing and Therapeutic Touch: A Testable Theory*, BEMI currents, Journal of Bio-electric Magnetics Institute 2: pp. 8–17, 1990. Seto, A., *Detection of Extraordinary Large Biomagnetic Field Strength from Human Hand*, Acupunture and Electro-therapeutics Research International Journal, 17: pp. 75–94, 1992.

[28] Rubik, B., *Energy medicine and the unifying concept of information,* Alternative Therapies, March 1, Vol. 1, No. 1, 1995. Rubik, B., *Bioelectric Medicine*, Administrative Radiology J., Vol. 16, No 8, Aug., 1997. Popp, F. A., Watnke, U., Koenig, H. L., Peschka, W., *Electromagnetic Bio-information*, Urban and Schwarzenberg: Baltimore, 1989.

[29] Fahrion, S.; Wirkus, M.; and Pooley, P.; *EEG amplitude, brain mapping and synchronicity in and between a bioenergy practitioner and client during healing,* Subtle Energies, Vol. 3, No 1, pp.19–53.

[30] Becker, R., *Evidence for a primitive DC electrical analog system controlling brain function*, Subtle Energies, Vol. 2, No. 1, pp. 71–87.

[31] Higucchi, Y., *Endocrine and Immune Response during Qigong Meditation*, Journal of International Society of Life Information Science, (ISLIS) Vol. 14, No. 2, Sept., 1996. One wonders whether the differences cited in this study are a function of exercise in general or Qigong in particular. This could be determined by further research which adds another exercise group and compares their endorphin levels to the qigong group.

[32] See The Qigong Computerized Database is available from the Qigong Institute of San Francisco, Contact Dr. Ken Sancier or Francesco Garripoli at www.qigonginstitute.org.

[33] Mayer, M., "Qigong Clinical Research," in Ed: Jonas, W., *Healing, Intention and Energy Medicine,* Elsevier Health Sciences, 2003. Also see, Mayer M., "Qigong and Hypertension: A Critique of Research," The Journal of Alternative and Complementary Medicine, Vol. 5, No 4, 1999.

[34] Articles related to External Emission Qigong are not included due to the focus of this book being on Self-Healing Qigong Practices. There is a wide body of research on the former, which can be found in various sources such as *Subtle Energies,* Journal of the International Society for the Study of Subtle Energies and Energy Medicine, Golden Co. Also see Yount, G., "Simulated Infrasound Component of External Qigong may enhance glioma cell response to chemotherapy" (unpublished, currrently in peer review).

[35] For a review of this literature please see my article, *Qigong and Hypertension: A Critique of Research,* The Journal of Alternative and Complementary Medicine, Vol. 5, No. 4, 1999, pp. 371–382. I conclude, after using rigorous research methodology criteria that, "The weight of evidence of 33 studies representing 5545 subjects suggests that practicing Qigong has a positive effect on hypertension; however, due to inadequate addressing of methodology issues, it is difficult to determine just how effective Qigong is, and what other factors may contribute to the positive effects reported in the studies reviewed. I also state in my abstract that, "Whether Qigong alone can affect hypertension is not necessarily the most important question. Further research will be required to better assess and understand the effect of adding Qigong into an integrated, multifaceted program that selectively incorporates diet, moderate aerobic exercise, relaxation training, and social and psychological dimensions." I have updated this review by reviewing 73 studies; please see Jonas, W., *Healing, Intention and Energy Medicine,* Elsevier Health Sciences, Mayer, M., "Qigong Clinical Research," 2003.

[36] Kuang, A., et al., *Research on "Anti Aging" effect of Qigong*, Journal of Traditional Chinese Medicine 11 (2): pp. 153–58, 1991.

[37] There was also significant difference in the total mortality rate in the Qigong group and in the control group (P < .01). Likewise there was a significant difference in death due to stroke in Qigong group compared with in the control. (P < .05). Ankun, K., 1991, pp. 154, op. cit. See Appendix 1 for a critique of this study.

[38] Wang, C., et al., Proceedings from the Second World Conference for Academic Exchange of Medical Qigong; Beijing, China, 1993, pp. 123–124. Quoted by Sancier, K., *Medical Applications of Qigong*, Alternative Therapies, Jan. 1996, Vol. 2., No. 1.

[39] Xing, Zh; Li, W.; Pi, D.R.; *Effect of Qigong on blood pressure and life quality of essential hypertension patients*, Institute of Combined TCM-WM, Human Medical University, Changsha, China, 7: pp. 413–414.

[40] Kuang, A.; Wang, C.; Xu, D.; Qian, Y., *Research on anti-aging effects of Qigong*, Journal of Traditional Chinese Medicine, 1991; 11 (2): pp. 153–158; and 1991; and continued 11 (3): pp. 224–227.

[41] Wang, C.; Xu, D.; Qian, Y.; Shi, W.; Bao, Y.; Kuang, A., *The beneficial effects of Qigong on the ventricular function and micro-circulation of deficiency in heart energy hypertensive patients*, Chinese Journal of Internal Medicine, 1995: (1): 21-23.

[42] Jing, G., *Observations on the curative effects of Qigong self adjustment therapy in hypertension*, Proceedings from the First World Conference for Academic Exchange of Medical Qigong, Beijing, China, 1988, pp. 115-117.

[43] Kuang, A.; Wang, C.; Xu, D.; Qian, Y.; *Research on anti-aging effects of Qigong*, Journal of Traditional Chinese Medicine, 1991; 11 (2): pp. 153–158; and 1991; and continued 11 (3): pp. 224-227.

[44] Wang, C.; Xu, D.; Qian, Y.; Shi, W.; Bao, Y.; Kuang, A., *The beneficial effects of Qigong on the ventricular function and microcirculation of deficiency in heart energy hypertensive patients*, Chinese Journal of Internal Medicine, 1995: (1): pp. 21–23.

[45] Liu Yuanliang, He Shihai, and Xie Shanling, Zhejang College of Traditional Medicine, China, 1993. Reported by worldtaijiday.org.

[46] Sun, Q., and Ahao, L., *Clinical observation of Qigong as a therapeutic aid for advanced cancer patients*. Proceedings, First World Conference for Academic Exchange of Medical Qigong, Bejing, 1988: pp. 97–98. Reported in Sancier, K., Anti-Aging Benefits of Qigong, Journal of Internat. Society of Life Information Science, Vol. 14, No. 1, March 1996.

[47] Chen, K., and Yeung, R., *A Review of Qigong Therapy for Cancer Treatment*, Journal of International Society of Life Information Sciences, Vol. 20 (2), 2002.

[48] Trieschmannj, R., *Energy Medicine for Long–Term Disabilites*, Disability and Rehabilitation, Vol. 21, No. 5–6, 1999.

[49] Iwao, M., et. al., *Effects of Qigong Walking on Diabetic Patients: A Pilot Study*, Journal of Alternative and Complementary Medicine, Vol. 5. No 4., 1999, pp. 353–359, .

[50] Xu, D., and Wang, C., *Clinical study of delaying effect on senility of hypertensive patients by practicing "Yang Jing Yi Shen Gong."* Proceedings from the Fifth International Symposium on Qigong: Shanghai, 1994, p. 109. Reported in Sancier, K., Medical Applications of Qigong, Alternative Therapies, Vol. 2, No. 1, Jan. 1996,

[51] Singh, B. B.; Berman, B. M.; Hadhazy, V.A.; and Creamer, P., *A pilot study of cognitive behavioral therapy in fibromyalgia*, University of Maryland School of Medicine, Alternative Therapeutic Health Medicine, 4 (2), March 1998, pp. 67–70.

[52] Reuther, I., Dr. Med. and Aldridge, D, Ph.D., *Qigong Yangsheng as a Complementary Therapy in the Management of Asthma, A Single Case Appraisal*, Journal of Alternative and Complementary Medicine, Vol. 4, No. 2, 1998, pp. 173–183.

[53] Gaik, F. V., Merging East and West: *A preliminary study applying Spring Forest Qigong to depression as an alternative and complimentary treatment*, 2003. Adler School of Professional Psychology, 65 East Wacker, Chicago, IL. Frances V. Gaik can be contacted at ibitmog1@aol.com.

[54] See Jonas, W., *Healing, Intention and Energy Medicine*, Harcourt Publishers Limited, 2003. My article there is entitled, *Qigong Clinical Research*. Also see, Mayer, M., *Qigong and Hypertension: A Critique of Research*, The Journal of Alternative and Complementary Medicine, Vol. 5, No. 4., 1999.

[55] This new model is beginning to be practiced in leading-edge clinics throughout the United States such as the one I co-founded with a multidisciplinary team called The Health Medicine Institute in Lafayette,

California, www.healthmedicineinstitute.com. At centers like ours practitioners use their different areas of expertise and work together at a team. At HMI, a health guide leads patients through the process, and when appropriate, the whole team meets with patients in healing circles.

Appendix III

[1] Province, M. A., et al, *The Effects of Exercise on Falls in Elderly Patients: A Preplanned Meta-Analysis of the FICSIT Trials,* JAMA, Vol. 273, No. 17, May 3, 1995.
[2] For a review of the literature see The Qigong Database: http://www.qigoninsitute.org. Also see http://www.worldtaichiqigongassn.org.
[3] Prevention Magazine V. 42, May 90, pp.14–15.
[4] *American Geriatric Society,* Nov. 1995, 43 (11) pp. 1222–1227. Reporting research results on Tai Chi. Journal of the American Geriatric Society, 1999; 47: pp. 277–84. Lancet (Vol. 353) reports a randomized study and gives blood pressure numbers.
[5] Adler, P.; Good, M.; Roberts, B.; Synder, S.; *The Effects of Tai Chi on Older Adults with Chronic Arthritis Pain.,* Jour. Nursing Scholarship.,Vol. 32 (4), 2000, pp. 377–389. Reported by McCaffrey R., *Qigong Practice: A Pathway to Health and Healing,* Holistic Nursing Practice, March/April, 2003.
[6] The American Journal of Physical Medicine and Rehabilitation 70 (3), June, 1991, pp. 136–141. According to a studies reported by the American Geriatric Society (December 2000), called "Taiji Eases Osteoarthritis," it is beneficial for those suffering from osteoarthritis.
[7] Reference from McCaffrey, Holistic Nursing Practice, March/April 2003 to Lumsden, D. B., et al., *Tai Chi for Osteoarthritis: An Introduction for Primary Care Physicians,* Geriatrics, Vol., 53, 1998, pp. 84–6.
[8] American Journal of Physical Medicine and Rehabilitation 70 (3), June, 1991, pp. 136–141.
[9] The reports of support groups using Tai Chi comes from http://www.worldtaichiday.org.
[10] American Journal of Physical Medicine and Rehabilitation 70 (3), June, 1991, pp. 136–141.
[11] "Qigong and Hypertension: A Critique of Research, "The Journal of Alternative and Complementary Medicine, Vol. 5, No 4. 1999. Jonas, W., *Healing, Intention and Energy Medicine,* Elsevier Science, 2003. My article is entitled, *Qigong Clinical Research.*

Selected Bibliography and Suggested Readings

1. Achterberg, J., *Imagery in Healing: Shamanism and Modern Medicine*, Shambhala: Boston, 1985.
2. Becker, R., *The Body Electric: Electromagnetism and the Foundation of Life*, William Morrow: New York,1985.
3. Benor, D., *Spiritual Healing: Scientific Validation of a Healing Revolution*,Vision Publications, 2001.
4. Bienfeld, H. and Korngold, E., *Between Heaven and Earth: A Guide to Chinese Medicine*, Ballentine Books, 1991.
5. Bly, R., *Iron John: A Book about Men*, Addison Wesley, 1990.
6. Campbell, J., *Historical Atlas of World Mythology: The Way of the Animal Powers*, Perennial Library, Harper and Row, 1988.
7. Chandra, P., *The Sculpture of India*, National Gallery of Art: Washington, 1985.
8. Chopra, D., *Ageless Body, Timeless Mind*, Harmony Books, New York, 1993.
9. Chopra, D., *Quantum Healing: Exploring the Frontiers of Mind/Body Medicine*, Bantam Books, 1990.
10. Chuen, L.K., *The Way of Energy*, Gaia Books: England, 1991.
11. Chuen, L.K., *The Way of Healing: Chi Gung*, Broadway Books: New York, 1999.
12. Cohen, K., *The Way of Qigong*, Ballentine Books, 1997.
13. Cohen, K., *The Five Animal Frolics*, Video Tape, 1990
14. Diepersloot, J., *The Tao of Yiquan: Warriors of Stillness, Vol. I and II*, Center for Healing and the Arts: Walnut Creek, CA, 1999.
15. Dosey,L., *Re-inventing Medicine*, Harper Collins:San Francisco, 1999.
16. Dychtwald, K. and Fergusen, M., *Bodymind*, Pantheon Books, 1977.
17. Eliade, M., *The Forge and the Crucible*, University of Chicago, 1956.
18. Eliade, M., *Myth and Reality*, Harper & Row, 1963.
19. Eliade, M., *Shamanism: Archaic Techniques of Ecstasy*, Bollingen Series, Princeton University Press, 1972.
20. Feng, A., *The Five Animal Play-Medical Qi Gong*, Zhi Dao Guan, 2003.
21. Gach, M., *Acupressure Potent Points: A Guide to Self-Care for Common Ailments*, Bantam Books, 1990.
22. Gendlin, E., *Focusing*, Bantam Books, 1978.
23. Gerber, R., *Vibrational Medicine,* Bear & Co., 1996.
24. Goodman F., *Where the Spirits Ride the Wind: Trance Journeys and Other Ecstatic Experiences*, Indiana University Press, 1990.
25. Gore, B., *Ecstatic Body Postures*, Bear and Co., 1995.
26. Gwei-Djen, L. and Needham, J., *Celestial Lancets*, Cambridge University Press, 1980.
27. Ha, F., *Stillness in Movement: The Practice of Tai Chi Chuan*, Video, Vision Arts, San Francisco.
28. Huntington, S., *The Art of Ancient India*, Weatherhill, 1985.
29. Jahnke, R., *The Healing Promise of Qi*, Contemporary Books: A Division of McGraw Hill, 2002.

30. Jonas, W., and Crawford, C., *Healing Intention and Energy Medicine*, Elsevier Science, 2003.

31. Klatz, R., *The Anti-Aging Revolution*, Basic Health Publications, 2003.

32. Kohn, L., *Taoist Meditation and Longevity Techniques*, University of Michigan Press, 1989.

33. Kohn, L., *Daoism and Chinese Culture*, Three Pines Press, 2001.

34. Lade, A., *Acupuncture Points: Images and Functions*, Eastland Press, 1989.

35. Mayer, M., *Qigong and Hypertension—A Critique of Research*, Journal of Alternative and complementary Medicine, Vol. 5, (4), August, 1999.

36. Mayer, M., *Qigong Clinical Research*, Ed. Jonas, W., and Crawford, C., Healing Intention and Energy Medicine, Elsevier Health Science, 2003.

37. Mayer, M., *Find Your Hidden Reservoir of Healing Energy: A Guided Meditation for Chronic Disease*, Audio Tape, 2001.

38. Mayer, M., *The Mystery of Personal Identity*, ACS Publications, 1985.

39. Mayer, M., *Psychotherapy and Qigong: Partners in Healing Anxiety*, The Psychotherapy and Healing Center, 1999.

40. Mayer, M., *Trials of the Heart: Healing the Wounds of Intimacy*, Celestial Arts, 1994.

41. Rinpoche, S., *The Tibetan Book of Living and Dying*, Harper: San Francisco, 1993.

42. Rossi, E., *The PsychoBiology of Mind-Body Healing*, W.W. Norton and Co.: New York, 1986.

43. Sapolsky, R., *Why Zebras Don't Get Ulcers: An Updated Guide to Stress, Stress-Related Diseases, and Coping*, W.H. Freeman and Company: New York, 1998.

44. Seem, M., *Bodymind Energetics*, Healing Arts Press: Vermont, 1989.

45. Sha, Z.G., *Zhi Neng Medicine*, Zhi Neng Press: Vancouver, 2000.

46. Sha, Z.G., *Power Healing*, Harper and Row, 2001.

47. Sherman L., Zuckerman M., and Weil, A., *The Canyon Ranch Guide to Living Younger Longer: A Complete Program for Optimal Health for Body, Mind and Spirit*, Simon and Schuster, 2001.

48. *Subtle Energies*, Journal of the International Society for the Study of Subtle Energies and Energy Medicine, Golden Co.

49. Storm, H., *Seven Arrows*, Harper and Row: New York, 1972.

50. Teeguarden I., *Acupressure Way of Health: Jin Shin Do*, Japan Publications, 1978.

51. Wile, D., *Lost Tai-chi Classics from the Late Ching Dynasty*, State University of New York Press: Albany, 1996.

52. Wile, D., *Tai Chi's Ancestors: The Making of an Internal Martial Art*, Sweet Chi Press, 1991.

53. Yang, J.M., *Advanced Yang Style Tai Chi Chuan, Vol. 1*, Yang's Martial Arts Association: Jamaica Plain, MA, 1986.

Websites related to Qigong, Health and Longevity:

Web address: www.organization

1. aaom.org   American Association of Oriental Medicine
2. abodetao.com   Empty Vessel: Journal of Contemporary Taoism
3. acupressure.com   The Acupressure Institute of Berkeley
4. ahna.org   American Holistic Nurses Association
5. alternative-therapies.com   Alternative Therapies in Health and Medicine
6. aobta.org   American Org. for the Body Therapies of Asia
7. bodymindhealing.com   The Bodymind Healing Center
8. chilel.co   Chilel Qigong Site
9. eastwestqi.com   American Qigong Association
10. energypsych.org   Association for Comprehensive Energy Psychology
11. fongha.com   Integral Chuan Website
12. healerwithin.com   Dr. Roger Jahnke's site
13. healthmedicineinstitute.com   The Health Medicine Institute
14. holisticmedicine.org   American Holistic Medical Association
15. imaahe.com   Intern. Mart. Art Assoc. for Hlth. & Enlightenment
16. ions.org   Institute of Noetic Sciences
17. masaru-emoto.net   Dr. Masaru Emoto's site
18. mfsu.edu/~jpurcell/taichi   Tai Chi information site
19. nccam.nih.gov   Nat. Ctr. for Complimentary and Alternative Medicine
20. nqa.org   National Qigong Association
21. qigonghealing.com   Website of author Ken Cohen
22. qigonginstitute.org   Qigong Institute
23. qi-journal.com   Qi: Journal of Traditional Eastern Health and Fitness
24. redwingbooks.com   Redwing Books
25. tai-chi.com   Tai Chi Magazine
26. taichiproductions.com   Tai Chi and Arthritis Site
27. warriorsofstillness.com   Jan Diepersloot's Website
28. worldhealth.net   American Academy of Anti-Aging Medicine
29. worldtaichiqigongassn.org   World Tai Chi and Qigong Association

INDEX

X

Xiangzhai, Wang, 3-4, 19, 20, 71-72, 175
  origins of Yi Chuan, 19-20
Xin, heartmind, 117

Y

Yang energy, exercises for activating, 163-64,
  166
Yang Cheng Fu, 21, 25
Yang Linking Vessel, Yang Chang Mo. (See
  Great Bridge Channel)
Yang Lu Chan, 21
Yang Style Tai Chi, 151-80
YHVH, 54-55
Yi
  definition of, 43, 172
  exercises for developing, 108, 125
Yi Chuan, 17, 19, 43, 67, 135
  as method of self defense, 150
  eating ritual, 208-9
  Tai Chi and, 172-80
Yi Chuan Qigong. (See Walking Meditation)
Yi Chuan Walking Meditation. (See Walking
  Meditation)
Yin/yang
  balancing technique, 57
  Tai Chi and, 156
  Taoist sexuality and, 211-12
Yoga
  compared to Sitting and Standing Meditation,
    29-30
  research, 231

Zhan Zhuang (Standing like a Tree), 54-55, 92,
  94, 185

Z

This Triple-Offer Coupon Entitles the Bearer to:

❖ ONE COPY OF THE BODYMIND HEALING QIGONG VIDEO TAPE OR DVD-R for the discounted price of $19.95/60 min. (normally $24.95), plus $2.95 for shipping and handling (normally $3.95 for U.S. orders).

❖ FREE CONSULTATION: For a limited time, with my Bodymind Healing Video Tape/ DVD mail-in order, I can have a free 15-min. consultation (if long distance, I just pay phone charges) about how the exercises in the book and video can be tailored to my individual needs.

❖ DISCOUNT ON FIRST SESSION OF BODYMIND HEALTH COACHING: For a limited time, after the free 15-min. consultation mentioned above, I will receive a 50% discount on my first session of Bodymind Health Coaching.

Name: _____

Address: _____

Phone: _____

E-mail address: _____

**Please note: Michael Mayer, Ph.D., is not a medical doctor and therefore any advice about Self-healing exercises is not medical advice, nor is it a substitute for your medical doctor's care.

Please make check out to Michael Mayer, Ph.D. Send it to Bodymind Healing Center, 2029 Durant Ave., Berkeley, Ca 94704. 510-849-2878, or contact him through his e-mail address: drmichael@bodymindhealing.com, www.bodymindhealing.com.

Michael Mayer, Ph.D., is a licensed Psychologist, hypnotherapist and a Qigong/Tai Chi teacher in the San Francisco Bay Area who specializes in giving his patients self-healing methods for physical and mental health problems. Dr. Mayer presents his integrative approach to bodymind healing at hospitals, universities, national/international conferences and workshops. The First World Symposium on Self-Healing gave him an award for outstanding research and contribution to the advancement of mind-body medicine. He was perhaps the first person in the country to train doctoral level psychology students in the integration of Qigong and Psychotherapy. Dr. Mayer co-founded and serves as part of a multidisciplinary medical team called The Health Medicine Institute, which practices integrative healthcare. He has authored ten publications on bodymind healing, including books, audio-tapes on cancer and chronic disease and articles on chronic pain and anxiety. His peer reviewed article on Qigong and hypertension appeared in *The Journal of Alternative and Complementary Medicine*, and is updated in the book *Healing Intention and Energy Medicine* by Dr. Wayne Jonas, former Director of the National Institute of Health, Office of Alternative Medicine. Dr. Mayer's Bodymind Healing Qigong videotape synthesizes ten Qigong systems for a lifetime preventative medicine practice.